Soldier and Sailor words *and* phrases

Including slang of the trenches, the sea and the air force; British and American war-words and service terms and expressions in everyday use; nicknames, sobriquets, and titles of regiments, with their origins

Compiled by

Edward Fraser

Author of *The Soldiers Whom Wellington Led, The Sailors Whom Nelson Led, The War Drama of the Eagles, Napoleon the Gaoler, Famous Fighters of the Fleet*, etc., etc.

and

John Gibbons

12th Battalion, The London Regiment (1914–18)

Solis Press

Caution: this book contains words that are vulgar and offensive.

Obvious errors have been corrected; all other inconsistencies are as in the original edition.

"Tommy" by Rudyard Kipling on page 218 is an addition by the publisher.

"Quidquid agunt homines, votum, timor, ira, voluptas, Gaudia, discursus, nostri est farrago libelli".
[Whatever men are engaged in, their wishes and fear, anger, pleasures, joys, runnings to and fro, form the medley of my book.]

Juvenal, *Sat. 1.*, 85–6

"Our Armies swore terribly in Flanders."

Sterne, *Tristram Shandy*, ii., ch. 2

"It's very odd that Sailor-men should talk so very queer."

Ingoldsby Legends: Misadventures at Margate

First published in 1925. This edition published in 2018 by Solis Press

Typographical arrangement copyright © 2018 Solis Press

ISBN: 978-1-910146-35-4

Published by Solis Press, PO Box 482, Tunbridge Wells TN2 9QT, Kent, England

Web: www.solispress.com | *Twitter*: @SolisPress

Prefatory Note

This book was primarily designed as a Dictionary of War Slang at the instance of the authorities of the Imperial War Museum, using materials contributed by officers and men of all branches of the Service who had served with the British and Dominion forces. A large proportion of the slang of the war, however, comprised old pre-War Army and Navy expressions, which, in the War, were either adopted as they stood, so to speak, or else were altered and adapted to suit existing circumstances, and the enlargement of the original plan became unavoidable. The scope of the work has also been further extended to include a considerable number of Service terms, familiar among people in general, as being of interest in themselves or through their origins.

A number of American service words and expressions, particularly some that became familiar among British troops during the war, have been included.

Under the head of "Nicknames, Sobriquets, and Titles of Regiments", explanations in detail will be found of the origins and meaning of these, from, as far as they exist, authentic sources of information.

Special acknowledgment, with thanks, is due to Captain J. Murray Kendall, M.B.E., of the Imperial War Museum, for indispensable and invaluable help and advice given in the revision of the proofs.

Finally, as to the book as a whole, it is the only book on the subject published, and if in places the net may seem to have been cast rather widely, it is trusted that the book will be found the more interesting and entertaining on that account. That there are errors and omissions, in spite of infinite care and labour taken to ensure accuracy and completeness, goes without saying.

A (or Ack): The letter A in Signallers' vernacular: a word coined for clearness of expression and to prevent misunderstanding. Men's lives, even the fate of a battle, may depend on a signaller's message, on a signaller's pronunciation of a single word, even of a single letter. In the War, the words ordinarily used by the Signal Staff as substitutes for letters of the Alphabet in transmitting messages, particularly by telephone, were as follows:—

Ack (also Ak) — A
Beer   — B
Don   — D
Emma   — M
Pip   — P
Esses   — S
Toc   — T
Vic   — V

Ack, Ack, Ack (Ak, Ak, Ak) signified the close of a sentence or message. A.M. (Before Noon) was transmitted as "Ack Emma": P.M. (After Noon), as Pip Emma. How a message may be distorted in oral transmission through a number of men, the following Signal Service story of pre-War days, said to be true, exemplifies. The first man in an extended chain of signallers under instruction was given the message to pass along the line, "Going to advance—send reinforcements". It was delivered by the last man at the far end as, "Going to a dance—lend me three and fourpence!"

A.D.C.: The usual abbreviation for Aide-de-camp, or, according to *Punch,* "An Di Cap to a General".

A.D. Corps: Army Dental Corps.

A.E.C.: Army Educational Corps.

A.E.F.: The initials of the American Expeditionary Force, unkindly said in certain quarters to stand for "After England Failed", i.e., why America had to come in!

A.O.: Army Order.

A.O.C.: Army Ordnance Corps, made "Royal" in 1918 for "splendid work in the War".

A.P. and S.S.: Army Printing and Stationery Services. The department concerned with printing, photography, etc.

A.P.C.: Army Pay Corps; made "Royal" in 1920 for "excellent work performed in the War".

A.P.M.: The initials stand officially for Assistant Provost Marshal. Unofficially sometimes rendered "A Permanent Malingerer".

A.S.C.: Initials for Army Service Corps. Also for "Ally Sloper's Cavalry". (*See* Nicknames of Regiments.) The Army Service Corps was made "Royal" in 1918 for "splendid service performed in the War".

4

A.V.C.: The initials of the title of the Army Veterinary Corps: otherwise occasionally in jest, "All very cushy". The Army Veterinary Corps was made "Royal" in 1918 for "splendid service performed in the War".

Abdominal Crash: An Air Force term for an aeroplane smash. A bad fall. (*See* Gutzer.)

Abdul: The usual term on Eastern Fronts in the war for a Turkish soldier.

About Turn: Army vernacular for Hébuterne, a village on the Western Front.

Ace, An: (*French*—"As"). Originally applied as a slang term in the French Service to a smart cavalry man (an Ace being, of course, the best card in a suit), it was extended in the war as a familiar term for an airman whose name was cited in an "Ordre du Jour" as having brought down at least five enemy aeroplanes. Passing into English Air Force vernacular, it acquired the rather derogatory meaning of a showy airman, one with a tendency to "play to the gallery".

Ace, Guarding the: A Navy expression: the protection of a battleship under way in the open sea by a cordon of destroyers, the battleship being the ace or principal card.

Acid, Coming the: Stretching the truth: making oneself unpleasant: trying to pass on a duty: exaggerating one's authority.

Ak Dum: (*Hind.*—Ek Dam). At once: instantly. (Old Army.) In the war on the Western Front the German notice or warning boards bearing the word "Achtung" (Beware), come upon in captured positions, were often called "Ak Dums" by our men.

Acting Rabbit Pie: A pie made of fresh beef and bacon. (Navy.)

Adam and Eve: Believe. E.g., "Could you Adam and Eve it". (Rhyming slang.)

Adam and Eve on a Raft: Eggs on toast.

Adam and Eve Wrecked: Scrambled eggs.

Addressed to: Aimed at. A shell, for instance, was often said to be "addressed to" some special target.

"Admiralty to all ships. Commence Hostilities at Once with Germany": The message broadcasted by wireless to all British fleets and warships at 11 p.m, on August 4th, 1914, immediately war was declared. Following on that the King's Message to the Fleet (*see* King) was wirelessed round, and then the official notification that Sir John Jellicoe had been appointed Commander-in-Chief in British waters.

Admiralty Ham: Tinned Corned, or "Bully", Beef.

Adrift: Absent without leave. (Navy.)

Afters: The second course, when there was one, of the mid-day meal. E.g., "Any afters to-day?"—"Is there any pudding to come?"

Agamemnons, The Old: *See* Nicknames of Regiments.

Aggie: Formerly a familiar name among bluejackets for the late Dame Agnes Weston, the foundress of the Seamans' Temperance Hostels at the naval ports. Also the familiar nickname of H.M.S. *Agamemnon.*

Agony, An: A term among the rank and file for some young newly-joined officer, confused, or showing nervousness in shouting out words of command.

Ah Wee: (*French*—"Ah oui"). Oh! Yes. A colloquial expression in the *lingua franca* of the Western Front, and a convenient stop gap in a possibly inadequate vocabulary in conversation.

Aiglers, The: *See* Nicknames of Regiments.

Air Flapper, An: A Signaller. (From the flag-wagging motions in transmitting messages.)

Air Pills: Bombs dropped by aeroplane.

Air Torpedo: A universal name in the War for a type of elongated trench mortar bomb, fitted with balancing planes or "fins", which gave the projectile something of the appearance of a torpedo. (Torpedoes contain, and are actuated by, self-propelling mechanism.) The naval service torpedo dropped by aeroplanes. Its course and depth for running below the surface are set before being dropped. Employed by the present "Dart" type of sea-plane, R.N. (*q.v.*) "Torpedo", as a word, was the name originally given to a species of fish which defends itself by giving an aggressor an electric shock. (From *torpere,* to benumb.)

Ak: *See* "A".

'Alf a Mo, An: Australian slang for an incipient or "tooth brush" moustache of the Charlie Chaplin pattern.

"'Alf a Mo, Kaiser!": One of the most popular recruiting posters of the early part of the War bore these words, with the picture of a "Tommy" lighting a cigarette prior to unslinging his rifle and going into action. The catch phrase was widely adopted in England.

"Alice": The nickname given to a certain imitation tree on the Western Front, cased with iron and set up as an observation post in the Fauquissart sector. It was designed by a Royal Academician and constructed at a considerable cost, only however to prove a failure from being badly placed.

All Arms and Legs: Government ale, as having no "body". Also, weak tea.

All Callio: Happy. Content. (Navy.)

All Cando: All right. (Navy.)

All Cut: Upset. Confused: excited. A man struggling to put his equipment together within a few minutes of an inspection, would describe himself "All cut".

All Highest: (*German*—"Aller Höchst"). A phrase quoted in the Press in the earlier months of the War from addresses and official reports to the Kaiser, which many people in England condemned as deliberately "blasphemous". The expression is really a very old Prussian form of address to the Sovereign, in particular in his capacity as Head of the Army—the "Supreme War Lord".

All Kiff: All right. All correct.

All of a Doodah: An expression used of an aeroplane pilot getting nervous in mid air (Air Force). Pre-War ordinary slang.

All out: Eager. Straining, every effort. Exhausted after extra exertion. E.g., "All out to beat them"; "Going all out".

All Over Oneself: Extremely pleased. Overconfident; e.g., "He's all over himself because he's got leave". "He used to be all right, but now he s promoted he's all over himself".

All Spruced Up: Said of a man smartened up unusually to meet someone, or "walk out". Originally from the words of a music hall song. Variants were "All poshed up" or "Togged up".

"All Very Cushy": *See* Nicknames of Regiments.

Alley (or Ally): (*French*—Allez). Go away. Be off.

Alley at the Toot: (*French*—"Allez tout de suite"). Get off quickly.

Alleyed: Gone away.

Alleyman: (*French*—Allemand). A German. Alleuman and Fritz were the usual army names for the enemy in the earlier days of the War. They gave place later to Jerry. (*See* Fritz; Jerry.)

Allumettes: (*French*). Matches. Originally in the War meaning French matches in particular. The word continued to be used for all matches when with the general establishment of British canteens, it became possible to buy English matches (*see* Asquiths).

"Ally Sloper's Cavalry": *See* Nicknames of Regiments.

Ammo: Ammunition, e.g., Ammo depot, Ammo store, etc.

Ammos: Ammunition boots. The Army regulation pattern boots.

Andrew, The: The bluejackets' universal term for the Royal Navy.

Angel, An: A wireless telegraphist. From the wings forming part of the badge. (Navy.)

Angel Face: Air Force slang for any young, or boyish looking, Probationary Flight Officer.

Angels of Mons, The: An extraordinary legend of the earlier days of the war was to the effect that the British Forces in the Retreat from Mons had been super-naturally aided. It was widely declared that many men at the front owed their escaped from death or capture to Angelic Intervention, and widespread public interest in England was aroused, a newspaper controversy also starting. The "Angels of Mons" became an article of faith to hundreds of people. The legend, it finally came out, originated with a contribution to the *Evening News* under the title of *The Bowmen*, a piece of realistic fiction by Mr. Arthur Machen. Apparently the idea was suggested by the chronicled narratives of super-natural appearances in the sky before old-time battles; as, for instance, before the Battle of Edgehill in the Civil War, and, according to local legends, on several occasions during the Wars of the Roses.

Angel's Whisper: An old Service phrase, originally, for the Defaulters' bugle-call and also for the Reveille or "Rouse"; the awakening bugle-call in the morning.

Angry Cat, The: The lower-deck name for the French battleship *Henri Quatre*, serving with the British in the Mediterranean in the War.

Annie's Room, In: An expression by way of jesting answer to an enquiry for someone who cannot be found, e.g., "Where is Private Smith?" "In Annie's room" (*see* Barbed Wire).

Ante-up, To: To give up or hand over anything. A term from the game of poker, originally from America.

Anticks: Navy tactical evolutions. "Steam anticks" was a term for Fleet exercises at sea.

Antonio (or Tony): A Portuguese soldier. In the War a colloquial term at the front for any man of the Portuguese Contingent.

Antwerp Expresses: A German army name in the War for big high-explosive shells.

Anty: Sugar.

"Any More for Any More?": A meal-time call by mess-orderlies to signify that enough food was left over for a second helping.

Anzac: A word popularly applied in the war for any member of the Australian or New Zealand Forces, the name being formed from the initials of the title Australian and New Zealand Army Corps. As to the origin of the word Sir Ian Hamilton in his foreword to "Crusading at Anzac", claims to have been "The man who first, seeking to save himself trouble, omitted the five full stops of the official designation of the Corps and brazenly coined the word Anzac." Credit for the introduction of the word is also claimed by General Birdwood, who has said" When I took over the command of the Australian and New Zealand Corps in Egypt, I was asked to select a telegraphic-code address and adopted the name Anzac." According to the Australian official war-history, a British Army Service Corps officer, Lieut. A.T. White, Superintending Clerk at the Australian and New Zealand Corps headquarters at Cairo, first suggested the name for telegraphic code purposes as an abbreviation of the long, cumbrous title, and a staff-officer, taking it from him, proposed it to General Birdwood. The heroic feats of the Australians and New Zealanders on Gallipoli made Anzac a term of the highest honour, specially associated with the Dardanelles operations. It had eventually to be officially notified that "Anzac" was restricted to men who had fought at Gallipoli; owing to the loose way people in general used the word often for Australians and New Zealanders who had never been there at all.

Anzac Cove: The name given to the Anzacs' landing place at Gallipoli to commemorate the heroism displayed on the occasion. Anzac Cove was so named by General Birdwood.

Apples and Pears: Stairs. (Rhyming slang.)

Apree La Gare: (*French*—Après la guerre—After the War). A colloquial Army phrase meaning Never. An expression of weariness at the apparently interminable continuance of the War. A hopeless soldier would often be heard to say for instance: "When shall I see my happy home again? "or" When shall I get my back pay?—Apree la Gare"—i.e., Never!

Archie (Archibald): A universal name for an anti-aircraft gun or shell, and sometimes for a member of the Anti-aircraft Force. The word is said to be derived from a music-hall song with a catch-word "Archibald, certainly not". It came into vogue apparently at first as expressive of the ineffectiveness of our earlier anti-aircraft gunnery efforts.

Archie, To: To shell aircraft.

Archie Barrage, An: A barrage (*q.v.*) against air raiders of anti-aircraft guns.

Area Shoot, An: A widespread bombardment over a whole district to make it untenable by the enemy.

Arminteers (or Arm-in-Tears): Army. Vernacular for the name of the town of Armentières. "Mademoiselle of Armentières", was the title of a very popular song at the Front, giving extremely personal details of the adventures of an apocryphal young lady of Armentières.

Armadillo Scout: The name of a type of aeroplane with several unique features introduced by Armstrong-Whitworth in 1918.

Armstrong Hut: A small, collapsible structure of wood and canvas, put to a variety of uses.

Army: The term "Army" had this specific Western Front meaning in the Great War. The original British Expeditionary Force of seven divisions was, early in the War formed into three Army Corps. As additional troops arrived these were formed into additional Army Corps. On December 25th, 1914, the term "Army" was specially introduced and two Armies were formed by grouping the existing Army Corps. The "First Army", comprising the 1st, 4th and Indian Corps, was placed under Sir Douglas (now Earl) Haig; the "Second Army", comprising the 2nd and 3rd Army Corps and the 27th Division, was placed under Sir Horace Smith Dorrien. To prevent confusion thenceforward what had been known as Army Corps, dropped the "Army" and were termed "Corps" simply. In September, 1916, the British Western Front forces were organized into Five Armies, sufficient troops being then available. This organization was retained till the Armistice. It was customary to write the numerical designations of each Army in letters, e.g., "FIRST ARMY"; to use Roman numerals for Corps, e.g., "XI Corps"; and to use Arabic numerals for Divisions, e.g., "5th Division". The term

9

"Army" for a group of divisions all under one command originated in the French Revolutionary War, between 1795 and 1800, when there were, on different Fronts, the "Army of the Sambre and the Meuse"; the "Army of the Rhine"; the "Army of Italy" (in command of which "General Bonaparte" first made his mark), each Army being composed of several divisions. "Army Corps" as a term first made its appearance in the French service in 1804, for the component parts, each under a marshal, of Napoleon's "Army of England", the invasion-force assembled at Boulogne. We adopted the term" Army Corps" first tentatively for the Waterloo Campaign. In the Great War, as far as possible, the units (Battalions, Batteries, etc.) forming a division, were altered, or transferred, as little as possible. Many Battalions thus fought throughout in the same division, and a strong feeling of comradeship between units, and, so to speak, an *esprit de* division, in many respects peculiar to the War of 1914–18, came into being.

Army Safety Corps: *See* Nicknames of Regiments.

Arrival, An: A term for the sound of an enemy shell bursting in our lines. As the report could easily be mistaken for the firing of one of our own guns, the question was often asked, "Is that an arrival?"

Ash Can: A U.S. Navy term for a Depth Charge, used for attacking enemy submarines. Suggested by its shape. A Depth Charge was a steel cylinder, filled with high explosive and fitted with a simple firing appliance, set off by the pressure of the water and adjustable to explode at any desired depth. Every anti-submarine vessel, destroyers, etc., carried a number of depth-charges, dropped over the side at the place where the submarine was believed to be. "Ash Can" is the ordinary American term for what we call "Dust Bin".

Asiatic Annie: A nickname for a Turkish heavy gun at the Dardanelles. "We saw the great flash blotted out by the night and heard the warning 'G' on a bugle sounded, and full of foreboding, we began to count the twenty-seven seconds which 'Annie' gives one to think about one's ins before she drops her shell." ("Letters from the East", by Ivan Heald, in the *Daily Express.*)

Askaris: Armed native levies in the East African Campaign, in particular those serving with the Germans. The name is the local vernacular word for natives employed by big-game sportsmen in East Africa as armed watchmen over their camps.

Asquiths: A name on the Western Front for French matches. The purchaser had to "Wait and see" whether they lighted or not. (From the celebrated answer given to a question in Parliament by Mr Asquith.)

Assayes, The: *See* Nicknames of Regiments.

As You Were: The ordinary military word of command, used colloquially by way of acknowledging a mistake in anything said, e.g., "I saw Smith—as you were—I mean Brown."

Atkins: *See* Tommy Atkins.

Attaboy: A contraction of the expression "That's the boy". American slang used by players and lookers on at Base-ball matches. It became popularized in England during the later stages of the War.

Says Mr. G. Bernard Shaw, in describing a Base-ball match at which he was a spectator: "Even those players who had no gift of eloquence expressed their souls in dithyrambic cries like the Greek Evoe! which sounded to me like Attaboy! I confess that I am not enough of a Greek scholar to translate Attaboy, but it is a very stimulating ejaculation."

Aussie, Aussieland: Australians; Australian Troops; Australia.

Avec: Spirits. Spirits being forbidden for the troops at the front in the War, their purchase. was always difficult. The usual way of getting over the difficulty was by diplomacy. One would ask in an *estaminet* for a *"Café Avec"*, stress being put on the *"Avec"*. The customer's meaning was obvious and liquor was forthcoming. As a colloquialism among ourselves in this way the word *"avec"* used by itself, came to stand as a general term for alcohol in due course.

B.A.B.: Initials of "Bab Code". The name of a confidential Army Telephone Code Book brought out in 1916. It contained groups of figures representing technical phrases. Being somewhat complicated, occasional resulted through hasty or inadvertent misreading of the figures. On one occasion, it is told, an officer meaning to telephone the numerals "46778652", signifying "Extra Rum Ration Required", hastily telephoned instead "46798654", signifying "Enemy about to attack". The book was sometimes spoken of as "the Adjutant's nightmare". It was small and easily mislaid, also, every other day, the authorities made perplexing alterations of code-numbers and additions.

B.B,'s.: British Blues. A bluejackets' term for themselves.

B.E.: The initials of "Biplane Experimental". A type of tractor aeroplane of Royal Air Factory design.

B.E.F.: British Expeditionary Force. Primarily the first Seven Divisions sent to France at the outset of the war and forming the "Contemptible Little Army". (*See* Contemptibles.) "Expeditionary Force" was the term officially adopted some time before the War for the British contingent nominally available for service overseas in the event of an European War, its normal strength being fixed at three Divisions. It replaced the original term for the contingent, "The Striking Force", and in the War was applied to overseas contingents everywhere, e.g., "Egyptian Expeditionary Force", "Mediterranean Expeditionary Force", etc., according to destinations.

B.F.: The initials of "Bristol Fighter, a Lewis-gun armed aeroplane, described as "perhaps the most efficient of all in the war". Also, of course, ordinary contemptuous slang: e.g., "He's an out and out B.F.!"

B.I.O.: Branch Intelligence Officer. An officer of an Army or Corps Staff under the G.S.O.I. (*see* I) "attached for rations and discipline" to the R.A.F. reconnaissance squadron of his Army or Corps, as a channel of communication from observers and air photographers between the Air Force and the Army.

B.L.: Breech Loading. Used in the British Services to indicate a gun with which the charge is made up in cloth bags. (*See* Q.F.)

Baa Lamb: A nickname for H.M.S. *Barham*.

Babbler, The: An Army Cook. A contraction of the rhyming slang word Babbling Brook.

Baby: The name given a small Sopwith 100 h.p. aeroplane used largely by the Royal Naval Air Service in the war. This and names such as "Camels", "Kangaroos", "Snipes", etc., were nicknames given either by aeroplane pilots or the manufacturers of the various types, because of some peculiarity in appearance or behaviour in flight.

Baby Crying, The: An old Army term for the Defaulters' Bugle Call. (*See* Angel's Whisper.)

Baby's Head: Meat Pudding. Suggested by its round, smooth appearance. (Navy.)

Baby Killers, The: The term applied by Mr. Winston Churchill when First Lord of the Admiralty, to the German Raiders at Scarborough, December, 1914. Writing to the Mayor of Scarborough he said, "Whatever feats the German Navy may hereafter perform, the stigma of the 'Baby Killers' will brand its officers and men while sailors sail the seas."

Baby Monitors: A Dover Patrol name in the war for the Monitors of the small "M" Class.

Back-Chat: (*Hind.*—Batchit). Gossip. Argument.

Back Numbers, The: *See* Nicknames of Regiments.

"Backs to the Wall" Order, The: The special Army Order issued on April 12th, 1918, by Earl Haig at the crisis of the great German "Push". It ran: "Every position must be held to the last man. There must be no retirement. With our backs to the wall, and believing in the justice of our cause, each one of us must fight to the end", American official statistics show that the German superiority over the Allies on the Western Front in rifle-strength amounted to 324,000 rifles on April 1st, 1918. The Allies did not attain superiority in rifle strength until the end of June; and then came the turn of the tide.

Backwash: An airman's term for the air disturbance in rear of aircraft in motion.

Badgy: An enlisted boy. "Badgy Fiddler"—a boy Trumpeter. (Old Army.)

Bag Of, A: Sufficiency. Plenty: e.g., a bag of beer.

Bag of Rations: A term of contempt, referring to some over-zealous, fussy, or domineering superior.

Baggies: An old Army term for seamen—from their wide-bottomed trouser legs.

Bagonet: A common Army corruption for Bayonet. Curiously "Bagonet" and "Baggonet" for Bayonet are forms often met with in old 17th-Century documents and letters contemporary with the introduction of the Bayonet.

Bags, The: The familiar term for the trench parapet, constructed with sand bags. "Mounting the bags", "Over the bags", were usual synonyms for the opening of an attack, going "Over the Top".

Bake: Head: e.g. "He got it on the Bake", i.e., a head-wound.

Baker: *See* Nicknames.

Balb, To: An airman's colloquialism, meaning the manoeuvring of an opponent into a bad position. Of American origin, meaning to get round somebody. The word is possibly derived from the Balbus of old Latin grammars who "was building a wall".

Ball and Bat: Hat. (Rhyming slang.)

Ball of Lead: Head. (Rhyming slang.)

Balloo; Ballyhooly: Army vernacular for the name of the French town of Bailleul. Bailleul was at one period of the War outside the fighting area, and was a military centre. As such it was also a centre for social gatherings and diversions, through which the phrase "A trip to Balloo", i.e., a pleasure trip, came to be a colloquialism. In 1918, in the great German breakthrough, Bailleul was entirely destroyed by the enemy, the houses, Cathedral, fine Town Hall—everything being blown up or burned to the ground.

Balloon, The: A colloquial term used of any event, e.g. "What time does the Balloon go up?" the speaker meaning, "What time is the parade?" Usually referring to a Pay Parade. *Cf.* the Theatrical slang expression: "When does the Ghost walk?"

Balmorals, The: The name of the Concert Party of the 51st (Highland) Division. Practically every Division in the War, particularly in the New Armies, had its Concert Party, or troupe of entertainers, picked out from men who in civilian life had been professionals. These were organized to provide entertainments for their comrades when resting "Out of the Line". There was considerable rivalry and sometimes inter-divisional jealousy in connection with the Concert Parties over the possession of some "star" performer. The Divisional Parties were quite distinct from the Concert Parties from England, such as those of Miss Lena Ashwell, whose tours were confined to areas in rear. The Divisional Concert Parties' *cast* had, of course, to rely on men for ladies' parts, and many performers acquired a widespread reputation from their skill. It may be interesting to recall that much the same thing was done in the Peninsular War by some of Wellington's Divisions, particularly the famous "Light Division", when in Winter Quarters in 1811, the performances of which attained widespread popularity. Some of their programmes are still in existence and treasured in various Regiments.

Band, To Follow the: To belong to the Creed of the majority of a Battalion:—Church of England in an English regiment, Presbyterian in a Scottish, Roman Catholic in an Irish regiment (previous to the general disbandment of Irish regiments in 1922). *See* Band Party; Drum, To follow the. In Highland Regiments it is usual to march to church without music.

Band Party, The: The Old Army term in English regiments for members of the Church of England. These of course were usually more numerous than members of other religious bodies, and the band consequently headed their march to Church on Sundays. This story is told in this connection. "What's your religious persuasion?" asked a sergeant of a new recruit before Church Parade. "My what?" "Yer what. Why what I said; what's yer after o' Sundays?" "Rabbits mostly!" "'Ere stow that lip. Come now, Church Chapel, or 'oly Roman?" After further explanation from his questioner, the recruit replied: "I ain't nowise pertickler Sergeant. Put me down Church of England; I'll go with the Band". (*See* Drum, To follow the; and Fancy Religion.)

Bandagehem: A name coined in the War for a certain Hospital Station in Flanders. Two others were named Dosinghem and Mendinghem. The names are specimens of official humour, and were suggested apparently by place-names on the Northern France and Belgian border, such as Blaringham (near Aire) a rest-billet, and Ebblinghem.

Bandook, Barndook, Bundook: (*Hind.*—Banduq, musket). A rifle. (Old Army.) The word is traceable back to a Perso-Arabic name for a pellet-bow and then for a cross-bow. (*See also* Vandook.)

Bandstand: A Cruet. From its shape. (Navy.)

Bangalore Torpedo: A device for dealing a pathway through a barbed-wire entanglement. A tube of sheet-iron with conical wooden head, filled with high explosive, thrust in advance into the obstacle and exploded by a safety lighter or electric lead. Several tubes (each 6 feet long and 4 inches in diameter) can be jointed together, according to requirements. Bangalore, in Mysore, is the Headquarters and Depôt of the Q.V.O. Madras Sappers and Miners. Introduced on the Western Front early in 1915.

Bangers, The: *See* Nicknames of Regiments.

Banjo: Shovel. Entrenching tool. (An Australian term.)

Bankers' Battalion, The: The 26th (Service) Battalion of the Royal Fusiliers, raised early in 1915 mainly from Bank Clerks and Accountants.

Bantams, The: The name given in the War to certain battalions especially recruited from men under the minimum army height of 5ft. 3ins. At first not accepted, such men during 1915 were formed into separate Bantam Battalions, the two Birkenhead Battalions, the

15th and 16th Battalions of the Cheshire Regiment, leading the way. Bantam Battalions were recruited afterwards all over the country—one Division, the 35th, being at one time composed entirely of "Bantams". Later, owing to the necessities of the situation, some battalions were "de-bantamized", and made up with men of any size.

Baralong Fate, A: A German submarine-service expression for being trapped by a British Decoy Ship. (*See* Decoy Ships, Mystery Ships, Q Ships.) These were commonly called in the German Navy "Trap Ships". The expression "A Baralong Fate" originated after the memorable surprise and sinking of the German submarine U27 on August 19th, 1915, off the South of Ireland by the "Mystery", or "Q ship", *Baralong*. The *Baralong*, disguised as a "tramp steamer", came upon U27 while attacking the Mule-Transport *Numidian*, and hoisting the White Ensign disclosed her guns and opened fire, with ultimate disastrous results to the submarine, whose survivors tried to board the *Numidian*, and were knocked on the head by the Yankee muleteers.

Barbed Wire, On the: Primarily meaning killed. Also used familiarly of any absent man; e.g., "Where is Robinson?" "Hanging on the barbed wire". Every attack, of course, left a number of men killed in getting through the enemy's wire entanglements and literally hanging there.

Barber's Cat, A: A gossip: tale bearer: chatterbox.

Barishny, A: (Russian). An unmarried girl, character not guaranteed. A Murmansk Expeditionary Force term.

Barker, A: A revolver. Also a sausage, with reference, of course, to the ancient joke embalmed in the once popular Dutchman's song, "Oh vare, and oh vare, is my leedle vee dog?"

Barn Owls, The: The Divisional Concert Party of the 37th Division.

Barnabas, The Guild of St.: A Guild which, since the Armistice, has organised parties from Great Britain to visit the graves of their dead across the Channel. Founded by the Rev. M. Mullineux, M.C., who originally worked his way as a deck-hand from San Francisco to New Zealand to join the forces. St Barnabas was, of course, "The Son of Consolation". In 1923 upwards of 2,000 poor relatives of the fallen were taken to France and Flanders under the auspices of the Guild, and the kindly work continues.

Barnstormers, The: The Divisional Concert Party of the 60th Division.

Baron, A: An Army Commander.

Barpoo, to Go: To lose one's nerves. To go off one's head in panic. To crash. (An Air Force colloquial term.)

Barrage: (*French*—Barrage). A barrier formed by Artillery fire (Army). An anti-submarine Net and Mine barrier (Navy). In land warfare to "put down" a barrage meant to concentrate artillery fire to clear ground on a line parallel to the front of an infantry attack and paralyse the defence. The main Naval barrage in the War was across the Straits of Dover and was designed to keep enemy submarines from interfering with the passage of transports across, and merchant traffic in general. One extensive mine-barrage system stretched across between Folkestone and Cape Grisnez, and from the Goodwin Sands to off Dunkirk. Another was the vast Northern Barrage, practically extending across the North Sea from the Orkneys to off the coast of Norway. The North Irish Channel Barrage was another, where many enemy submarines met their fate.

Barrage, Box: *See* Box Barrage.

Barrage, Creeping: *See* Creeping Barrage.

Barrell's Blues: *See* Nicknames of Regiments.

Base Wallah: Anyone employed at a Base, or having a job behind the front lines. (*Hind.*—Wala—meaning Fellow, etc.). (*See* Wallah.)

Bashi-Bazook: A Bluejackets' name for a Marine. [Bashi-bazooks actually are a species of Turkish irregulars, brutal ruffians and marauders as a rule.]

Bat: (*Hind.*—Bat). Language: e.g., To sling the bat. To speak the language.

Bat Boat: The nickname given a Sopwith flying boat with tail board and fixed tail fin and rudder not integral with the hydroplane as in other flying boats.

Bats in the Belfry: Of defective intellect. Not quite sane.

Bat out of Hell, To Go Like a: To go at extreme high speed. (Air Force.)

Batchy: Mad. Silly.

Bath Mats: The flooring of wooden battens laid over the mud of trenches. (*See* Duckboards.)

Batman: An officer's servant; personal attendant. Used occasionally contemptuously of any sycophantic private, currying favour with a N.C.O. by running errands, etc.

Batter, To Go on the: To indulge in a drinking bout. (Old Army.)

Battle-Axe Company: *See* Nicknames of Regiments.

Battle-Bag A: A slang term for the big naval rigid airship designed in the War for service with a fleet.

Battle-Bowler, A: The steel shrapnel helmet. Tin Hat (*q.v.*).

Battle Honours of the Great War: The "Honours" allocated were published in monthly instalments of twenty or thirty, accompanying the monthly issues of Army Orders. The first appeared in February, 1924.

Battle Surplus: The officers and men of a unit or brigade left out of action and retained to replace casualties. (*See* Lifeboat Party.) Before an attack Operation Orders provided that a certain proportion of Officers and Other Ranks in every unit to be engaged was not to accompany the unit into action. Usually styled "First Reinforcements", they were retained to make good casualties and in case of disaster form a nucleus for reconstructing the unit. Meanwhile they were employed during the action on special work of various kinds close behind the fire zone.

Battling L's. (also 'Ells), The: A familiar name for the flotilla of destroyers of the "L" Class, the *Lance, Lennox, Legion, Loyal* and others, active in the North Sea during the War. The "L" Class of destroyers were being Introduced into the Service when the War broke out and were our newest and most powerful destroyers to date, built under the 1912–13 programme.

Battling Third, The: A familiar name for the Third Destroyer Flotilla of the Harwich Force in 1914, noted for its part in the action off Heligoland, in August, 1914.

Bayonet, Spirit of the: "The Spirit of the Bayonet must be inculcated into all ranks so that in the attack they will go forward with that aggressive determination and confidence which assures the success of a bayonet assault; and which during moments of danger and exhaustion and the varying circumstances of battle, will enable the soldier confidently to seek close combat with his opponent". (*Musketry Regulations,* Part I, "Bayonet Training", Sec. I., par. 6.)

Bayonet Trench: *See* Tranchée des Baïonnettes.

Bays, The: *See* Nicknames of Regiments.

Bazaar Motor Vans: A "Tommy" name for the French village of Autos Bazars.

Beach, On the: Discharged. Set aside. To be beached. To be turned adrift. Put out of employment. (Navy.)

Beachy Bill: The name given to a Turkish big gun by the men at Gallipoli. An officer wrote, "At Anzac we knew almost every gun by name. ... 'Did you hear old Beachy pooping off this morning?' was a frequent question."

Beat It: Clear off. Run away.

Beat, My: A bluejacket's fancy term for a sweetheart.

Beaucoup: Plenty of. The French word was adopted as an every-day expression in the War; e.g., "There were beaucoup cigarettes. There was beaucoup beer", etc. A man who was very drunk would be said to be "beaucoup drunk".

Beef Trip, On the: A Navy term in the War, used of the vessels carrying meat to the Grand Fleet at Scapa.

Beer: The letter "B" as pronounced by signallers for clearness of expression and to prevent confusion. (*See* Ack.)

Beetle-off, To: Air Force slang. To fly straight. To go off direct, as a beetle flies; e.g., "I just beetled off home".

Behemoths, The: A Navy term in the War for the original Third Battle Squadron of the Grand Fleet, comprising eight battleships of the *King Edward VII.* Class. They were also called the "Wobbly Eight" (*q.v.*).

Belgeek: Belgium: A Belgian.

Bellied: A Tank Corps term for being stuck fast owing to a tree-stump, or other obstruction, catching the underside of the tank and so putting the treads out of action. In soft ground this might happen through the treads working their way under the surface.

Belly Band: The flannel cholera belt issued to the troops.

Belly Flopping: A term for the sectional rushes of troops in an attack in which the men advance in a crouching posture.

Bender, A: A yarn. (Navy.)

Bert: Albert, the town of the Leaning Virgin (*q.v.*).

Best, To give it: To give up. To acknowledge defeat; e.g., "I couldn't get on with it, I gave it best."

Bevvy: Beer. Any drink. (Beverage.)

Biff, To: To hit or punch.

Big Bertha: A nickname for a big Krupp gun. Originally a German soldier's nickname for any heavy gun; German ordnance coming from the Essen Works owned by Frau Bertha Krupp. "Busy Bertha" and "Fat Bertha" were German Army variants. The nickname was widely used by men of the Allied armies and in the Press at home. It was also specifically applied for the heavy German guns which bombarded Paris at immense range in March and April, 1918. "La Grosse Berthe" was a Parisian nickname. No "dud" projectiles were found. and the guns were destroyed by French airmen. It is considered that the immense range with abnormal velocity was due to the increased length and long hollow head of the projectile.

Big Boys: Large guns. "Heavies".

Big Noise, A: A General, or other important personage. (Of American origin.)

Big Willie: The Kaiser. (*See* Willie, Big and Little.)

Big Stuff: Heavy Shells.

Bilge: Foolish talk. (Navy.)

Bill Harris: The Army name for Bilharzia, a scourge of Egypt, the name of a parasite found in water, against which Special precautions have to be taken. The pipe-line from the Sweet Water Canal to the Palestine front had to be fitted with gauze strainers which trapped the snails on which the parasite exists.

Bill Jim: An Australian. (Australian slang.)

Billet: The usual term for quarters in a private house, or other building. Also the document requiring a householder, innkeeper, etc., to receive a soldier or soldiers. A term for the area of sea allotted to a submarine for patrolling. Also, familiarly: a job, a position,: e.g., a Staff billet.

Billy Wells, A: A big gun, or big shell. From the name of Bombardier Wells, the heavyweight boxer.

Binge: Drink. A carouse.

Bingham's Dandies: *See* Nicknames of Regiments.

Bint: (*Arabic*). Girl. Woman. Also prostitute. In colloquial use among troops in Egypt.

Bint, The: A familiar term for a man who played a female part in a Divisional Concert Party or Troupe.

Bird: Sweetheart. Any girl; e.g., to walk out with a Bird. Compare the French soldier's term for his sweetheart, "Ma Poule, my chicken". Also, a Navy term for an old offender, a man habitually in trouble.

Bird, To Get the: To fail in a request. To be "shut up"; e.g., "I went and asked for leave, and got the bird properly." (Originally theatrical slang, meaning to get hissed.)

Birdcage: At the Front the colloquial term for the enclosure, surrounded by barbed wire, where prisoners of war were herded together during action previous to being marched to camps in rear. The name was also used for any military prison or detention quarters.

"The Birdcage" was the name universally given to the elaborately entrenched position, north of Salonika, constructed in 1916 to serve as a final stronghold in the expected event of an overpowering attack. It was designed for the same purpose that Wellington constructed the Lines of Torres Vedras.

Bird Catchers, The: *See* Nicknames of Regiments.

Birdseed: Chocolate, sweets:—something nice for the "Bird".

Biscuits: The squat, square-shaped mattresses used in barracks and in hospitals. Three went to a bed. In shape and "softness" they rather resembled huge ration biscuits, which suggested the name.

Bit, To Do One's: To play one's part, to do one's duty. The phrase was not much heard at the Front in the War, although at home it was of universal application, and is now established in the language as a colloquial expression.

Bivvy: A Bivouac. Also, any temporary lodging, from an improvised shelter to a dug-out.

Bivvy, To: To halt for the night. To put up anywhere.

Bivvy Sheet: Waterproof sheet carried by each man. Two with short poles, rope and pegs, make a shelter-tent in which two men can lie down.

Black Cow, The: A German spy signalling device, according to the newspapers, during the German advance into France and Belgium in 1914. Peasants in German pay drew in charcoal, it was said, black cows on walls, gates, etc., in varying sizes and attitudes, each of which had a special significance in regard to the presence and force of the Allied troops. The size and shape of the horns had special meaning, as had the direction in which the cow was looking, and so on. In addition to the Black Cow there were, of course, many other German spy devices at that time; the moving of the sails of windmills spelled out certain information; the method of driving flocks of sheep similarly had a significance; all in accordance with a prearranged code.

Black Cuffs, The: *See* Nicknames of Regiments.

Black Hand Gang: A colloquial term at the Front in the War for a party volunteering or told off for some "forlorn hope" venture or risky enterprise, such as a trench raid. The term was sometimes applied in a mock heroic manner to themselves by men such as Bombers, Stretcher-bearers, and others whose duties were of a specially dangerous kind. [Originally suggested by the villains' role in a film melodrama.]

Black Horse, The: *See* Nicknames of Regiments.

Black Maria, A: An enemy shell of large calibre, from its dense black smoke on bursting. Possibly the name was suggested by the big black London Police Van. The Germans, curiously, had a similar term "Schwarze Maria", for our heavy shells.

Black Watch, The: *See* Nicknames of Regiments.

Blanco: *See* Nicknames.

Blank-Ed: Drunk. (A word coined from the French Vin Blanc; White Wine.)

Blankets: The "Tens" in a pack of cards. Suggested by the regulation method of folding or rolling Army blankets in tens before removal for convenience of transport.

Blayney's Bloodhounds: *See* Nicknames of Regiments.

Bleat, To: To grumble. (Navy.) Similar to the Army word "Grouse".

Blighty: England: Home. (*Hind.*—Belati.) Formerly an everyday word with the old Army in India. It came from early in the War into general currency in England, and was used on the Western Front with every kind of application. A "Blighty wound", for instance, was one that necessarily involved returning or being "evacuated" to England; "Blighty food" was tinned food and so on. The Hindustani word "Belati" is derived from the Persian "Wilayat", meaning a province, a country at a distance.

Blighty Bag: The name given at the Front to the small Stuff bags made in England in immense quantities and sent out to soldiers at the Front. A wounded soldier, on reception at a Casualty Clearing Station, parted company with his kit, with the result that no receptacle was left him for his personal belongings, pipe, etc. On this being made known in England, numbers of ladies made and sent out stuff-bags for the purpose, which were issued at the Casualty Clearing Stations. They got the name of "Blighty Bags" as having come from "Blighty".

Blimp: A small semi-rigid Coastal-Patrol airship, or Submarine Scout, introduced in 1915 for keeping watch along the coast, and locating enemy submarines cruising submerged, or lying temporarily concealed on the bottom. The name was probably suggested by the corpulent, stumpy shape of the "Blimp".

Blind: A "blind" shell, i.e., one failing to burst on impact.

Blind Half Hundred, The: *See* Nicknames of Regiments.

Blind-O: Drunk.

Blink, A: A cigarette stump or fag end.

Blinking: A word used as a euphemism for "Bloody", to qualify anything and everything, and on any occasion: "Halt! Who comes there?" challenged an outpost sentry, on a mounted patrol approaching his post at night. "12th blinking Lancers" came a shout in the darkness. Satisfied, the sentry simply answered "Pass 12th blinking Lancers and all's well!" This story also is told of a smart young Staff Officer in the South African War. Riding up one day to a party of dusty infantrymen wearily tramping over the veldt he called out "Are you the West Riding?" "No, me lord", came the reply from the ranks, "we ain't. We're the blinkin' Buffs—walkin'".

Blip, To: To switch an aeroplane engine on and off.

Blister: The familiar Navy name from its appearance for the "bulge" or longitudinal protuberance, somewhat like an elongated cushion, on the hull of Monitors and Battleships below the water-line, to minimize damage to the structure of the hull from mine explosion, or torpedoes. It formed an outer skin or exterior hull plating, thus saving the main structure of the vessel from damage. "Bulges" were first fitted in building the *Royal Sovereign* class. They have been discontinued since the Great War.

Bloater, The: The name given to the "B.E.8" type of aeroplane of 1914–15.

Blob, A: A glass of beer.

Block: Head: face. "Off his block"; angry, off his head.

Bloke, The: In the Navy the Lower Deck term for the Commander. In the Army used of anyone. An officer's batman, for instance, would be spoken of as his Bloke, and the batman himself would refer to his master as his Bloke.

Blood, A: A third-class shot. (Old Army.)

Blood Boat, The: A Navy term for the morning boat sent to fetch fresh meat from shore for a man-of-war. The term was largely in use before ships were fitted with refrigerating chambers.

Blood Money: Compensation for wounds. The term, common now to both Army and Navy, is originally a very old Navy term dating back to the 18th Century. The name given to an indefinite sum which the French were popularly supposed to be going to present at the end of the War to every British soldier who had served in France.

Blood on the Bullet: A phrase used to impress on soldiers undergoing musketry training that the rifle is meant to hit and kill, not as "Something somehow to be let off".

Blood Spirit, Getting up the: An Army instructor's phrase in bayonet fighting exercise. Sacks stuffed with straw serve as dummies, and the men have to attack them not only in scientific form, but with suitable ferocity—the "blood spirit". The phrase was invented during the War at the musketry school at Hardelot. (*See* Bayonet, Spirit of The.) The exercise forms part of the Army training course. The "enemy" (dummy sacks), are placed in alignment. The assailants are drawn up in front of a parapet or wall, which they scale and then rush forward to tackle the dummies, afterwards pressing on as in pursuit.

Bloodsuckers, The: *See* Nicknames of Regiments.

Bloody: Probably the commonest expletive used among the English speaking races of the world, and as such it found its place in the language of the War afloat and ashore with universal application. The derivation of the word is generally understood to go back to the adjuration "By our Lady" of the "Middle Ages", whence it gradually degenerated into the current expletive through the dramatists of the 17th and 18th Centuries. Shakespeare uses it over 200 times. Dryden and the Restoration Dramatists popularized it, and "Men of refinement and high culture adopted it as an article of scholarly adornment." Possibly also, from associations of drunkenness and folly among those called in the 17th Century "Bloods", it came to have unpleasant associations as an intensive: "It was bloody hot walking to-day." (Dean Swift in a Letter to Stella, *Journal*, 22.)

Bloody Eleventh, The: *See* Nicknames of Regiments.

Bloody Flag, The: The old Navy name for the Red Flag hoisted as the signal to commence action, and so employed from Blake's time until the end of the 18th Century.

Blotto: Drunk. Possibly from the idea of soaking up liquor like blotting paper. There is also a suggestion of the effect of over-indulgence in blotting things out from memory.

Blow in: To arrive—usually unexpectedly.

Blow off the Line, to: To lose, e.g., "He looked like winning, but blew off the line in the last round".

Blow, To: To have too much to say.

Blue, In the: Failure. Something gone wrong. An attack that broke down, or troops who got out of touch, would be said to be "in the blue".

Blue Caps, The: *See* Nicknames of Regiments.

Blue Cross, The: The Auxiliary Veterinary Service organized in the War by "Our Dumb Friends' League". The first Blue Cross Hospital was established in France between Dieppe and Paris at the end of 1914.

Blue Cross Gas: "Sneezing" gas, so-called from the Blue Cross marked on the shells. Introduced by the Germans in 1917. Its technical name is "diphenyl-chlorodysine".

Blue Devils, The: The universal name for the French Chasseurs Alpins, first given by the Germans in the fighting in the Vosges.

Blue-Eyed Boy: A Friend. A Pal. A Pet. Often used to imply favouritism on the part of a superior officer, e.g., "He does as he likes; he's the Major's blue-eyed boy."

Blue Horse, The: *See* Nicknames of Regiments.

Blue-Lights: Gunner R.N., as being responsible for the ship's supply of port-fires, rockets, blue-lights, etc.

Blue Marines, The: *See* Nicknames of Regiments.

Blues: The usual term for the regulation hospital dress of invalided men able to leave their beds, and allowed out-of-doors, wearing a blue armlet attached round the sleeve of the khaki overcoat as a protective mark in the streets.

Blues, The: *See* Nicknames of Regiments.

Boa Constrictor: Naval Instructor. (Old Navy.)

Boat, To Push out the: To pay for drinks all round; to stand treat.

Bob-a-Day Gunner: A Navy term for a lieutenant granted an extra shilling a day pay for carrying out gunnery duty in place of a regular gunnery officer.

Bob-Down Man, A: An anti-aircraft sentry, whose duty it was, on the approach of hostile aircraft, to give warning to all to get under cover.

Bob Tack: Cleaning gear. Brass polish.

Bobbajee: (*Hind.*—Bawachi). A cook. (Old Army.)

Bobber, A: A tale bearer. A man given to report everything he hears to a N.C.O.

Bobbery, A.: A noise: row. A squabble, e.g., to kick up a bobbery—to create a disturbance. An old Army colloquial term, derived from the Hindustani exclamation of surprise or grief, "Bap-re!" (literally, "Oh, my father!")

Bobbing Drill: Aiming Drill. Target practice.

Bobbing on: Anticipating or expecting something. Equivalent to "Sweating On" *q.v.*), but with the sense of looking forward to something unpleasant. A man would be "sweating on" leave; he would be "bobbing on" punishment.

Bobby's Job, A: A safe job: a "soft" duty. Meant usually by way of a reflection on the comparatively "safe" duties of a military policeman in war-time. This, however, was Earl Haig's opinion of the Military Police and their work in the War, as recorded in his "Final Despatch" of March 21st, 1919. "In the battle-zone, where frequently they had to do duty in exposed positions under heavy fire, and suffered severe casualties, the Military Police solved an important part of the problem of traffic control by preventing the unavoidable congestion of troops and transport on roads in the vicinity of active operations from degenerating into confusion. In back-areas their vigilance and zeal have largely contributed to the good relations maintained between our troops and the civilian population."

Boches: The universal French name in the War for the Germans, taken up in England by the public in general and the Press. The nicknames Jerry and Fritz were more usual terms with Army and Navy, and Hun with the Air Force. The word Boche first appeared, apparently, about 1860, as low-class Parisian slang, meaning "bad lot", *mauvais sujet,* and it was not until some time after the Franco-Prussian War of 1870–1, during which the enemy were always spoken of as "les Prussiens", that the word Boche came to be generally applied in France to a German. It was applied then first to those in Alsace, in the form Alboches or Allemands Boches. Zola in *L'Assommoir* uses the term "Les Boches" with particular reference to Alsatian concierges. *Bocheser,* to Germanize; *Bochonnie,* Germany; *Bochonnerie,* German foul play; *Bochirie,* German cruelty; *Bochiser,* to spy; *Bochisme,* German "Kultur"; are derivatives of Boche current in France during the war.

Bodger: *See* Nicknames.

Body Snatcher: A stretcher-bearer, either regimental or belonging to the R.A.M.C. Used occasionally also of a sniper. In the Navy sometimes, a Ship's Corporal. (Naval Police.)

Bogey: A mistake. A blunder.

Bold Fifteenth, The: *See* Nicknames of Regiments.

Bollicky, A: A Bluejacket (an old Army nickname, said to come from an old and crudely improper song—"Bollicky Bill").

Bolo, A: A Spy. In allusion to Bolo Pasha, the French adventurer executed for espionage and treason in 1918. Also meaning "Bolshevik". In use among men serving with the Expeditionary Force in North Russia in 1918.

Bolo House: An Air Force nickname for the Hotel Cecil, while occupied in the war as the Air Ministry's Headquarters. The term was in use among some Airmen who professed to believe that their Headquarters' Staff were not only incompetent and useless, but that their activities tended to benefit the enemy rather than the Allies.

Bolo to: (*Hind.*) To speak: e.g., To bolo the Bat—to speak the language.

Bombardier Fritz: Fried potatoes. (Perverted French for pommes de terre frites.)

Bomb-dodger: A term of contempt which came in during the War for people who left their houses in London and took season tickets to places at a distance, such as Maidenhead and Brighton, in order to be out of the way of danger during night Air Raids.

Bomber: How the term "bomber" came to be officially adopted in the War is curious. When, after the first Battle of Ypres, hand-grenades came into general employment, the parties of men trained to use them—a certain number in each battalion—were given the name of "grenadiers". The Grenadier Guards objected, claiming that they had a prescriptive right exclusively to the name, as having been specially conferred on them after Waterloo to commemorate their part in over-throwing Napoleon's Grenadiers of the Guard. The Guards, says Sir Frederick Ponsonby, in his *History of the Grenadiers in the War*, were "much perturbed", considering it as "an infringement of their privileges and misleading". The Colonel in command of the First Battalion Grenadier Guards protested to the War Office against the "usurpation". After a protracted controversy a final appeal was made to the King, and in May, 1916, it was officially announced that "at His Majesty's 'expressed wish' the word 'Bomber' should be universally substituted for 'Grenadier' ".

Bomb-proofer: A man given to scheming methods of evading duty on dangerous occasions.

Bomb Proofs, The: *See* Nicknames of Regiments.

Bombing the Chat: Practising trickery: exaggerating: "telling the tale": plausible deception.

Bon Drop, A: A composite expression meaning complete satisfaction: as much of anything as wanted, e.g., A bon drop of sleep.

Bon for the Bust: Good to eat.

Bon Sonty: (*French*—Bonne Santé). Good Health. Good Luck. A common expression on hearing an unusually heavy cannonade by our guns. The words were sometimes chalked on shells by our gunners.

Bonce: Head.

Bonfire: A cigarette.

Bongo Boosh: A tasty morsel of anything. At the Front in the war, any occasional "luxury", such as cold sausage on toast! A perversion of the French bonne bouche.

Bonza (also Boshta): Good. Excellent.

Boob, The: A military prison. Guardroom. Also a boob (booby), a stupid fellow. The word is of American origin.

Booby Hutch, A: A dug-out. Any underground shelter.

Booby Trap: The name given at the Front in the War to the devices, often of fiendish ingenuity, employed by the Germans, in particular after evacuating positions and occupied districts. They were of every kind and form. A helmet, for instance, would be left lying about in a deserted trench, and when one of our men anticipating a souvenir went to pick it up, a bomb, secretly attached to the helmet, would go off and kill the man. Pianos were left in German officers' dug-outs or quarters with wires attached secretly connecting the keys with an infernal machine. Mines were buried at cross roads in many cases timed to explode at a certain time or number of days after the enemy had withdrawn. A story which had a wide circulation on the Western Front related to a wretched kitten which some Germans had left nailed alive to a barn door. A soldier was said to have hastened to take down the poor creature, whereupon the unfortunate man was blown to pieces by a concealed bomb, secretly attached to the kitten. An American writer vouches for the story in a book—*Small Things* (p. 218), but its authenticity has been doubted. At any rate, however, the kitten story was very widely believed among our men. It was the same on all fronts. In Palestine, for instance, after the taking of Beersheba and Gaza, "booby-traps" were found connected with the wells and all over the public buildings, with trip wires in the streets, etc., attached to in one case a mine of 600 lbs. of high explosive. Sentries were always posted where booby-traps were suspected, until investigation could be made.

Booka: (*Hind.*—Bhukha). Hungry.

Bookri: Crooked: out of line: wrong.

Books: Playing cards.

Boost, A: A raid. An attack. A heavy bombardment. As a Navy phrase: To boost—to support anything, a statement, without adequate reason. A booster—one who by false or misleading statements bolsters up a case. (Originally American colloquialism—to lift, or shove up.)

Bootneck, A: A Bluejacket's nickname for a Marine. From the tab closing the tunic collar, the modern representative of the old leather stock.

Booty Men: The group of men in a trench raiding party for collecting and bringing away captured documents and papers, identification details, etc., for the use of the Intelligence Department.

Bosky: Mildly drunk. Dazed.

Bosom Chums: Vermin.

Bounce: A Navy ship-dog's name with historic traditions. One of the first Bounces was Collingwood's dog-companion at sea, to whom the Admiral wrote some quaint verses. Bounce was at Trafalgar, and did not exactly distinguish himself, according to Collingwood. He was notorious for his way of swaggering objectionably as "the Admiral's dog" over other dogs in the fleet, and finally disappeared overboard one dark night. A more recent naval Bounce figured before the King one day at Scapa as an officer relates. At the King's inspection on July 8th, 1916, at Scapa, Bounce followed his ship's company on board the flagship for the parade before His Majesty. At the supreme moment, when everybody was standing at attention, Bounce suddenly burst into the midst in deadly combat with a German dog which had been rescued from a sinking prize and named Fritz. There was general consternation on the quarterdeck until the King made everybody easy by saying with a laugh: "Ten to one on the bull terrier!"

Bounce, A: A perquisite. A "squeeze". A transaction more or less illicit, e.g., "Forty lots of cigarettes were drawn for thirty men: somebody got the bounce". Dismissal, e.g., "He got the bounce this morning".

Bounce, On the: On the spur of the moment. At the critical moment.

Bounce, To: To "bluff" anyone.

Bow Bells: The Divisional Concert Party of the 56th (London) Division.

Bowler, To be Given One's: To be demobilized and returned to civil life.

Box Barrage: An artillery technical term. A barrage (*q.v.*) put down on three sides (in front and on either flank) of attacking troops, to box them in as it were from interference by the enemy, leaving the rear side open for reinforcements and supports.

Box, The: A coffin.

Box, To: To manipulate the figures of returns, particularly musketry returns, for purposes of deception.

Boys in Blue, The: A familiar name for the permanently crippled ex-service men from the Great War, inmates of hospitals in the London area, upwards of 7,000 in number. On their behalf all the year round the "Not-Forgotten" Association, of which Princess Mary is patroness, does a splendid work of practical remembrance. (*See also* Not Forgotten.) Originally, and for long before the War, the familiar name for all soldier patients undergoing hospital treatment, from the colour of the hospital dress worn. "Boys in Blue" was also, years ago, a familiar phrase for the Navy, brought into vogue by a popular music-hall song.

Brads: Cigarettes.

Braggs, The: *See* Nicknames of Regiments.

Brahma: Something good. Also a flashily dressed girl.

Brass Before and Brass Behind: *See* Nicknames of Regiments.

Brass Hat, A: In the Army; a pre-war term for a General or Staff Officer. In the Navy; an officer of Commander's rank and upwards. From the gold lace embroidery on the peak of the cap.

Brass Heads, The: *See* Nicknames of Regiments.

Brass Neck: Impudent, e.g., a brass neck lie.

Brass off, To: To grumble.

Brass Rags, To Part: A lower-deck expression meaning to sever friendship; to quarrel. Bluejacket chums always share the cleaning rags, etc., which they use in polishing up brightwork on board ship. To "part brass rags" thus means to cease being on intimate terms, to become unfriendly. (*See* Raggie.)

Brave Fifteenth, The: *See* Nicknames of Regiments,

Breamy, That's: That's bad.

Breeze, To: To boast. (Old Army.)

Breeze Up, To Have the: To be nervous, to have the "Wind up" (*q.v.*).

Breezer, A: A breather. A rest.

Breezy: Nervous. Easily frightened. (*See* Wind up.)

Brickdusts, The: *See* Nicknames of Regiments.

Brief: A Discharge Certificate.

Brig, In the Dutch: Placed in irons. Under arrest.

British Legion, The: The Central Association in which most of the Officers' and Men's ex-Service combinations. are now merged. It works in co-operation with the British Empire Services League and the Inter-Allied Federation of ex-Service Men, and was formed in 1920 to relieve distress among ex-Service men, help them to get work, ensure provision for widows and orphans and to obtain increased pension allowances, etc. The Benevolent Department disturbed £289,712 in 1923. The British Legion has branches throughout the Empire;—upwards of 2,488—and is affiliated to over 50 Regimental Associations. Earl Haig is the President, and the Prince of Wales, Patron.

"British Official": A familiar war-time phrase often used at the Front as implying untrustworthiness. In the early stages of the war "British Official" was considered as synonymous with reliability, in connection particularly with published Army intelligence. Later, however, certain official reports, notably, after the Battle of Loos, were published in so misleading a form that among those at the Front who knew the facts the phrase became a by-word. Matters improved in this respect later, during 1918, and the term regained its original character.

British Red Cross Enquiry Dept., The: A War organization of the British Red Cross Society established, in London for the purpose of tracing men posted as "missing". Unless a man's fate was officially notified definitely, British Red Cross Volunteers set to work to trace him by questioning men in hospital, comrades of the missing, as to the circumstances in which they had last seen the missing man. In not a few cases, satisfactory results were obtained.

British Warm: The short thick overcoat worn generally by officers in the war, although not officially recognized as uniform until 1918. The name was usual for the khaki pea-jacket worn by officers in the South African War over 20 years ago. First introduced in India for wear at hill-stations, two kinds being issued: "Coats Warm-British", and "Coats Warm-Native".

Brock's Benefit: A usual name at the Front for the nightly display of Véry Lights, star-shells, etc., sent up to illuminate the surface of "No Man's Land" (*q.v.*) and the front line trenches. The name comes from the annual framework display at the Crystal Palace.

Broken Spur, The: The historic badge adopted as "Divisional Sign" by the 74th Division, as commemorating their self-sacrifice in assenting to be transformed from Yeomanry into an Infantry Division for service on Gallipoli and in Palestine. Painted on a board the sign was displayed swung from a staff at Divisional Headquarters.

Broody: Lethargic. Sleepy. Slack. A frequent expression on the drill-ground by drill-sergeants to liven men up, e.g., "You there, don't get broody, get a move on".

28

Brownies, The: Originally a nickname for the Land Army girl workers during the. War, from their being garbed in brown. Also the girl-messengers in Government offices from the brown overalls when on duty.

Bubbly: Rum. (Navy.) The name also for the look-out man posted by men gambling or playing some prohibited game, such as "Crown and Anchor".

Bubbly Jocks, The: *See* Nicknames of Regiments.

Buck: (*Hind.*—Bâk). Exaggeration. Too full of talk, e.g., "Shut up there, not so much of your buck." Originally old Army and to some extent general slang for tall-talk or bragging. A U.S. Army term for a Private, a smart soldier—a Buck Private.

Buckshee: (*Hind.*—Bakshish). Free. Gratis. Extra. Of old Army origin from India, the word acquired in the War all kinds of applications. For instance: A usual enquiry at meal time among the rank and file was "Is there any buckshee?" meaning is there anything over, anything to spare. "Buckshee Leave" was a term for special leave, not counting as the ordinary leave, A "Buckshee Corporal" would be an extra one over normal strength. A man wanting a smoke would say to another, "Have you a buckshee cigarette about you?" i.e., one to spare me. The word of course is in ordinary everyday use in the Services for any "catch" or windfall.

Buckshee King, The: A Paymaster.

Buddy: A recruit. A chum.

Budmash: (*Hind.*—Badmash). A rascal. A thief. (Old Army.)

Buff Howards, The: *See* Nicknames of Regiments.

Buff Stick: Orderly man. A Buff-Stick is a polishing instrument and the man appointed daily to take charge of a hut or barrack room, being exempted from certain parades in consequence, is supposed to employ his time with his Buff-Stick.

Buggly, To: To exchange or swap.

Bug Hutch: A small hut or sleeping place.

Bulge: *See* Blister.

Bull, The: A nickname given to Lord Allenby. Says a writer in the *Morning Post*: "It was Tommy's way, not only from his leader's physical proportions (he is reputed to be the biggest of our fighting Generals) but from his blunt simplicity and directness." The nickname was officially recognized in the "Sign" or Badge of the Third Army, when commanded by Lord Allenby, which had a black bull's eye on a white disc, on the usual black bar on a red field of the "Army Sign".

Bulldog Corps, The: An occasional name in the War for the Sixth Army Corps, suggested by the Corps Sign, a Bull-dog, The tenacity of the corps in heavy fighting in 1917–18, under the command of Sir Aylmer Haldane, added point to the nickname.

Bullet, A: A nickname for a type of small aeroplane, introduced in 1915 by Vickers.

Bullet with a Name on it, A: A familiar phrase with reference to the chances of a man being killed in action, e.g., "I was all right; I knew there wasn't a bullet with my name on it".

Bullock, A: A bluejacket's term for a Marine.

Bully, or Bully Beef: The canned corned beef which forms ordinarily a considerable part in Service rations. Originally a Navy term and probably derived from the French *bouillon*.

Bully the Troops, Don't: An expression by way of rebuke to anyone talking too loudly or too much.

Bummer: Bombardier. Also, officer's batman.

Bumming the Chat: Having too much to say. Doing all the talking.

Bump, Give Your Head a: Pull yourself together. Wake up. Bestir yourself.

Bump, To: To shell, e.g., "The gunners are doing a lot of bumping to-day". "That village looks well bumped".

Bun Strangler, A: Teetotaller. (From their supposed predilection for a bun diet. Old Army.)

Bun Wallah: A man given to frequenting a Temperance bar in preference to the "wet" canteen.

Bunce: Something for nothing.

Bundabust: (*Hind*. Band-o-bast—a tying or binding). Preparations: preliminary arrangements for anything. (Old Army.)

Bundle, A: A wife. (Navy, *see* Bundle-man.)

Bundle-Man, A: A Lower Deck phrase for a married man, apparently suggested by the small bundle tied up with a blue handkerchief which married seamen in a Rome Port usually take ashore with them when going on leave.

Bundle or Ten: A packet of ten cigarettes. The tens of various suits in a pack of cards. Also, Army blankets, always rolled in tens.

Bundook: A rifle (*See* Bandook.)

Bung, Bungy, Bung-Hole: Cheese.

Bung in it, Put a: Shut up. Stop talking. Also (in a hut or barrack-room), Close the door.

Bungs, Jimmy: The cooper on board ship. (Navy.)

Bunjee: The Officer Instructor of Physical Training. (Navy.)

Bunker Plate with Spanner, A: A tin of sardines fitted with a patent opener. (Navy.)

Bunkey Boo: A nickname for General Sir J.M.S. Bunker, Inspector of R.H.A. and R.F.A. A sentence in the Royal Artillery War Commemoration Book (p. 286) runs thus: "The Battery Commander had two jobs to do. He was early told that to say 'Bunkey Boo' to a young subaltern was enough to keep him awake all night, and he found it perfectly true, and that this dark saying had a most important moral attached".

Bunting Tosser (also Bunts or Buntin'): Signalman. (Navy.)

Bunty: *See* Nicknames.

Burbury: Army vernacular for the French town of Burbure.

Burglars: Bulgarians.

Burgoo: Porridge. (Old Army but originally a Navy word, dating from the 18th Century.)

Burney Gear: The Paravane and its gear. (From the name of the inventor, Lt. Commander C.D. Burney, R.N.)

Burnt Cinders: Windows. (Rhyming slang.)

Burnt Offering, A: A dish of meat baked with potatoes round it. A bluejacket's term; from the state in which the meat sometimes arrives at the mess-table owing to the cook's want of attention.

Bus: In the War, "Bus" had a wide popularity at first among airmen generally, when speaking of their own machines. Latterly, however, the word came to be regarded as rather bad form from its becoming a hackneyed expression and being taken up by outsiders.

Business: Army vernacular for the French town of Busnes.

Butterfly Boat: A familiar term for the cross-Channel leave boats, principally on the Southampton–Havre service.

"Butt in": Motto of the T.B.D. *Sportive*, whose ship's badge is a goat.

Butt in, To: To interrupt. To interfere.

Butt-Notcher, A: A familiar War term for a sniper, who, as some did, kept tally of his victims by cutting notches on the butt of his rifle.

Button Loose, A: Silly. Soft headed.

Buy, To: To have something not desired, such as a job, thrust on one unexpectedly, e.g., "Just as he was going out, he ran into the Corporal and bought a fatigue". Also to obtain something by craft (*cf.* Click, *also* Wangle). Another meaning: to be scored oft or victimised. Of a man getting an answer to a question which made him ridiculous: "He bought it that time".

Buzz, A: A rumour: e.g., It's all the buzz. Used also of a report which started activity. In the Navy, on board ship in the Grand Fleet at Scapa, for instance, the arrival of an urgent message as to enemy movements would always result in a "buzz" i.e., general activity and preparation for sea. On that would follow a "Flap" and then a "Panic", as the preparations for putting to sea 'progressed at ever increasing pressure. (*See* Flap and Panic.)

Buzz off: Get away.

Buzz to: To telephone on the Buzzer machine (*q.v.*).

Buzzed, To be: To be killed (probably from the sound of a bullet in flight.)

Buzzer: A Naval Wireless Signalman. A Member of the Royal Engineers Signal action, known collectively as "The Buzzer", from the name of the original Army standard-type "Buzzer Telephone Machine", known as the Buzzer. It was Superseded in 1916 by the "Fuller-phone" from the name of the officer, its inventor.

Buzznagger, A: A man who talks too much.

Byng Boys, The: The name adopted by the Canadian troops, so brilliantly distinguished under Lord Byng In 1917, being suggested by "The Bing Boys are Here", a *revue* in London very popular among men on leave. The Canadians, it is recorded, in one action, on capturing a German second-line, signalled back to the artillery, barrage-firing immediately ahead, to let the gunners know their position and lift the barrage further on, "The Byng Boys are here".

C.O.D., A: A common War expression, used of any extra large shell on being fired, or of one from the enemy. The initial are the ordinary commercial abbreviation for "Cash on Delivery", and as used at the front meant that when the big shell hit there would be the deuce to pay.

C. of E.: The Service abbreviation for Church of England; in the War stamped on Identity Discs (*q.v.*), so that in case of death men should be buried with the rites of their Creed. "R.C." stood for Roman Catholic and "NC." for Nonconformists in general.

C3: The classification for conscripted men under the Military Service Act of 1916, implying unfitness for active service overseas. The term "C3" has since practically established itself in the language as a term implying inferiority of type.

C.B.: The usual abbreviation for Confinement to Barracks the punishment for minor offences, extending over a number of days, according to the offence.

C.O.: Commanding Officer, employed colloquially perhaps more often than "O.C." An officer of whatever rank, though referred to familiarly as the "C.O.", or the "O.C.", would sign officially "O.C." this or that whatever his command might be.

C.I.V.: The initials of the name of the historic "City Imperial Volunteers" of the Boer War. The Navy adopted the initials as a nickname for the five years' service men, specially entered under Lord Selborne's *régime* at the Admiralty not long after the Boer War. They were alternatively called, "Selborne's Light Horse". (*See* Ticklers.)

C.M.A.R.: "Can't Manage a Rifle". The initials R.A.M.C., read backwards. R.A.M.C. men were unarmed and the term was applied in jest.

C.M.B.: Coastal Motor Boat. *See* Scooters.

Cadet: A new Military significance was given to the word in the War. The Cadets of the War were a temporary emergency organization formed to make good the shortage of officers through casualties. They were mostly selected from N.C.O. ranks at the front and O.T.C.

youths nearing military age, and underwent a course of intensive training at special centres, in due course receiving Temporary Commissions and being drafted to units overseas. They wore officer's uniform, without rank badges, and with a white cap band. There was also a special Mercantile Marine Cadet establishment with schools at Chatham, Portsmouth, Cardiff and Greenock, for training apprentices and officers in gunnery, and methods of dealing with submarine attack.

Cady: The "Kilmarnock" or "Balmoral" caps worn in Scottish Regiments.

Cag, A: Gossip: argument. (Navy.)

Cagnas: Barracks. (A French Army term used by certain Canadian regiments.)

Cain and Abel: Table. (Rhyming slang.)

Cake Walk, A: An easy task. E.g., Of an easily carried out operation—"We did a cake walk over".

Calm-Laylas, The: A nickname for the men of the native Egyptian Labour Corps, derived from the refrain of the droning chant of the men leading camels on the march—"Kam Layla, Kam Yom!" "How many nights, how many days?" (i.e., "before this weary task will be over!")

Calvert's Entire: *See* Nicknames of Regiments.

Camarhas, The: *See* Nicknames of Regiments.

Came Up, Before You: Before your time: before you joined up. A phrase used by way of sarcasm by an older soldier to a bumptious younger man.

Camel, The: The nickname of a type of Sopwith scout aeroplane carrying Vickers and Lewis guns. (From its distinctive appearance.)

Camel Corps, The: An occasional jocular name for Infantry, in allusion to their heavy packs.

Camelier: An Australian term for a member of the Imperial Camel Corps in Egypt and Palestine.

Camel-Wallah: Native Camel Driver. (*Hind.*—Wala.—A person in any employment, a fellow, etc. *See* Wallah.)

Camouflage: From the French word *Camoufler*, to blind or veil; also Italian *Camuflare*, to "make up". *Camoufle* was the term in the 17th and 18th Centuries for the screen in front (towards the audience) of the candles of the footlights in a theatre.

The word was first adopted in the War by the French, to express deceptive concealment—actually, the concealment of the fact that a deception is being practised, the essential feature being deception. On land, at the outset of the War, a simple method of concealment, in particular for gun positions, was employed; by means of boughs of trees and grass, etc., strewn over canvas screens or netting. This gave place to camouflage proper in an unlimited variety of forms, the general idea being to make the camouflaged object harmonize with its surroundings, and be either indistinguishable, or readily mistaken for something else. Devices were innumerable. Outlying snipers were camouflaged in canvas garments painted to tally exactly with their surroundings. Guns and limbers, transport wagons, railway carriages, all underwent various processes of treatment to that end. The head-dress of troops in chalky districts was whitened, and in muddy districts browned, steel helmets were covered with sandbag cloth; roads were camouflaged with stretches of screens along the sides painted with scenery in keeping with the natural features of the neighbourhood and so on. In France and England some hundreds of people were kept busy producing camouflage materials, etc., for every kind of deceptive purpose.

Most noteworthy perhaps of all the achievements of Camouflage in the War was the part played in the strategy of the autumn campaign of 1918 in Palestine by the 15,000 camouflaged dummy horses (sacks. of straw on sticks) set up in abandoned cavalry camps in the Jordan Valley, which, by completely deceiving the energy airmen, enabled Lord Allenby to transfer his entire cavalry forces secretly, right across the whole country to the sea coast, from one flank of the Army to the other, Without the enemy having the least idea of what was happening or where the attack was to be delivered.

In the Navy, at the outset of operations, a system of painting was adopted to make it difficult for the enemy to judge range in action. Then, the painting of an imitation bow-wave was adopted, to give the impression of speed. With the extension of German submarine activity "Dazzle" painting came in (*see* Dazzle Painting), With the idea of making it difficult for a submarine to make out the course of a proposed victim. "Etienne" in *A Naval Lieutenant* tells this story: "There is a letter from a Camouflage officer to a merchant skipper who protested against the vivid splashes of blue and green and red with which his ship was being decorated. The Camouflage officer wrote in reply: 'Dear Sir,— The object of camouflage is not, as you suggest, to turn your ship into an imitation of a West African parrot, a rainbow in a naval pantomime, or a gay woman. The object of camouflage is rather to give the impression that your head is where your stern is.'"

Beyond its Service use, the word Camouflage came into vogue as an expression implying any deception. A prevarication or half-lie would be "camouflaged truth"; a doubtful patriot might find himself called a "camouflaged Hun"; Private Jones, whose smartness was questionable, would be referred to as "Jones camouflaged as a soldier".

The official post-War definition of "Camouflage" is, "the art of concealing that something is concealed". (*Manual of Field Words*, 1921, p. 23.)

Canard: the name given to a type of aeroplane with the elevator In front and without a tail, so having a duck-like appearance In the air.

Canaries, The Old: *See* Nicknames of Regiments.

Canary, A: A name for any soldier wearing a yellow brassard; an Instructor at a gas school, or one of the Sanitary Corps of the R.A.M.C.; also the battalion Sanitary Orderlies attending to incinerators latrines etc., work for which men were usually detailed for punishment. Canaries (the birds) were used in the War by the Royal Engineer Tunnelling Companies as Gas Detectors, being quickly affected by the presence of gas, otherwise imperceptible, in the mine galleries. An officer tells this story of one bird: "Twice a particular bird gave the necessary warning by dropping off his perch. Having recovered on both these occasions, he evidently considered he had 'done his bit,' as, on the next and future visits, he habitually fell off his perch immediately he entered the gallery, although there was no suspicion of gas. Consequently the bird had to be relieved of future duty, and took his place as the Commanding Officer's pet".

Cane, The: Punishment. E.g., "Smith got properly caned at the Orderly Room this morning", i.e., got a stiff sentence of C.B.

Cane, To: To damage severely; to shell heavily.

Canned Up: Drunk.

Cannon Fodder: (*German*—Kanone Futter). German cavalry slang used contemptuously for infantrymen of the Line. The term itself is said to have originated with Frederick the Great, in the same spirit. *Cf.* The French "Chair aux Canons" sometimes attributed to Napoleon.

Canteen Eggs: A Gas Attack. The age of eggs used at the canteen was not guaranteed.

Canteen Medal, A: The Good Conduct Medal awarded to men with four good conduct stripes. Being sometimes gained by men who were hard drinkers, but had sufficiently strong heads to avoid betraying themselves and so escaping a charge of being drunk, the medal acquired often jestingly the name of Canteen Medal. Also, an old Army term for beer stains on a soldier's tunic.

Canteen Stinker, A: A cheap cigarette. A "gasper".

Canuck, A: A Canadian. (The term was known in Canada and the United States for years before the War.)

Cap Badge, A: A piece of bone. After distributing the meat ration the mess orderly might say, "Does anyone want a cap badge?"

Cape of Good Hope: Soap (rhyming slang.)

Caprete: (*Arabic*). Matches.

Carfindo: A ship's carpenter. (Old Navy.)

"Carl the Caretaker's in Charge!": A phrase on the Western Front among both British and American troops when finding themselves in a "quiet" sector with few indications of enemy activity. "The trenches opposite", writes an officer, "were said to be in charge of Carl the Caretaker, a methodical old man whom the Kaiser had left in charge while the troops were elsewhere. Many were the stories told about him in different parts of the line; sometimes he was credited with a family, a 'Missus' and 'three little nippers.' Sometimes he was 'Hans the Grenadier,' owing to an occasional fancy for a night bombing party. Sometimes he was called 'Minnie's husband!' " (*See* Minnie.)

Carney: Artful. Sly.

Carry On: Originally a naval word of command, meaning "Continue as before". Used universally in this sense in the War alike in the Army and at home. "Carryon" is, of course, now an everyday phrase.

Cart, A: A bed. (Old Army.)

Carving Knife: Wife. (Rhyming slang.)

Casabianc: The last one left. E.g., "Have you any cigarettes?" "Sorry, old man, this is Casabianc". (The allusion is, of course, to the poem of the boy on the burning deck, "Whence all but he had fled".)

Cashed In: Finished. Dead. From card slang: To cash in one's "chips" at the end of a game and settle up.

Cast Iron Sixth: *See* Nicknames of Regiments.

Castor Oil Artist: A Surgeon. A Doctor.

Castor Oil Dragoons: *See* Nicknames of Regiments

Casualties of the Great War: According to an American official estimate (1923), the casualties of the belligerent nations in killed and missing (exclusive of wounded and only dealing with combatants) were, in round numbers, as follows:—

Great Britain	1,000,000
France	1,385,000
Russia	1,700,000
Germany	1,600,000
Austria	800,000
Italy	364,000
Turkey	250,000
U.S.	50,000
Serbia	125,000
Roumania	100,000
Bulgaria	100,000
Belgium	102,000
Greece	7,000
Portugal	2,000

The toll of the War in human life, counting in both combatants and non-combatants, is thus graphically set forth by another American statistician. He pictures the vast host of fallen passing a given spot, ten abreast, day and night. To pass the spot it would, he says, take the British dead ten days, the French dead eleven days, the Russian dead five weeks. All the Allied fallen would take two and a half months; the enemy dead six weeks; and a column of all the killed in the War four months.

Casualties of the British Empire in the Great War

	Military Forces	Royal Naval Division	Royal Navy	Royal Air Force	Mercantile Marine	Followers	Total
United Kingdom	696,293	8,723	38,859	5,695	15,168	94	764,832
India	63,056	–	271			–	62,327
Canada	56,639	–	174			63	56,813
Australia	59,330	–	147			2	59,540
New Zealand	16,711	–	16			3	16,729
South Africa	7,121	–	6			–	7,130
Newfoundland	1,204	–	120			–	1,324
Other British Possessions	5,022	–	–			45,551	50,573
	904,376	8,723	39,593	5,695	15,168	45,713	1,019,268

Graves: 550,000 identified; 150,000 unidentified. Missing (not known graves): 300,000.

Category Man: A man medically pronounced unfit for Overseas Service. One capable of light duties on Home Service, or employment at a Base, on Lines of Communication, in Hospital Ships. "Category" acquired at the Front a general meaning of something inferior, second or third rate, and was used in that sense colloquially, e.g., "This is a category sort of road", "Without actually Calling you a liar, I would put you down as a Category Man—C3 in veracity".

Cats, The: The name given to the four Battle-Cruisers of the *Lion* and *Tiger* Class of the First Battle-Cruiser Squadron of the Grand Fleet. They were: the *Lion, Tiger Queen Mary,* and *Princess Royal.* Also, colloquial for Caterpillar Tractor Lorries, a four-wheel drive, powerful type used for hauling heavy howitzers.

Cat, Not Room to Swing a: A very old Navy phrase, in allusion to the confined space between-decks on board old-time men-of-war, so cramped that there was no room for a bo'sun's mate to swing a cat-o'-nine-tails. It fell to the bo'sun's mates to administer floggings.

Cat Stabber: Bayonet. The soldiers' clasp knife.

Cat Walk, The: A Western Front name for the brick-paved pathway, usually one brick (nine inches) wide, laid down across farm fields in Flanders.

Caterpillar: A familiar name for the tractors fitted with "girdles", or flat slabs of metal, round their wheels, employed to haul heavy guns and large vehicles on soft ground.

Catsood: Drunk. (A corruption of the French Quatre Sous.) "Catsoos" was the usual soldiers' name for a drink at an estaminet, the price being four sous in the earlier days of the War. The price was raised later but the term remained without regard to price.

Cauliflowers, The: *See* Nicknames of Regiments.

Caulk, A: A nap, a short sleep. (Navy.)

Ceiling: The Air Force technical term for the highest flying level an aeroplane can reach at minimum safe speed; the highest point to which it can climb.

Celestials, The: *See* Nicknames of Regiments.

Cells: The Official Service term for solitary confinement, the punishment awarded for comparatively minor offences.

Cenotaph, The: The National Memorial to those who fell in the War. Designed by Sir Edwin Lutyens, R.A., the modelling being executed by Prof. F. Derwent Wood, R.A. The original plaster model was set up for the Peace Procession of 19th July, 1919. A portion of this is still preserved in the Imperial War Museum. On each side of the Cenotaph were displayed the Union Jack, the White, Red, and Blue Ensigns, the only inscription being the dates, "1914–1918" and the words "The Glorious Dead". The permanent monument was unveiled by the King on the 11th November, 1920. It bears a similar inscription and similar flags are displayed. Wreaths are deposited at the base on certain anniversaries, and a Commemorative Service is held round the Cenotaph by the British Legion. It is customary for men passing the Cenotaph to remove their hats.

Chain, Who Pulled Your: Who asked you to interfere, to "chip in". (Addressed to someone intruding on a conversation.)

Chainy Tenth, The: *See* Nicknames of Regiments.

Chalky: *See* Nicknames.

Challenge Ships: The name given in America to the two ships (*Orleans* and *Rochester*) sent in May, 1916, to France to dare molestation by German submarines in the "Blockaded Area".

Chance One's Arm, To: To take a risk: to try one's luck. Of a N.C.O. doing anything that may mean a court-martial and consequent deprival of his arm-stripe and reduction in rank.

Chancer, A: A prevaricator: a "half-truther". One taking the chance of being found out.

Char: (*Hind.*—Chhah). Tea. (Old Army.)

Char D'assaut: The French official term for a Tank.

Charles O'Malley's Own. *See* Nicknames of Regiments.

Charley: A familiar name for the Infantry soldiers' pack. Suggested by the hump-backed appearance of a soldier in heavy marching order laden with the whole field-service equipment. Derived from an old saying that a hunchbacked man was carrying his little brother Charley on his back. "Young Charley", or "Little Charley"—a haversack.

Charley Pope: Soap. (Rhyming slang.)

Charlie Noble: An old Navy name for the galley-stove funnel. Charlie Noble is said to have been a Commander in the Mediterranean Fleet about 1840, one of whose fads was the keeping the copper cowl of the galley funnel extra bright and shiny.

Charming Wife: Knife. (Rhyming slang.)

Chat, A: Vermin, in particular a louse. As vermin was one of the greatest personal afflictions among soldiers at the Front, "Chat" was one of the regular everyday words.

Chat Up, To: To strip off one's clothes to search for vermin.

Chat, Bombing the: Making up a story. Lying.

Chatham Rats: A Ship's Company from Chatham. (Navy.)

Chatty: Verminous. A possible derivation of the word Chat is that it is a cognate of Chattel or Cattle, live-stock. *Cf.* the French Chatouiller, to tickle.

Chatty but Happy: A Navy term used for a ship not very smart in appearance.

Cheese It: Stop it. That's enough. Used also as the schoolboys' "Cavé", i.e., "Look out!" E.g., "Cheese it, here's someone coming!"

Cheeses, The: *See* Nicknames of Regiments.

Check, A: A certificate of discharge. E.g., "I am hoping to get my check at the next Medical Board". Also meaning killed, e.g., "Poor old Bill got his check last night." (*Cf.* The American term, "handing in one's checks".)

Cheerio!: A very general greeting, toast, or valedictory expression, dating from before the War.

Chef: Ship's cook. (Navy.)

Chemist, The: A Surgeon. Doctor.

Chemozzle: A row. A little unpleasantness.

Chequers, The: The Divisional Concert Party of the 34th Division. [From the Divisional Sign.]

Cherry Nobs: Military Policemen. (From their red cap covers.)

Cherry Pickers, The: *See* Nicknames of Regiments.

Cherubims, The: *See* Nicknames of Regiments.

Chest, To Chuck a: To attempt to exercise undue authority: to "throw one's weight about".

Chestnut Troop, The: *See* Nicknames of Regiments.

Chestnuts: Bullets. (*Cf.* The French Army slang words, "Chataignes", "Prunes", meaning bullets.)

Chew the Fat, To: To talk too much. To argue. To grumble. Also, to spin a yarn. (Navy.)

Chewed Up, To be: To be reprimanded or told off.

Chicken, The: The U.S. Army colloquial term for the national "Eagle" badge, Worn on caps and uniform.

Chicot: Verminous. Chicot was apparently a French mispronunciation of the word "Hitchy-Khoo", originally a word in an American popular song. As to the employment of Chicot, a French woman in a billet behind the Line, desired to wash a soldier's shirt, would enquire first if it was chicot. If not verminous the man would reply, "No Hitchy Koo".

China, or Old China: Chum. (A contraction for China Plate, which is rhyming slang for "Mate".)

China Tenth, The: *See* Nicknames of Regiments.

Chinese Attack, A: Not strictly speaking an attack as the word is usually understood. Artillery would put down a bombardment on an enemy trench exactly as though the prelude to an infantry assault, while the troops in front shouted, showing dummies and an array of bayonets over the parapets. The bombardment would then be "lifted" over the enemy's trench further to the rear, and after that suddenly come back heavily on the enemy's front line, in that way catching his infantry, who would, on the bombardment moving on, have issued from their shelters and be again manning their front trenches in expectation of infantry attack. Heavy casualties to the enemy were usually the result.

Chinese Rolls-Royce: A Ford car (R.A.S.C.).

Chink, A: In the War the usual term for a man of the Chinese Labour Corps: also any Chinaman. Chink is an old pre-War name for a Chinaman, long current in the East-End of London and the Chinese quarters of Liverpool, Cardiff, etc., and in America.

Chinny: (*Hind.*—Chini). Sugar.

Chin Wag: Talk: voluble discussion.

Chip In, To: To interfere. To intervene.

Chippy: *See* Nicknames.

Chippy Chap, A: A man of carpenter's rating. (Navy.)

Chips: Ship's carpenter. (Navy.) Pioneer sergeant. (Army.)

Chit: (*Hind.*—Chitthi). A letter. Note: Official Form. Voucher, etc. "Chit", as an adopted word, dates back to the old East India Company times, and is over 150 years old, being originally used for Club and Mess vouchers. It early became a Service word for correspondence, official and other, and is fully established nowadays. At the Front in the War, everything written was colloquially a "chit", from private letters to official correspondence.

Choker, A: A cigarette.

Chokey: (*Hind.*—Chauki). Service colloquial for prison.

Chow up, A: A squabble. A row. A hot argument. E.g., "There was a regular chow up over it".

Christians Arise: A nickname given to a Turkish big gun, and its shell, at the Dardanelles. Also, a name for the early morning *réveille* bugle call. *See* Angel's Whisper.

Christmas Tree Order, In: Heavy marching order. Suggested by the laden appearance of a soldier as it were "hung round" with the paraphernalia of his complete service equipment.

Christmas Truce, The: The exceptional occurrence of Christmas Day, 1914, in some sectors of the Western Front. A sort of fraternization took place here and there in front line trenches between British and Germans, and men met in the intervening "No Man's Land" and exchanged cigarettes, etc. "It began", Lord French, in his book, "1914", says, "by individual unarmed men running from the German trenches across to ours holding Christmas trees over their heads". The British authorities issued stringent orders against the recurrence of anything of the kind, and certain officers in charge were severely called to account for what had happened. On Christmas Day, 1915, at one or two points the Germans sang carols and tried to come out into No Man's Land, calling on our men. Staff Officers, however, had been posted in our trenches to prevent fraternization and shells from our artillery quickly made the enemy run back.

Chuck: Bread. Food.

Chuck a Dummy, To: To faint on parade (with a suggestion of malingering). To report sick without reasonable cause.

41

Chuck One's Hand In, To: To refuse or stop doing anything.

Chuck One's Weight About, To: To appear unduly important, e.g., Of a newly promoted officer:—"Now he's got two pips up, he does chuck his weight about".

Chuck Up, A: A salute. From the act of throwing up the hand to the forehead in saluting.

Chum, Long Eared: A Mule.

Chum, Long Faced, or Tailed, A: A horse.

Chum, Long Haired, A: A girl. Sweetheart.

Chummy Ship, A: A naval expression when the Ship's Company of one ship in a fleet or squadron is on specially friendly terms with that of another. Each ship would be the "Chummy Ship" of the other. On a foreign squadron visiting our ports, as on the occasion of a Naval Review, those on board certain British ships are told off to see to the entertainment of the Ship's Companies of corresponding ships of the visitors, and the ships become "Chummy Ships".

Chuprow, Chub-a-Row, Chipperow: (*Hind.*—Chuprao). Shut up. Cease talking.

Church-by-Hand: An emergency or makeshift performance of Divine Service on board ship on Sunday, when the regular service cannot be held. (Navy.) *See* Stand-up Prayers.

Churchyard Clock, As Many Faces as a: Used of an unreliable man. (Old Navy.)

Cinch, A: An absolute certainty. Something easy to do, e.g., "It's a dead Cinch". Apparently derived from the Mexican word "Cincha", a belt or girdle, a saddle-girth. (The "C" is pronounced soft, as in Cinders in Mexico and the American Southern States. In Canada and the Northern States it is pronounced hard, as "K".)

Cinch, To: To grip or fasten.

Cinema: In the War, behind the Line, on at least the Western Front, Cinemas were often to be met with being generally "run" by the Expeditionary Force Canteens (*q.v.*) by way of affording relaxation for the men from the strain of war. (The writer of this entry particularly remembers on one occasion, on "coming out" of Havrincourt Wood, seeing with a sense of great relief, Charlie Chaplin featured just behind the Line.)

Circus, The (also Richthofen's Circus): The name given colloquially in the Air Force in the War to any specially selected squadron which cruised from one point on the Front to another whenever offensive air strength was required. "Richthofen's Circus", undoubtedly the most widely known of all, comprised a group of German aeroplane squadrons, the scourge for months of the Western Front in 1917, led by the celebrated German airman, Baron von Richthofen. This "Circus" numbered from 15 to 20 machines per squadron and made a showy display, all the machines being painted glaring colours. Some had scarlet bodies, ringed yellow blue and white; others silver planes and gold noses; red bodies and green wings; blue bodies and red wings, etc. Brilliant colouring was characteristic of German aeroplanes on all Fronts. Richthofen led in a vivid vermilion-coloured plane. Voss and Wolff, leaders of other "Circuses", affected similar distinctive colours, the former usually leading in a conspicuous black and white chequered machine.

Civvies: Mufti or "plain clothes", the latter being the Cavalry and Navy term for civilian clothes: Mufti is usually an Infantry word. "Civvies", universally used in the "New Army" in the War for Civilian clothes, is a Service term at least 70 years old.

Civvy, A: A civilian.

Civvy Kip, A: (Civvy—civilian, Kip—the old Army word for a bed). A real bed, as contrasted with a "shake-down". During the War, in French villages behind the Front Line, feather beds were usually to be found and a man speaking of his Rest-Billet where one was available, would refer to it as a "Civvy Kip".

Clack A: Gossip. A rumour.

Clacker, A: A chatterer. A man given to spread rumours. A loose talker.

Clean and Polish—We're Winning the War: A war-time sarcastic phrase often heard at the front among men grumbling when too much importance seemed to be paid by their officers to appearances, or "Spit and polish"; the keeping buttons, etc., bright and so forth, a detail that was insisted on, for disciplinary reasons in some battalions almost up to the fighting line.

Clean as a Button Stick: A smart soldier. Spick and span.

Click, To: To meet with good (or bad) luck. A word in universal use and with every kind of meaning at the Front in the War. To "click" might mean for instance, that a man had succeeded in something, had secured a good job, had made good his advances or "got off with a girl", or that he had got into trouble and been punished. That he had been wounded and even killed, e.g., "Poor old Tom got clicked by a sniper this morning". "To click a Blighty" was a usual term for a wound which meant a man being sent to England. A possible derivation of the word is from the clicking or "engaging" of wheels in machinery, as in the gear of a motor-car.

Click, With a: Smartly. A phrase adopted in allusion to a drill-ground word of command that in certain exercises the heels should come together with a "click" which was parodied variously. For instance, of someone showing pleasure at getting good news, it would be said, "His ears went back with a click".

Clickety Click: 66 in the game of "House".

Client, A: Anyone. A fellow, e.g., "He's a rum old client".

Clink: Cells. The Guard Room. Prison. "I've sat in clink without my boots, admiring how the world was made" (Kipling). "Clink" is a survival of 18th Century thieves' slang, a name for Newgate and other jails, suggested by the clanking of the fetters and leg-irons of the prisoners. "The Clink" in particular, was the name of a large prison in Southwark, which was burned down in the Gordon Riots of 1780.

Clinker: A Prisoner.

Clobber: Uniform. Clothing. General equipment. (Romany and East End slang.)

Clod, To: To shell heavily, e.g., "Jerry is clodding hard to-day." Suggested by the heaving up of the earth as shells burst on impact.

Clods: Copper coins.

Clout, To: To do anything with eagerness. To eat greedily, e.g., "That fellow clouted six eggs this morning for his breakfast".

Clutching Hand, The: Applied sometimes to a Quartermaster Sergeant, as being popularly supposed—unjustly often probably—to benefit personally when there was a shortage of anything, rations, etc. The phrase would seem to have originated with a certain film melodrama of an exceptionally lurid kind. Also, an Air Force nickname for the "D.H. 6" (De Havilland) aeroplane in use in 1917–18 as an elementary training machine.

Coal Box: A German heavy shell. From the dense black smoke at its bursting first familiarized the public in England with the word. The Germans had a similar term for the same thing: "Kohlenkasten".

Coal Heaver, A: A Penny (Game of "Crown and Anchor".)

Cobber, A: Comrade. A friend or chum. (An Australian word.)

Cockpit: The Observer's compartment in an aeroplane, fitted with fighting equipment—machine-gun and ammunition, Véry Light pistol, etc.

Coffee Cooler, A: A shirker (U.S. Army slang.)

Coffin Nail: A cheap cigarette.

Coggage (Coggidge): (*Hind.*—Kaghaz). Paper. Writing paper. A newspaper, etc. (Old Army.)

Coil up One's Ropes, To: To die (Navy.)

Colco-Pari: A Bulgarian word used everywhere on the Salonika Front, meaning "How much?" In everyday employment in bargaining with natives in villages, it acquired a special significance in connection with the illicit traffic that sprung up; soldiers selling biscuits, chocolate, tinned fruit, etc., bought at the canteens at low prices, to the local people at often considerable profit. In the end the authorities intervened and stopped the traffic, but the word Colco-Pari, as synonymous with bargaining, continued in use. To prevent similar practices going on among the American Troops on the Western Front, everything sold in American Army Canteens was marked and stamped "This is U.S. Property and Cannot be Sold".

Cold Feet: Nervousness. Cowardice. (Originally an Air Force phrase.)

Cold Meat Ticket: The soldier's Identity Disc (*q.v.*). It bore his name, regimental number and creed, and was worn under the uniform to serve as the means of identification in case of the wearer being killed.

Cold, To have Someone: To be master of the situation, e.g., "We had Jerry cold in that last affair".

Cold, To Leave One: To annoy or bore. Presumably from the French colloquialism, "*cela me laisse froid*", i.e., "It's a matter of complete indifference. It doesn't interest me."

Colours, The: In the British Army the Colours have not been taken into the field by regiments since 1881. The Canadian "Princess Pats" were the only regiment that had regimental colours with them on the Western Front in the War. In British regiments eventually Company Colour were round necessary by many units, and were often improvised to serve as guiding points to the artillery in barrage firing. They were either improvised on the spot, or else, as with the Royal Scots, specially made at home and sent out. After the Armistice, the Battalions occupying Cologne and the Rhine districts had their Colours sent out to them from the depôts and places such as Churches, Town Halls, and other public buildings where they had been deposited during the War. In 1919 a King's Colour (a Union Flag) was presented to each Service Battalion engaged in the War, on the understanding that on disbandment it should be deposited in a Church or public institution locally connected with the Unit.

Colours, Bayonets and Drums in the City of London: The following corps alone of the Forces of the Crown have the privilege of marching through the City of London with Colours flying, Drums beating and Bayonets fixed:

The Grenadier Guards.

The Buffs (East Kent Regiment.)

The Royal Marines.

The Royal Fusiliers (City of London Regiment.)

The Honourable Artillery Company.

The 3rd Battalion Grenadier Guards, the Buffs, the Royal Marines and the 7th Battalion (Territorial) of the Royal Fusiliers have possessed the privilege ever since Charles II's reign, owing to historic and traditional connections with the old City Trained Bands and certain recruiting arrangements of former days. The privilege was specially extended in the Great War to all battalions of the Grenadier Guards, and in October, 1924, to all battalions of the Royal Fusiliers and to the Honourable Artillery Company. The H.A.C. formally availed themselves of it first on "Remembrance Day", 1924 (November 11th), when marching to the Service at the City War Memorial in front of the Royal Exchange.

Columbus, The Knights of: An American Roman Catholic organization, somewhat similar to the Y.M.C.A., which, on the entry of the United States into the War, established canteens, rest-hostels, etc., in England and France, wherever U.S. troops were stationed.

Column, To Dodge the: To shirk a duty. To absent oneself from Parade, etc.

Comb, The: The popular newspaper term used in the War for the process of obtaining men for the Army by compulsorily thinning out from the professional classes and trades and Government Offices all physically fit. At the Front the non-combatant branches were also dealt with.

Come it, To. (To Come the Old Soldier; to Come the Old Man): To attempt to shirk anything. To try to bluff someone. Also, to be domineering.

Come the Double, To: To take more than one's share.

Comic Business: An Air Force term for Flying.

Comic Cuts: A colloquial term for the "Intelligence Summary", issued daily by Headquarters of Corps, Divisions and Brigades, displayed on notice boards and read publicly in orders. As a certain amount of the information given was mere propaganda, and often of a somewhat romancing nature, it was generally received more or less derisively among men at the Front in the War. (The phrase came from the name of a popular comic paper.)

Commandeer: To annex. To take forcibly. An old Cape-Dutch word which came into Army language in the Boer War.

Commo: Communication Trench.

Compo: Pay. Money.

Compree: (*French*—Compris). Understand! See!

"Comrades of the Mist": A term for the Grand Fleet of American Navy origin, recalled by Lord Beatty in his farewell speech to the American Squadron serving with the Grand Fleet, on their departure after the Armistice.

Conchy: Conscientious Objector.

Conk (or Conk out), To: An Air Force term for the engine of an aeroplane failing or giving out.

Consolidate, To: To take measures for holding a captured position to meet a counter attack. The word was used colloquially with a variety of meanings: in courting, for instance, to make good one's advances to a girl.

Contemptibles (also Old Contemptibles), The: This now historic phrase originated with the Kaiser's address to the German Army issued at Aix la Chapelle on August 19th, 1914. The Kaiser's words were as

46

follows:—"It is my Royal and Imperial command that you concentrate your energies, for the immediate present, upon one single purpose, and that is that you address all your skill, and all the valour of my soldiers, to exterminate first the treacherous English and then walk over General French's contemptible little army." The men of the Old Army, who stopped the German onset before Ypres, accepted the sneer as a title of honour, and after their practical annihilation facing the enemy, their successors of the New Army applied the name "Old Contemptibles" to them in admiring memory of their heroism. There is a curious historical parallel. In the Netherlands War of Independence, in the 16th Century, Philip of Spain gave the name "the Beggars" (Gueux) in contempt to the Flemish nobles who led the revolt, and the name was adopted as a title of honour and their own name by the nobles and their followers. *Apropos* the Kaiser's sneer, what Bismarck once said of the British Army may be recalled. There was at the time friction over a colonial question between England and Germany, and someone suggested to Bismarck that it might be possible for the British Army to land on the German coast. "Bah!" was the reply, with a contemptuous reference to its small size, "If it did I would ring for the police and have it locked up!"

Contour Chasing: An Air Force term for an aeroplane flying very low, and as it were following the slopes and rises of the ground.

Contract, To Mess up the: To spoil or wreck anything.

Cook of the Grot, The: A Mess Orderly. (Navy.)

Cook's Tour, A: A colloquial phrase for the customary tour round the trenches by officers and N.C.O.'s of relieving, or newly arrived, units, before the newcomers "went in" in order to gain knowledge of local Conditions, the "Cook's Tourists" being guided by the previous holders of the position. Also, used of the trips round the trenches, permitted on occasion to foreign Allied Officers, Politicians, Journalists, and certain Civilians, under official guidance. The "Conducting Officer" taking such a party round, would speak of himself, sometimes, as a "Cook's Guide".

Cooker, A: A travelling field kitchen. Also a perversion of kukri, the Gurkha knife.

Cookhouse Official: A general term for any unreliable or baseless rumour. The Cookhouse had the reputation of being a centre of idle gossip among mess-orderlies and people whose duties took them there.

Cookies, The: *See* Nicknames of Regiments.

Cooler, The: The Guard Room. Cells. (As being a place where a disorderly or drunken man had the opportunity of "cooling his heels".)

Coop, The: The Guard Room. Cells.

Coopetty Coop: Money. (Navy.) The term is said to be derived from a story of a sea-captain who put an unruly apprentice into a hen-coop and fed him out of a trough, malting the lad call out "Coopetty Coop!"

The lad's father sued the skipper and got heavy damages. The money was paid in court, and as he picked the notes up, the father called across to the captain, "Coopetty Coop—what about it now!"

Cooshy, A: (*French* Coucher). A sleep.

Cooter Goosht: (*Hind.*—kutta—dog; gosht—food or meat). Bad food. Contemptuously "Dogs' meat".

Coots, Cooty: Vermin. *See* Chat, Chatty.

Coppa Dah: Catch this! Take hold of this! (Suggested by the thieves' slang word "Cop".)

Corned Dog: Canned beef.

Cornstalks, The: The Australians. The nickname originally meaning persons of European descent born in Australia (particularly New South Wales), is at least sixty years old.

Corps: *See* Army.

Corpse Ticket: The Identity Disc, worn round the neck of every officer and man on active service. *See* Cold Meat Ticket and Identity Disc.

Cosh: The bludgeon carried by night patrols men and trench raiders. A cosh is the name for the stick carried by London professional roughs when out for mischief.

Cot, On the: A man of a bad character, trying to amend his ways—i.e., in a moral hospital, so to speak. (Old Army.)

Coughing Clara: A nickname for a heavy gun.

Couple o' Doorsteps: A sandwich.

Courrier de l'Air, The: The propaganda journal issued from April, 1917, to November, 1918, at Adastral House, London, to give people in occupied territories in France and Belgium accurate news of the War from the Allied side. It contained also extracts from German Socialist papers, suppressed in Germany, containing news of the discontent and privations there. It was dropped by aeroplanes at first, and later, owing to the maltreatment by the enemy of airmen captured while on their errands, distributed by means of paper hydrogen balloons released whenever the wind served. The Germans inflicted a £150 fine on any person found in possession of the "Courrier de l'Air".

Cow Climbed up a Hill, There was a: A retort, equivalent to telling a man that he is a liar.

Cow Feed: Raw vegetables, Salad, etc.

Crab, A: A Midshipman (Navy.)

Crab, A Land: A Military Policeman. Also, a nickname for a type of aeroplane.

Crab Grenade: The name for a type of German hand grenade, oblong and flat, with detonating studs round the edge, and bearing a resemblance to the shell of a crab.

Crackers, To Get the: To go off one's head. Mad.

Cramp One's Style, To: To render useless. To put off one's stroke.

Crappo, A: (*French*—Crapaud). The name of a type of improvised French trench-mortar.

Crash, A: The Air Force term for a fall. An aeroplane brought down out of control. Any failure or misfortune.

Crash Dive, A: The sudden submersion of a submarine on being surprised, or in imminent danger of being rammed. (Navy.)

Crawl, To: To cadge. To cringe.

Crawling With: Full of. Alive with. Used with reference to anything from vermin upwards, e.g., "The place fairly crawled with Staff Officers".

Crawling on One's Eyebrows: Exhausted. Dead beat. An expression used of men returning thoroughly worn out—e.g., "They came in crawling on then eyebrows".

Creased, To be: Fainted. Laid out.

Creating: Grumbling. Making a fuss.

Creeping Barrage: The name given to an artillery method of covering infantry in attack by a moving wall of fire, shelling each successive enemy position immediately ahead, sweeping the ground over which the troops had to advance, according to the infantry rate of progress. The barrage moved forward by "lifts" usually fifty yards at a time, the shelling between "lifts" usually lasting a minute and a half. Watched from a distance, in rear, the barrage seemed to "creep" forward, hence the name. First used at the Battle of the Somme, 1916.

Crib, To: To grumble.

Cricket Ball, A: A type of hand grenade. From its size and shape.

Crime, A: The Service term for any kind of wrong-doing involving punishment; practically from the typing of a bootlace in a non-regulation manner to striking an officer, or murder.

Crime, To: To charge a man with a "Crime". In the Army: for instance, on a soldier being formally charge with an offence, an entry is made by a N.C.O. on a "Crime Sheet" (Army Form 256), on which in due course follows the delinquent's appearance before authority.

Criq: Brandy. (French Canadian term.)

Crown The: Colloquial for Sergeant-Major: from the badge of a crown on the Sergeant-Major's sleeve. A Company S.M. wears a crown by itself; a Regimental S.M., a crown with the addition of the Lion and Unicorn badge—e.g., "To get the Crown"—to be promoted Sergeant Major.

Crown and Anchor: The popular, though officially prohibited, gambling game in the Services, played with dice and a coloured cloth marked out in squares. The Ace, a Crown, is usually referred to as "The Lucky old Sergeant Major", and the anchor called the "Mud-hook", (Navy slang for an anchor). The players put their stakes on the squares. Usually, two or three partners run a Crown and Anchor board, one man financing the board, a second acting as a sort of umpire, and the

49

third "minding out" or keeping watch for the approach of a military policeman. Luck invariably favours the board, and in the War, when the game was constantly played in out of the way places, it was sometimes said that men in Some cases "made hundreds of pounds" at Crown and Anchor, particularly the holders of the Board.

Crucifix Corner: A name given in the War to various places on French roads where a Calvary was set up, forming a conspicuous landmark over open ground. A widely known Crucifix Corner was near Lagnicourt. A curious belief, current among the troops on the Western Front, was that the Figure on the Cross was never hit, however enemy shells might devastate everything all round and close by. Many, all the same, did suffer mutilation, but probably the majority escaped through which the general belief originated. Wrote an officer on the Western Front in a letter home: "One thing I can't understand (or can in a Catholic way). You will find out here walls standing with a crucifix or other sacred image, or the wall on which they hang, part standing: the churches the same. A church may be shattered in bits, hut the crucifix and the part on which it stands is the only solid part left in the place. This happens nine time out of ten." A curious incident in this connection is recorded to have occurred on board the battleship *Warspite* at Jutland. A heavy shell burst just inside the door of the "Church" below decks. Everything inside, chairs, fittings, etc., was wrecked and smashed to pieces. Only the Cross remained undamaged on the shattered altar.

Crucifixion: The familiar name for the official "Field Punishment No. 1". The principal feature of the punishment was the spread-eagling of the delinquent on the wheel of a gun or limber, to which he was fastened with straps or ropes, to remain "crucified" for a certain number of hours. The punishment has now been abolished.

Crummy: Dirty. (Navy.)

Crump: The universal term for any heavy shell. From the sound of its "burst" on impact, Writes an officer: "The crump goes off with a terrifying double explosion and makes a great hole in the ground".

Crump, To: To bombard with heavy shells.

Crush, A: A body of troops. A colloquial term among soldiers, mostly in referring to their own regiments. An old Army word, used of units generally in the War—e.g., "The Berkshire's Crush", "The Canadians' Crush", etc.

Crusher: A Ship's Corporal, a member of the Naval Police. (Navy.)

***Crystal Palace*, H.M.S.:** The Royal Naval Division Depot at the Crystal Palace, Sydenham. "The Crystal Palace Army" was one of the nicknames of the R.N.D. The W.R.N.S. (Wrens) and D.A.M.C. crews, etc, were trained at the Crystal Palace during the War and the Palace afterwards (1920–24) was occupied by the Imperial War Museum, which during the period was visited by over 3,000,000 people.

Crystal Palace, The: The name in the War for the huge iron mine superstructure at Loos, taken on September 25, 1915. Its two tall pit-head erections joined by horizontal corridors at some distance had a resemblance to the Sydenham Crystal Palace with its two tall water-towers. (*See* Tower Bridge.)

Cubby Hole, Cubby Hutch: A Navy term used in the Army for any small billet or dug-out.

Cuckoo Plane: A newspaper name for a type of Sopwith Aeroplane, or "Torpedo Plane", designed for dropping torpedoes. The name was given in allusion to the Cuckoo's habit of laying eggs in other birds' nest.

Cuffer, A: A story. A yarn—e.g., "Spin us a cuffer". (An old Service term.)

Cully, A: A pal. A chum.

Cumshaw: Naval slang for something "extra"; something gratis; a perquisite; a gift, equivalent to Buckshee (*q.v.*). Apparently a Pigeon-English rendering of the Chinese word Kamsia (Kam—grateful; Sia—thanks). (Cumshaw goes back to the 18th Century and Hickey in his Autobiography mentions it as a current word in China ports *circa* 1775.)

Cup and Wad: Tea and a bun in the Canteen or a Y.M.C.A. hut.

Cushy: (*Hind.*—Khush—pleasant; also popularly said to be derived from Cushion). Comfortable. Easy. Pleasant. A universal colloquial term in the war—e.g., A cushy job, billet, etc. Now practically adopted into the language. Also, Army vernacular for the town of La Cauchie, near Arras.

Cut Out, To: To steal. (Old Navy.)

Cuthberts: A name in the War, coined by "Poy", the cartoonist of the *Evening News*, and colloquially adopted by way of contempt for fit men of military age, particularly in Government Offices, who had not been "combed out" for the Army. Also, for men who deliberately avoided military service, Conscientious Objectors, etc. In "Poy's" cartoon the "Cuthberts" were represented as frightened looking rabbits.

Cuts, To Have: To be excitable or eccentric. (Navy.)

D: Represented in the Signallers' vernacular by the word "Don".

D.C.M.: Distinguished Conduct Medal. Also, colloquially, "District Court Martial".

D.F.C.: Distinguished Flying Cross.

D.F.M.: Distinguished Flying Medal.

D.R.L.S.: Despatch Rider Letter Service. The initials franked by an officer on the envelope of a letter, causing it to be carried by the service of motor-cyclists organized for the purpose.

D.S.C.: Distinguished. Service Cross. Among men expecting to be demobilised the initials were sometimes colloquially used in jest for "Decent Suit of Civvies".

D.S.M.: Distinguished Service Medal.

D.S.O.: Distinguished Service Order.

Dabster, A: A skilful fellow (*Cf.* the schoolboy word a "Dab".)

Daddy, A Sea: The Navy term for the officer who takes charge of, and sees to the welfare and instruction in everyday matters, of a new arrival or junior on board ship, putting him "up to the ropes" of sea life. In the Grand Fleet in. the War, temporary officers, on joining, were usually given each a "Sea Daddy" from among the officers of the ship to which they were appointed.

Dado: The body-belt, or "cholera belt", issued to every man in the War.

Dados: A word coined from the initials of Deputy Assistant Director of Ordnance Services which, at the Front, were seen on notices as to where things could be got—horseshoes, for instance, at one place, shirts at another, and so on. A "D.A.D.O.S." was attached to each Division and served as Universal Provider of every kind of article (upwards of 20,000 were listed), from guns to toothbrushes and tin-tacks.

Dag, A: A funny fellow. A wag.

Dag Up, To: To smarten oneself up for guard or parade.

Dago: A sea term, not usually meant too politely; applied seafaring men of Southern European Latin races, hailing from along the Mediterranean littoral. The term is sometimes used among English people in India for various kinds of foreigners, mostly of an undesirable sort.

Dags: Cigarettes.

Dags, On the: At home on long leave. (Navy.)

Daisy Pushing: A common euphemism for dead. e.g., "Old Brown's been daisy pushing a year now".

Daisy Roots: Boots. (Rhyming slang.)

Dandies, The: *See* Nicknames of Regiments.

Dandy: Fine. Excellent. An Americanism adopted on the Western Front from Canadians and U.S. Troops.

Dandy Ninth, The: *See* Nicknames of Regiments.

Dark Night Patrol: During the War, throughout the moonless periods in the winter months, a "Dark Night Patrol", as it was called, was established off Scapa and at other naval bases; usually comprising a light cruiser and two destroyers, told off to patrol from sunset to sunrise, on guard against attempts to lay mines by enemy surface-craft.

Darky: *See* Nicknames.

Darts: (*French*—Flêchettes; *German*—Stahlpfeil). A device used in the earlier part of the War for attacking troops from an aeroplane. They were steel darts of about the size of a pencil, grooved and sharp-pointed, dropped in clusters with deadly effect. On one occasion one dart from a French aeroplane killed a German General and his horse, the dart passing through the body of each into the ground. In March, 1915, a British merchant ship in the North Sea, the *Teal*, was attacked by a German aeroplane with darts, which stuck all over the decks of the ship, in the words of one on board, "like pins in a pincushion". Also, the name of a type of small, very fast aeroplane, intended for attacking warships by diving down at high speed and dropping a torpedo when at close range and just clear of the water.

Date, To Have a: To have an appointment. An American cinema phrase adopted among British airmen mostly, in the War.

Daty: Soft-headed. Suffering from sunstroke.

David: The familiar Navy name for Admiral of the Fleet, Lord Beatty. At the Dogger Bank battle, on Lord Beatty (then Sir David Beatty) quitting his disabled flagship, the *Lion*, to hoist his flag in another ship, says Mr. Filson Young, in his *With the Battle-Cruisers*, "the stokers, who had come up from below, gathered round cheering, and in the enthusiasm of the moment one of them clapped him on the back as he stepped on to the destroyer's forecastle and shouted, 'Well done, David!'"

David (or Davy), Send it Down: A soldiers' greeting to a shower of rain likely to postpone a parade.

Day, The, "Der tag": "To the day", was the German Navy toast originating some ten or twelve years before the War, in confident anticipation of victory over the British Fleet when War should come. So it is generally understood, but it is only fair to say that many German officers have denied that the toast had special reference to the British Fleet.

Day's Pack: Defaulters' punishment; pack drill; often done at the double in heavy marching order.

Dazzle Painting: The system of painting ships invented in the War as a protective device by Commander Norman Wilkinson, R.N.V.R., the well-known Marine Artist, to baffle submarine attacks. The effect was produced by means of strongly-contrasted colours, usually in variegated patterns and combinations of stripes, breaking up in appearance the accepted form of a ship; the governing idea being to mislead the captain of an enemy submarine as to the course and speed of the vessel, and make it difficult to take up an attacking position. The striped style of design adopted used mostly black, white, blue and green colours, which were decided on as the most effective for the purpose after numerous studio experiments on small ship models, made to scale. "It made a ship look", described an officer, "like a cross between a zebra and a sea-serpent off for a week-end". One of the first dazzle-painted M.L.'s (Motor Launches), arriving at Southampton, so startled a burly stoker on board a merchant ship who happened to be taking the air on deck, that, we are told, he hastily shouted down to the engine room to call up a mate:—"Bill! Bill! Come up quick, 'ere's a b—y rainbow coming alongside!"

Dead Marine: An empty bottle. A "Marine" or "Dead Marine" used in the days of hard drinking to be an accepted synonym for an empty bottle. William IV, when Duke of Clarence and Lord High Admiral, at an official dinner, is related to have said to a waiter, pointing to some empty bottles, "Take away those marines!" An elderly major of Marines present rose and said: "May I respectfully ask why your Royal Highness applies the name of the corps to which I have the honour to belong to an empty bottle?" The Duke, with the unfailing tact of his family, saved the situation. "I call them marines because they are good fellows who have done their duty and are ready to do it again!" According to Grose's *Dictionary of the Vulgar Tongue,* under the word "Marine Officer", the following libellous explanation is given: "An empty bottle" (Sea Wit), "Marine Officers being held useless by the Seamen".

Dead, On the: A teetotaller. (Old Army.)

Death or Glory Boys, The: *See* Nicknames of Regiments.

De-bus, To: An official Army term, coined in the War, for the setting down of troops brought up by motor-'bus transport. "Debussing Point" was the name given to the place where the men left the vehicles. (*See* Embus.)

Deck, Going off the: Leaving the ground. (Air Force.)

Decoy Ships: A name for certain vessels (also known as "Mystery Ships" and "Q Ships"), introduced in 1915. They were vessels of all types and builds, given the appearance of "tramps", trawlers, etc., manned by picked naval crews and armed with concealed guns, which were sent out to cruise on the trade-routes to entice German submarines into attacking them. On a U-boat opening fire in attack, the "Decoy Ship" stopped, and part of the crew, called the "Panic Party", and specially trained in the rôle, hastily lowered boats and went off, as though abandoning their ship in panic. On the U-boat closing on the apparently deserted vessel to finish her off, the men left on board, as the submarine came within close range, hoisted the White Ensign, dropped the vessel's sham bulwarks, and opened fire, usually sinking the submarine. The fortune of war was, of course, not always one-sided. The U-boat commanders learnt to be wary in approaching possible "Trap Ships", as the Germans called the "Decoy Ships", and on the "panic parties" quitting, often shelled the vessel savagely at long range. The enduring heroism of the concealed gun crews on such occasions, as recorded, is almost incredible. Remaining at their posts, with their ships on fire, or partly blown up, they—the survivors—waited until the enemy ceased firing, and eventually sunk the U-boat, when, confident that nothing living could be on board, the Germans finally came near. On the other hand, in some cases, the "Decoy Ships" met their fate in these encounters. (*See* Mystery Ships; Q Ships; Trap Ships; Mystery V.C.)

Deep End, To go off the: To get excited. To be furiously angry. (The origin of the phrase seems untraceable. Possibly suggested by the natural nervousness, and often terror, of a swimming pupil on being first told to leave the shallow end of the swimming bath and go in off the deep-end.)

Defeatist: (*French*—Défaitiste). The term applied in the War to people in Allied Countries who desired defeat and worked to that end, Originally, the term was given to the earlier Bolsheviks in Russia by the Kerensky party. The term was taken up in France, and applied to certain writers in the Paris Press and to the notorious traitor, Bolo, and his associates. Thence it passed to England.

Degommy: (*French*—Dégommé). Ungummed. Unstuck. Used of officers relieved or removed from command for failure. Dégommer was a French army term before the War. In the War, it obtained special notoriety owing to Marshal Joffre's wholesale "retiring" of generals in September, 1914. Properly, the word means to take the gum out of silk fabrics.

Dekko: (*Hind.*—Dekho—the imperative of dekhna). Look. See.

Delhi Spearmen, The: *See* Nicknames of Regiments.

Delible: Incompetent. Useless.

Delousing Chambers: A war name for the places where the vermin infested clothing of men from the trenches was cleansed. "Disinsectors" was another name for the same thing.

Demies: Invalids, Convalescents. Half-fit.

Dennis: A seafarers' old nickname for a pig on board ship, In particular "Dennis" was the name given to the big white pig of the German cruiser *Dresden*, which, on that vessel being sunk off Juan Fernandez (Robinson Crusoe's) Island by the *Kent* and *Glasgow* in 1915, was picked up while swimming away. He was given the name "Dennis" at first, but was later re-named "Tirpitz". As "Tirpitz" the pig was sold in England on behalf of Service Charities, and realized a large sum. Later, "Tirpitz" was made pork chops of. His huge head, mounted on a board, is now an exhibit at the Imperial War Museum. (*See* Tirpitz.)

Deolali Tap (otherwise Doolally Tap): (*Hind.*—Deolali—a sanatorium and rest-camp in Bombay; tap—fever). Mad. Off one's head. Old Army.

De-Racks: A pack of cards. (Back Slang.)

Derby, A: A man enlisted under the recruiting scheme introduced in the autumn of 1915 by Lord Derby, as Inspector General of Recruiting. Lord Kitchener's Appeal of 1914, nobly responded to as it was at first, in the end failed to produce men sufficient to make good the enormous casualties of the war. To supplement it, Lord Derby's Scheme of "Group-recruiting" was introduced, as a last-hope effort under the Voluntary Enlistment system. It was heartily responded to, and in three months, to the end of 1915, brought in over two and a half million men. The ever increasing losses of the War, however, compelled, early in 1916, the passing of the Conscription Acts. Men of the "Groups" of "Derbies", awaiting their turn to be called up, according to in dispensability of occupation, wore armlets lettered "G.R." (General Reserve). The German newspapers made mock of the scheme and foretold its failure; one comic illustrated paper caricaturing Lord Derby as a drummer with a burst-in drum.

Derzy (*Hind.*—Darzi). A Tailor.

Desert, To Swing it Across the: To contrive or "work" one's way into hospital. To malinger. (An Egyptian Expeditionary Force phrase.)

Deuce and Ace: Face. (Rhyming slang.)

Devil's Own, The: *See* Nicknames of Regiments.

Devil's Royals, The: *See* Nicknames of Regiments.

Devil's Wood: The name given to Delville Wood, a stretch of woodland, 160 acres in extent, with dense undergrowth, the scene of terrific fighting in the Battle of the Somme. Delville Wood is now legally a part of South Africa. The title deeds of the whole area were, after the War, made over to the Government of the Union of South Africa, as containing the graves of the South African troops who fell there.

Dial: Face. (Old slang.)

Dick, Money for: Money for nothing.

Dicky Dirt: Shirt. (Rhyming slang.)

Dicky Flurry, A: A spree on shore. (Navy.)

Dicky Flutter, A: A bet.

Dicky Leave: Absence without leave.

Dicky Run, A: Short leave. (Navy.)

Diddlum Buck: A name for the game of Crown and Anchor.

Dido, To Cut a: To excel in some freakish way. (Navy.)

Die Hards, The: *See* Nicknames of Regiments.

Died of Wounds: An answer given sometimes in jest on an absent man being called by name. *See* Barbed Wire.

Dig in the Grave, A: A shave. (Rhyming slang.)

Dig In, To: To secure or consolidate one's own position in some desirable occupation or billet. Suggested by "digging in", or entrenching, by troops after capturing a position, to hold their capture against counter-attacks.

Dig Out, To: To move off. To strike camp. Also, to wash, or tidy up generally.

Digger, A: An Australian; also a New Zealander. The name originated for Australians in the old gold-mining days, at the "diggings", and for New Zealanders among the "gum-diggers". In the War, applied both to Australians and New Zealanders, and considered a title of distinction in both cases. Australians specially claimed it, it has been said, for their trench work at Gallipoli, and New Zealanders for the work at Gallipoli, and New Zealanders for the work of the N.Z. Tunnelling Company on the Western Front. "Digger", in the War was a common term of greeting among Australian, troops, as equivalent to "churn", eventually displacing "Cobber". (*q.v.*). It was often also heard among British troops in the same sense.

Digger, Up the: In the trenches. Up the Line.

Dimback: A louse.

Dingbat, A: A batman; officer's servant. (Australian). A swab for drying decks, made out of the frayed end of a hawser. (Navy.)

Dingy: Dengue; malarial fever.

Dinkum: Genuine. Smart. Excellent. An Australian term said also to have been current formerly in Lincolnshire with the meaning "honest". In the sense of "genuine", the word "Dinkum" in the War on one occasion proved the undoing of an enemy spy. It was on Gallipoli. Two Australian officers were talking in a trench, when a third, apparently a major, joined them, and advised them not to fire in a certain direction as patrols were out there. Doubting the statement, and noting a detail wrong in the major's uniform, one of the Australians asked: "Are you fair Dinkum?" "That's right", was the reply, "I am Major Fair Dinkum". He was shot dead on the spot.

Dinkum Oil: A colloquial phrase meaning "Correct Information".

Dinky, A: A mule.

Dipped: Failed. (Navy.) Probably originating in allusion to the hauling down of the ensign in surrender.

Dirty, To Do the: To behave shabbily. To take unfair advantage.

Dirty Half Hundred: *See* Nicknames of Regiments.

Dirty Shirts: *See* Nicknames of Regiments.

Disinsector: *See* Delousing Chambers.

Ditch, The: The sea. (Navy.) E.g., "He fell into the ditch", i.e., overboard.

Ditched: Done for. Specifically a Tank Corps term for a tank bogged or sunk in swampy ground. *Cf.* Bellied.

Ditty Box: The small wooden box in which a bluejacket keeps his private belongings, letters, photos, etc. It is provided with a lock and key, but by unwritten law the Ditty Box is never locked, as a point of honour among messmates. Their money bluejackets keep in a waist-belt, and under the pillow in their hammocks at night.

Division: The theoretical basis of Army Organization in the field; a self-contained formation of all arms capable of independent action. In practice, the Cavalry is usually formed into a Cavalry Division or Corps with its own Artillery, Engineers, etc., to give it power of independent action. In actual strength a division might vary between 20,000 and 10,000 of all ranks, according to the casualties it had sustained.

Divisional Sign: *See* Signs.

Dixie (Dixy): (*Hind.*—Degshi). The Army cooking pot.

Dizzy, A: A man easily flustered.

Do, A: An event. A stunt. An attack, etc. E.g., "When is the do coming off?"; "The Somme do"; "The Havrincourt do", etc.

Do an Alley, To: (*French*—Aller). To go off. To hurry away.

"Do its Damndest!": The phrase widely attributed to General Elles, the Commander of the Tank Corps, before the Battle of Cambrai. The Tank Corps Commander on that occasion is said to have issued this order: "England expects that every Tank to-day will do its damndest". Nothing of the kind, however, was uttered by the General, and the text of his address to the Tank Corps (Special Order No. 6) contains nothing to suggest the idea. Apparently the phrase was a newspaper correspondent's invention, taken up by the Press in England and made the most of.

Do One's Nut, To: To lose one's head.

Do Svidanya: Good-bye. Au revoir. (A Russian phrase adopted by our men in North Russia and pronounced according to ability.)

Dobbs: Pork.

Dobra: Good. (*Niet Dobra*, no good). *Russian:*—used by our men in Murmansk and North Russia.

Dobying: (*Hind.*—Dhobi—a washerman). Washing clothes. (Navy.)

Dock, In: In Hospital.

Docs, The: *See* Nicknames of Regiments.

Doctor, The: A common colloquialism for Pill No. 9 in the Field Medical Chest. A strong purgative and the usual prescription in cases of suspected malingering. Also No. 9 in the game of "House". (*q.v.*)

Dodger, A: A sarcastic term for a good conduct badge. Also a Sandwich.

Dog and Bonnet, The: An occasional nickname for the Lion and Crown badge (the Royal Crest of Scotland) of the King's Own Scottish Borderers.

Dog Biscuits: An old Army term for the Army mattresses; suggested by a certain resemblance in colour and shape.

Dog Fight, A: An aeroplane squadron battle. Its apparent reckless ferocity at furious speed, with wild manoeuvring and crashes, suggested the similarity to a confused *mêlée* of fighting dogs. (Air Force phrase.)

Dog Watches: The half-watches of two hours each, from 4 to 6 and 6 to 8 p.m. on board ship. Thus the daily watches are made uneven in number, seven instead of six in the twenty-four hours. Otherwise the same man would be on watch at the same time daily throughout a cruise. The term is over two hundred years old. Among suggestions for its origin are "dodge-watch" and "docked watch". Theodore Hook suggested that it is a watch which is "cur-tailed". Various others have been offered.

Dogs: Sausages. (*See* Barker.)

Dogsbody: A Midshipman. A humorous semi-sarcastic colloquialism for any junior officer, R.N. E.g., "He's only a dogsbody sub". Also, a blue-jackets' name for peas boiled in a cloth.

Dog's Leg: The single rank-stripe of a Lance-Corporal. (From its shape.)

Doing It: Army vernacular for the town of Doingt, near Péronne.

Doings, The: A word with every kind of meaning and application. E.g., In quarters, "Pass the doings", might mean bread, salt, a pack of cards, or anything at hand. "I'll have a drop of the doings" (i.e., whatever drink there is going). "Here comes Jerry with the doings". (I.e., An enemy aeroplane sighted). "The doings come off tomorrow". (I.e., An attack will take place tomorrow.)

Doings, In the: In the Guard Room.

Dolphin, The: The name given to the Sopwith 200 h.p., four-gun aeroplane.

Don: Signallers' vernacular for the letter "D". (*See* Ack.)

Done In: Spoiled. Destroyed. Dead.

Done to the Wide: Utterly beaten. At the last gasp.

Donkey's Breakfast: A straw mattress. (Navy.)

Doo Hicky: An airman's term for any small, detachable fitting (*cf.* Gadget.)

Dooly: (*French*—Du lait). Milk.

Dope: Medicine. Poison. False information. Aeroplane fabric varnish. Also, a fool: inefficient.

DORA: D.O.R.A. The Initials of the Defence of the Realm Act, which, promulgated in installments from time to time, gave the government despotic powers over everybody and everything during the War.

Dosinghem: *See* Bandagehem.

Dots on One, To Put: To bore or tire.

Double, To Come the: To try and get more than one's share of anything.

Double X's, The: *See* Nicknames of Regiments.

Dough: Pay. Money.

Doughboys: The U.S. Soldiers' name for themselves. The name was preferred by them in the war to the name with which first the British public greeted the Americans on arrival, "Sammies" (*cf.* Uncle Sam), which was much disliked by the Americans themselves. That and another name, "Teddies" (*q.v.*), was so disliked that it is said, Major-General Sibert, commanding the first U.S. Division landing in Europe, publicly asked for suggestions for a name to correspond to the British "Tommy Atkins"; Doughboys was the result. "Doughboys" was apparently first used among the Federal Soldiers about 1862, during the War of Secession, suggested by the large globular brass buttons of the uniform which had a fancied resemblance to dumplings or "doughboys". Another suggested derivation ante-dates the origin of the word to the Mexican Campaign of 1846–7, suggesting that it originated from the adobe huts in which the U.S. Infantry were usually quartered.

Doughcock, A: A weak brained, "soft-headed" person. (Navy.) A Devonshire word—*cf.* Doughcooked—"soft" or partly cooked.

Dough Nuts: A Navy name for the "Carley Floats", life-saving rafts of circular shape, carried on board ships of war, capable of holding eight men each.

Dovecote, The: An old Army term for the quarters allotted to officers' wives on board the old Indian troop ships.

Dover Patrol, The: The Naval Force in the War based on Dover. It safeguarded the passage across the Straits of Dover of Army transports, hospital ships and mercantile traffic in general; and also the vessels carrying over the King, Ministers, Ambassadors, etc. between England and France. The Belgian coast bombardments were carried out by the Dover Patrol, whose crowning achievement was the attack on Zeebrugge on St. George's Day, 1918. (*See* Fred Karno's Navy.)

Dozen, the Old: *See* Nicknames of Regiments.

Dragged: Late for duty. (Old Army.)

Drogheda Light Horse, The: *See* Nicknames of Regiments.

Drowning Flotilla: The name given in the Dover Patrol to the German Flanders Coast submarine flotilla in consequence of its severe losses at our hands. Hardly any of the U-boats survived its third cruise. Practically all met their fate at our hands. One of the last was U.B. 116, which, manned by a crew entirely of German Naval Officers, made a forlorn-hope attempt, ten days before the Armistice, to enter Scapa and attack the Grand Fleet. Detected at the entrance, it was blown up on the mine-field and all on board perished. Colonel Repington in his "First World War", Vol. II., p. 290, visiting Admiral Sir Roger Keyes at Dover, in April, 1918, saw a chart showing Where the U-boats bad been dealt with. He says: "His graveyard shows the spots where twenty Boche submarines have been sunk since he took command in January. The trawlers and drifters fired on the U-boats, and small destroyers attacked them with depth-charges and drove them down upon the mines."

Drum, To Follow the: (*See* Band, To follow the; and Band Party). To "Follow the Drum", in its origin, is a very old Army expression, equivalent to enlistment, from the historic custom, going back centuries, of drummers being sent into towns and villages to "beat up" for recruits by marching through beating their drums to attract young fellow, who followed after the music and were enlisted by the accompanying recruiting officers.

Drum Up, To: To collect.

Drummy: The Sergeant Drummer. (Old Army.)

Duay: Mine. My own. A phrase originating in the War. Used usually in reply to some question of ownership. The word is said to be derived from the Royal motto "Dieu et mon Droit". To "come the Duay" was an occasional phrase in reference to someone making an over-display of authority.

Dub, Dub-Dub, A: A complete failure.

Dubs, The: *See* Nicknames of Regiments.

Duck Shoving: Evading a duty.

Ducks' Disease: Short legged.

Duckboards: The slatted timber paths, or walks, laid down in trenches, camps, etc., at the Front from a resemblance to the sloping hoards leading up to duck houses at the edge of a pond.

Duckboard Glide: A common term for after-dark movements along the trenches, when secrecy and quietness was essential, the men passing along as stealthily as possible.

Duckboard Harrier, A: A dispatch "runner" or messenger, whose duty took him along the duckboards in the trenches.

Dud, A: A shell that falls blind, and fails to burst. Anything that fails. Used of a man; worthless incompetent, stupid. A "dud affair", an action that failed. The word is of pre-war origin in commercial circles (e.g., "A dud cheque", i.e., dishonoured). Probably of American origin.

Duff: Pudding. Any sort of "sweet" following a meal—*cf.* "Afters".

Duffos: Ships belonging to, or commissioned at, Devonport. A Navy term, originating probably from the supposed liking of Westcountrymen for pudding or duff. Also used of bluejackets from Devonshire and Cornwall.

Dufter, The: (*Hind.*—Daftar, i.e., Office). The Orderly Room.

Dug-out: A protected place of shelter in the trenches. Also, familiarly a term not always kindly meant, for elderly officers returning to temporary service. It first came in apparently during the South African War of 1899–1902, for pensioned or retired officers who came back to service in consequence of the depicting of the active establishment through casualties in the field. In the War hundreds came forward as volunteers and served in every capacity both naval and military, in most cases filling subordinate posts, regardless of former rank. Retired admirals and captains did duty in auxiliary craft of all kinds, or trained and disciplined ashore the men of all callings who came forward to serve at sea. On the Army side, retired Generals and Colonels rendered equally invaluable service in training units and recruits for the New Armies.

Duke of Fife: Knife. (Rhyming slang.)

Duke of York: Fork. (Rhyming slang.)

Duke's, The: *See* Nicknames of Regiments.

Dukies, The: The familiar name for the boys (soldiers' orphans) of the Duke of York's Royal Military School established in 1801 in Chelsea, and removed in 1909 to Dover. In the War 2,427 "Dukies" were killed, 215 obtained commissions, and 185 won decorations. including a V.C. "Sons of the Brave" over the White Rose of York is the badge of the school, and the chorus of the school song runs:

"Be it peace or be it war;
  As your fathers did before,
  For the honour of your name
  Take the torch and fan the flame,
  Play the game, play the game,
  Play up 'Dukies.' "

Dullmajor: (*German*—Dolmetscher, i.e., interpreter). The name for an interpreter in British prisoner of war camps in Germany.

Dumb Insolence: A charge-sheet term entered in the case of a man who without saying anything "looked saucy" at his sergeant. Also: Breaking wind on parade.

Dum-Dum Bullet: An unofficial name, originally used for the Mark IV Lee-Metford bullet with a cavity in the head, introduced after the Chitral Campaign of 1895 in consequence of the lack of stopping power in the small-bore bullet hitherto in use. The Hague Tribunal, at the instance of Germany, interdicted its employment in European warfare, but in the Great War allegations were made on both sides that the other side was using such bullets, the term being used loosely for any bullet so tampered with as to increase its wounding power. The name comes from the Indian Arsenal at Dum-Dum, a few miles from Calcutta, where the small-arms ammunition of the Indian Army is principally made.

Dummy Ships, The: The squadron of converted merchant ships or wooden "Dreadnoughts", which Lord Fisher introduced in 1915 for "bluffing" the Germans in the North Sea and purposes of strategical deception. They were exact duplicates of, and given the same names as, corresponding Grand Fleet ships. One of them, the *Tiger,* was later torpedoed by a German submarine in the Mediterranean, and the sight of her wooden turrets and wooden guns floating about on the waves, the story goes, brought on an attack of "D.T." with the hard-drinking German U-boat Commander.

Dump: A place where war *materiel* of every kind was stacked or stored as a depôt to be drawn upon as required. Usually in the open, and when near the front at cross-roads, by road-sides, at rail-heads; also at base camps, etc.

Dumpies, The: *See* Nicknames of Regiments.

Dun Cow: One of the nicknames of the *River Clyde* at Gallipoli. (*See* Horse of Troy.)

Dunnage Bag: Kit Bag. (Navy.)

Dunsterforce: The official title of the force under Major General L.C. Dunsterville, sent to support the Russian Loyalist troops making a stand in the Caucasus in 1918 against the Bolshevik and Pan-Islam combination. *See* Hush Hush Army.

Duration, The: The term of service for which the men of the "New Army" were recruited, as contrasted with the regulation period for Territorials.

Duration, For the: A phrase often used colloquially to express weariness and impatience. It had all kinds of applications. Men, for instance, whose relief was long overdue might be heard complaining, "Are we going to stop here for the duration?" The expression had reference to the term of enlistment: "For four years or the duration of the War."

Duster, The Red: The Red Ensign; flown in the Mercantile Marine.

Dustman: Stoker. (Navy.)

Dusty: *See* Nicknames.

Dusty Boy: Ship's steward's assistant. (Navy.)

Dutchman, A: The British seafarers' name for sailormen in general, natives of Northern Europe: Dutchmen proper, Danes, Swedes, Russians, Germans. Finns are excepted. They keep their name of Finn and are credited by old tradition with having Black Art powers and capabilities of making themselves unpleasant as magicians, *cf.* Dago.

E.E.F.: Initials standing for Egyptian Expeditionary Force.

E.F.C.: Initials of the "Expeditionary Force Canteens", the vast official supply organization providing canteens, messes, clubs, rest camps etc., on all Fronts in the War from Flanders to Mesopotamia, from early in 1915 onwards. It had its own bakeries, laundries, butcheries, breweries, mineral water factories, depôts, etc., everywhere. The Treasury financed it to the extent of upwards of three quarters of a million sterling. Everything, practically from binoculars to bootlaces, could be obtained at the cheapest possible price. The E.F.C. formed the Central Supply Depot for the canteens of units throughout the war areas.

Eagle Takers, The: *See* Nicknames of Regiments.

Eagle Troop: *See* Nicknames of Regiments.

'Eaps: One of the Army colloquialisms for Ypres. (*See* Wipers.)

Earhole, On the: Cadging. Trying to borrow.

Earl of Mar's Greybreeks, The: *See* Nicknames of Regiments.

Earn, To: To acquire by dubious means. To steal. (*See* Win; *also* Wangle *and* Make.)

Ears Put Back, Get Your: Colloquial at the Front for "Get your hair cut". As men were compelled by regulation to keep their hair closely trimmed, cut quite short, for reasons of health and cleanliness, the regulation was strictly enforced and orders to men to "get their ears put back" were heard almost every day at parades.

Earthed: Used of an aeroplane brought down. (An Air Force expression.)

Eatables (also Eat Apples). Army vernacular for the name of the town of Etaples.

Edna: *See* Nicknames.

Egg, An: A bomb. Specifically, the name of type of small German grenade. Also, a sea mine. Suggested by its shape. Bombing aeroplanes and mine-layers at sea would be said to "drop" or "lay eggs".

Egg Shells: Nickname of H.M.S. *Achilles.*

Eggs-a-Cook. A Cairo street-sellers' cry when hawking eggs. Applied to themselves by Australians serving in Egypt in a complimentary sense of their being hard-shelled, or "hard nuts to crack".

Egypt: Bread.

Eight, One Over the: One drink too many. Slightly intoxicated, the presumption being that an average "moderate" man can safely drink eight glasses of beer—e.g., "You look as though you had one over the eight last night". Now a common phrase.

Elegant Extracts, The: *See* Nicknames of Regiments.

Elephant (and Baby Elephant) Dug-out: A dug-out made with semi-circular linings of heavy corrugated iron. The two names refer to the two sizes issued.

Elephant, The: The name of a type of Martinsyde aeroplane. (*See* Baby.)

Embus: To enter troops on board motor omnibuses for transport at the Front. The places where the troops boarded the buses were marked with notice boards bearing the officially coined words, "Embussing Point". *See* De-bus.

Emden, Sank the: A catch-phrase, applied sarcastically on occasion to men of certain battalions which it was thought got too much "advertised"—e.g., "It was your crowd, wasn't it, that sank the *Emden?*" (referring to the notorious German corsair of 1914, destroyed by the Australian cruiser *Sydney* at Cocos Island).

Emma: *See* Ack.

Emma Gees: Machine guns. Machine gunners. From the initials M.G., the letters being rendered as pronounced in the signallers' vernacular.

Emma Pips: Military Police. From the initials "M.P.", pronounced as in the Signallers' vernacular. (Emma—M; Pip—P.)

Emma Q: M.Q. A signaller's code-term, meaning "Wait a bit".

Emperor's Chambermaids, The: *See* Nicknames of Regiments.

Empire Battalion, The: The 17th Battalion of the Royal Fusiliers, raised in August, 1914, by a committee of wealthy men styled "The British Empire Committee". It was raised to full strength in ten days, and was completely provided, equipped, and hutted at the expense of the Committee.

Emsib: The familiar name for the "Eastern Mediterranean Special Service Intelligence Bureau, an organization established at Cairo for counter-espionage.

'Erb: A wag. A funny fellow.—e.g., "He's a regular 'Erb". Used also colloquially in addressing any man whose name was unknown to the speaker, equivalent to "fellow"—e.g., Here you 'Erb, I want you". From the typical Cockney pronunciation of the name Herbert.

Erfs: (*French*—Oeufs). Eggs. Where pronunciation failed, as it often did, recourse had to be had to pantomime. This is a true story officially recorded in a War Diary. The mess-sergeant of a regular battalion of the Queen's, out to buy eggs, was unable to make the village shopkeeper understand. No eggs being visible he picked up a turnip, put it on the floor, and sat on it, clucking like a hen. He got his eggs!

Erk, An: A rating. (Navy.) Lower deck colloquialism for any "rank" not that of an officer.

Ersatz: (*German*—Ersatz, the official term for reserves, reliefs, substitutes, etc.—e.g., Ersatz Truppen, Ersatz Kleider, etc.) The term was sometimes colloquially used at the Front among our troops for anything by way of substitute, generally in a depreciatory sense.

Esma: Listen! (An Arabic term used colloquially in the E.E.F.)

Esses Emma: "S.M." The initials for Sergeant-Major, as rendered in Signallers' vernacular.

Evacuate, To: To leave. To quit. To be removed. As a Medical Officer's term in the War, to denote that a patient was to be removed from the Front to a Base Hospital, or to England. In urgent cases a ticket marked "E" was issued, meaning the man's immediate evacuation was necessary.

Ever Since Adam was an Oakum Boy: A colloquial Navy phrase to indicate that something goes back to ancient history.

Ever Sworded, The: *See* Nicknames of Regiments.

Evergreens, The: *See* Nicknames of Regiments.

Excellers, The: *See* Nicknames of Regiments.

Eyeful, To Take an: To have a good look at.

Eyes, The Old: *See* Nicknames of Regiments.

Eyeties: Italians.

Eyewash: Humbug. Sham. Deceit. Flattery. Any merely complimentary outward show. "Eyewitness", in one of his letters from the Western Front refers to the term as being used by way of derision, in particular with regard to certain official circulars and memoranda dealing with trivial matters of dress and ceremony.

Eye-witness: The original "Eye-witness" of the Great War in 1914–15 was Lieut.-Colonel (now Major General Sir) E.D. Swinton, R.E., D.S.O, He was succeeded by Earl Percy, who similarly supplied the British public with what information the authorities thought fit to allow them, until, in the later stages of the war, increased facilities were accorded to the Press representatives at the Front, when "Eye-witness's" "Letters" ceased. Mr. Winston Churchill when First Lord of the Admiralty, in the autumn of 1914 proposed to appoint a selected journalist as naval "Eye-witness" with the Grand Fleet, but Lord Fisher objected, and the idea was dropped. The term "Eye-witness" for an official war-correspondent, first appeared three centuries ago, during the Great Civil War, in 1644, when the Lord Mayor and Corporation of the City of London employed a special writer to accompany and report on the doings of the London Trained Band regiments in Sir William Waller's Army, on the Commonwealth side, his letters being printed in the newspapers of the time usually with the heading "From an Eye-witness".

F.A.: Field Artillery. Also: Nothing at all—e.g., "We did F.A. all day". The initials of a vulgar expression, disguised or euphemized as "Fanny Adams" (*q.v.*). It figured on one occasion in print in the Trench Journal of the 58th Division, the "Direct Hit".

F.I.D.A.C.: Federation Inter-Alliée Des Anciens Combattants. An association for the promotion of good understanding and friendship among ex-combatants of nations that took part in the War. It held its first London Congress in 1924.

Fag Issue: The official ration of cigarettes (fags) allowed to troops serving overseas in the War. (*See* Red Hussar, *also* Ruby Queen.)

Fairy Light: Véry Light, named after its inventor. Véry Lights were flares or fire balls fired from a pistol, employed everywhere in the trenches and by airmen.

Faithful Durhams, The: *See* Nicknames of Regiments.

Fan Tan: The name officially given in the War to a Tank provided for the British Army by a wealthy Chinese resident and public man in the Malay States, Mr. En Tong Sen, at a cost of £6,000. It was built at Lincoln by Messrs. Foster and then taken to France, where it served throughout the War. The donor, being a Chinaman, "Fan Tan" had an eye painted on each side forward, in accordance with the Chinese junk practice:— "No eye, no can see. No can see, no can go", as the Chinese sampan man explained. (Fan-Tan is the universal gambling game among Chinamen, played with a *croupier* and numbered counters.)

Fancies, The: The Divisional Concert Party of the 6th Division.

Fancy Greens, The: *See* Nicknames of Regiments.

Fancy Religion, A: A very old Service colloquial term in both Navy and Army for a creed or denomination not Church of England, Roman Catholic or Presbyterian, before the War the three authorized creeds.

Fanny, A: A name for the receptacle holding the bluejackets' "tot" of rum.

Fanny Adams: Tinned boiled mutton. Fanny Adams, whose name is thus commemorated, was in real life a young woman, murdered by a solicitor's clerk named Baker a hundred years ago (*circa* 1812) who cut her up and flung the pieces into the river at Alton in Hampshire. Seamen of the period applied the name "Fanny Adams" by way of grim jest to the pieces of salt-junk or pork supplied as rations. Later, when tinned meat became a naval ration, the name was transferred to that. In the Mercantile Marine, in a similar way, the names "Harriet Lane" and "Jane Shaw" were given to the tinned meat rations, Harriet Lane being derived from the name of the ill-fated Whitechapel woman murdered by Wainwright in 1874, her body being chopped up. Tinned meat came into the mercantile seaman's dietary about that time.

Fannys, The: A name suggested by the initials F.A.N.Y. of the First Aid Nursing Yeomanry Corps, organized in 1909 as a Territorial unit to assist the R.A.M.C. in case of emergency. In the War they served both at Home and Overseas, largely as Motor Ambulance Drivers and on Ambulance Convoy Work. 16 Military Medals were awarded to Women Drivers of the F.A.N.Y. for heroism during an air raid in France in May, 1918.

Fashy: (*French*—Faché). Angry—e.g., "Don't get fashy".

Fatted for the Slaughter, Being: A colloquial expression for the intensive training during a "Rest" (*q.v.*) period in readiness for the next move back to the trenches.

Faugh-a-Ballagh Boys, The: *See* Nicknames of Regiments.

Feather, The: A term for the white wave-track made by the periscope of a submerged submarine under way.

Fed Up: Had enough of it. Bored. Utterly disgusted. The expression, now ordinary slang, originated as Service slang over fifty years ago. It is the exact equivalent of the word "weary" in Proverbs XXV, 17:—"Withdraw thy foot from thy neighbour's house, lest he be weary of (Hebrew 'full of') thee, and so hate thee". Also, by way of emphasis: "Fed up to the teeth".

Feel Out, To: Of Artillery "ranging" until a desired target or objective is attained.

Felix, A: A man who stands another a drink. (Old Army.)

Female Tank: A Tank mounting only machine guns, as distinguished from a "Male Tank" mounting only guns, i.e., cannon. Female Tanks were specially designed to deal with infantry by getting astride of and enfilading their trenches. (*See* Male Tank.)

Fernleaves, The: A familiar term for the New Zealanders. (From the New Zealand badge.)

Fetch Up, To: To arrive.

Fiddler: A Trumpeter. A Bugler. (Old Army.)

Fiddler's Green: The traditional Sailor's paradise, where there was unlimited fiddling and dancing, and liquor. A very ancient Navy phrase, date of origin unknown.

Field Rats: A Prussian Guard contemptuous term for ordinary Linesmen.

Fighting Fifteenth, The: *See* Nicknames of Regiments.

Fighting Fifth, The: *See* Nicknames of Regiments.

Fighting Fortieth, The: *See* Nicknames of Regiments.

Fighting Ninth, The: *See* Nicknames of Regiments.

Finee: (*French*—Fini). No more: all gone! An everyday term at the Front, applied indiscriminately to anything and everything. It originated from the usual experience of late-coming troops, arriving after others at some village behind the Line, and finding the small local shops "sold out" as was almost invariably the case. The shopkeeper's reply on being asked for anything was always "Fini, Monsieur, Na Poo (il n'y en a plus). Fini!" Thus the word "finee" came to be a stock phrase among the troops.

Finger and Thumb: Rum. (Rhyming slang.)

Fireworks: The familiar name for the display of search-lights, star-shells, rockets, etc., over the frontline and No Man's Land, on the occasion of night bombardments (*See* Brock's Benefit.)

First of the Moon: A bluejacket's phrase for settling day on the Lower Deck, when private accounts and debts are squared up.

First Post: *See* Tattoo.

First Tangerines, The: *See* Nicknames of Regiments.

Fitch's Grenadiers: *See* Nicknames of Regiments.

Five Pence Halfpenny: Something not visible; not there. A derisive term among men at the Front referring to the Government messing allowance. To supplement the men's rations, drawn in kind by Quartermasters, an expenditure of five pence halfpenny a day was allowed, to be laid out at the Quartermaster's discretion. As the money was never actually seen by the soldier, the phrase "fivepence halfpenny" came to be used as a sort of by-word.

Five and Threepennies, The: *See* Nicknames of Regiments.

Fix, At the Word: Be very punctual. Be sharp about it. (Suggested by the Drill Book word of command, "Fix Bayonets".)

Fixed Bayonets: An old Army name for a brand of Bermuda rum, the effects of which were often disastrous, if not deadly.

Flag-Wagging: Signalling. Hand signalling with flags. A Navy term adopted into the Army.

Flamers, The: *See* Nicknames of Regiments.

Flaming Onions: A colloquial name for a German anti-aircraft projectile. It had the appearance, on igniting, of a string of free-balls, and was shot up to set fire to an attacking aeroplane. The name was suggested by the row of onions carried by the Breton street onion-sellers, who go round hawking onions in English towns. The device describes an officer, consisted of "about ten balls of fire, shot from some kind of rocket-gun". "You can see them coming all the way from the ground, and they travel fast, too fast to make it possible to dodge them. ... The effect of these balls of fire reaching for you is most terrifying".

Flanker, A: A Shirker. "The Flankers", a title of distinction, was the old Army name for the "grenadier" and "light" companies of a battalion—except in Fusilier battalions—down to 1859, when the designation was abolished. They were all picked men, selected from the other or "battalion" companies. The "grenadiers", who paraded on the right of the line, comprised the tallest men in the regiment, and the "light company", the smartest and most athletic.

Flap A: The familiar Navy term for the sudden "liveliness" on board ship on the arrival of an emergency order involving general activity at extreme high pressure. A "Flap" was the second stage, following on a "Buzz" (*q.v.*). *See* Panic *and* Stunt. Also, an airman's term for an air-raid.

Flapper's Delight, A: A familiar war-time expression for the young subaltern, who during the War had the time of his life among very young ladies.

Flat Foot, A: A Sailor.

Flattening out: An airman's expression. The raising of the nose of an aeroplane after a nose-dive in order to make it resume the normal level of its flying path.

Flesher: A Shirt. (Old Army.)

Flight: The Air Force term for a tactical unit of five or six machines. Usually four or six Flights made up a Squadron.

Flimp, To: To swindle.

Flip, A: A Flight. To Flip. To fly. (Air Force.)

Floaters: Dumplings in a stew.

Floating L's (or 'Ells): A familiar term for the flotilla of "L" class destroyers which in 1914 served in the Harwich Force; the *Lance, Legion, Lennox,* and others. (*See* Battling L's.)

Flog, To: To sell something not the vendor's own to dispose of. To beat any one down or "do" him. To worry. To walk; go on foot.—e.g., "There was no train so we flogged it".

Florrie Ford, A: A motor car or lorry. A combination of the names or the American cheap car manufacturer and of Miss Florrie Forde, the actress.

Fluff, To: To brag. To boast. To lie.

Fly Boys: A name used contemptuously in Ireland for the English "refugees" who crossed over to Ireland to evade conscription. It was often heard in Dublin during the War.

Fly-catchers: A fast type of aeroplane, officially rated as "Fleet Fighters". Their duty is to protect reconnoitring, or spotting aeroplanes, or to attack torpedo-carrying aircraft.

Fly Slicer, A: An old Army term for a cavalryman. Suggested by the cuts of his sword in the air at sword exercise.

Flying Bedstead, A: A familiar name for a military bicycle or motor-cycle.

Flying Kite, A: A colloquial Air Force term for an aeroplane.

Flying Matinée: A trench raid.

Flying Pig: A name given to a type of large (9.45 inch) heavy trench-mortar shell. From its corpulent elongated form (2 feet long) and tail with steadying vanes which suggested the appearance of a pig in the air.

Fokker: The name of a type of German monoplane, armed with a machine gun firing through the propellor, the scourge of the Western Front in 1915–16. So called from its inventor, a Dutch engineer. He invented his machine in 1910, and offered it to the British Government, who rejected it because of certain defects. He made good the defects and the Germans took over the machine.

Follies, The: The Divisional Concert Party of the 47th (London) Division.

Football: The name given to a large type of spherical trench-mortar shell (60 prs.).

Footslogger: Infantryman.

For It: In trouble, On the "Crime Sheet"—e.g., "You will be for it tomorrow, Private Smith."

Force D.: The official designation of the Indian Expeditionary Force sent to Mesopotamia in 1914. "Force A." was the Indian Corps sent to the Western Front; "Force B." comprised the Indian contingent employed in German East Africa.

Fore and Afts, The: *See* Nicknames of Regiments.

Forking the Beam: A naval custom, originating with the usage on board the old-time men-of-war of sticking a fork into a beam in the gun-room, or midshipmen's quarters, as a sign to youngsters to clear out and leave the seniors to themselves.

Forty Thieves, The: *See* Nicknames of Regiments.

Four Bag: The old Navy bluejacket's term for a flogging—four dozen lashes. "Four bag and a Blanker" was the phrase when the flogging was followed by a discharge, the "Blanker" being the man's discharge certificate, which was returned to him with one corner cut off.

Four by Two: The term for the piece of flannel issued as a "pull through" for cleaning a rifle. From its size, four inches by two. Occasionally also a term for an army biscuit.

Four-Flusher, A: A cheat. A braggart. Originally a card term.

Fourteen, On His: A term used in reference to demobilized men after the War. Such men on demobilization were given fourteen days' leave without the necessity of reporting at its conclusion, the object being to give them an opportunity of finding civilian employment. When the men's accounts were finally settled they were credited with pay and ration allowances inclusive of the fourteen days.

Frangine: Brother. (French Canadian.)

Fred Karno's Army: A War-time expression suggested by the name of the popular comedian, Fred Karno, noted for his troupe of whimsical oddities and caricaturists. Practically every unit in the "New Army" invented its own marching song, and these in most cases included lines running:—

"We are Fred Karno's Army,
  A rag-time crowd are we."

Fred Karno's Navy: A nickname given to the Dover Patrol, suggested by its being made up of an extraordinary mixture of ships; every kind of craft—Battleships, Cruisers, Destroyers and Monitors, Submarines, Trawlers and Drifters, Motor Launches, Minelayers and Mine-sweepers, Troop Ships, Colliers, Oilers, and so on down to Rafts—being represented.

Free Gangway, A: On board ship in harbour, when, after the day's work and the watch has been detailed for duty, the rest of the ship's company are free to go ashore.

Free Tank, A: An old Service term for a "wet" canteen where unlimited beer could be got.

Freeman's, It's Harry: Gratis. Free. Nothing to pay. (Navy.)

Friday While, A: A bluejacket's term for a long week-end leave—from Friday to Monday.

Friendly, A: A trench phrase in the War, used of a shell heard either passing high overhead or one falling short in our lines, meaning in that case one of our own shells.

Frightfulness: The German War policy (*German*—"Schrecklichkeit"); wanton ruthlessness; primarily among civilians, and deliberately employed to force a decision by inspiring sheer terror. "You English", said a Prussian Officer to a British Officer during the Boer War, over twenty years ago, "do not know the rudiments of War. When the day comes for us to go to war you shall see how we deal with the men, women, and children. With us, terror is our greatest weapon". The word "Frightfulness", was so persistently used in the Press in England and Allied countries in the early part of the War that it became a word of jest in the Services, being used in all sorts of connections, and of anything, however trivial. A man, for instance, appearing for the first time with an incipient moustache, or wearing a new pair of trousers, or with anything at all unusual in his appearance or get up, would be chaffingly told that he was displaying "frightfulness".

Frigo: Frozen or Chilled Meat.

Fritz: The usual Service name in the early part of the War for the Germans. Later "Jerry" largely replaced Fritz. "A Fritz" was also a naval name for a German submarine.

Frog and Toad: Road. (Rhyming slang.)

Frogging It: Walking. Marching.

Frontiersmen, The Legion of: In the War the 25th (Service) Battalion, Royal Fusiliers. Originally founded in 1906 by Mr. Roger Pocock, and designed to include British subjects who had had experience as explorers, mining engineers, seafaring men, etc., the idea being to raise a body of men, who, by keeping in touch through mutual interest, might be of service to the Empire in an emergency. At the outset of the War in 1914 efforts were made to induce the Government to accept the services of the "Brotherhood" as an independent force, but unsuccessfully. In February, 1915, however, Colonel Driscoll (of "Driscoll's Scouts" in the South African War), obtained leave to raise a battalion from the Frontiersmen who had not meanwhile joined various branches of the Service on their own. The new unit was styled the 25th (Service) Battalion of the Royal Fusiliers (Frontiersmen), and within a few days of recruiting being opened, had reached the strength of over 1,100 of all ranks. It served with distinction in East Africa, suffering such severe losses from the climate that it had to be heavily reinforced by drafts before the end of 1916. Enrolled in the corps were, among others, F.C. Selous, the famous big-game hunter and naturalist, and Cherry Kearton.

Frying Pans: Hands. (Rhyming slang.)

Full Con: Flattery. Deceptive praise or compliment.

Full Pack: Carrying full Service equipment.

Function, To: To act as intended. To work satisfactorily. Applied variously, e.g., "That machine seems to be functioning at last". "The company were not up to much, but they seem to be functioning right now". "This cigarette won't function" (i.e., draw).

Funk-hole: A colloquial term for any small shelter or dug-out; usually one in the trenches. Any place of refuge. Also for a more or less safe job away from the firing line, e.g., "Billy Brown has found a fine funk-hole for himself in the Records Office at Rouen".

Funky Villas: Army vernacular for Fonquevillers, near Hébuterne.

Funny Party, The: The theatrical troupe, nigger minstrels, etc., on board a ship of war. (Navy.)

Furious Joy: An old Army term for "Feu-de-joie", the running fire of three rounds of blank cartridge up and down the ranks of infantry in line, usual at military festivities, special celebrations, etc.

Furphy, A: A rumour. An Australian term, suggested by the name of the maker of the sanitary carts at Broadwater Camp, Melbourne, seen going about everywhere when, at the outset of the War, all sorts of rumours were current as to the destination of the Australians. The camp rumours came to be called "Furphies", and the word was carried among the men to Egypt and spread thence through the forces.

Furphy King, A: A man given to spread rumours.

Fusilier: The official designation for a private in a Fusilier Regiment.

G.H.Q.: General Head Quarters.

G., Q. and A.: The main divisions, together with I (Intelligence), of Staff Duties. "G" (or "General's Branch") deals with the planning and directing of operations. "Q" (or "Quarter Master's Branch") deals with everything to do with equipment or *materiel*, from siege guns' examination to forks and spoons and food. "A" (or "Adjutant's Branch") deals with *personnel*, numbers, training, discipline, etc. The work of the branches may be summarized as supplying the answers to the questions "What shall I do?" "With what shall I do it?" "With whom shall I do it?"

Gadget: An everyday word applied colloquially to any mechanical contrivance or detail, usually small and easily removable. Also, a make-shift, substitute word for anything, when the right word does not readily occur to a speaker. For instance, a man fumbling with the buckle of a strap might say he couldn't get "this—gadget to work!" Originally, a Navy word and then adopted in technical branches of the Army, and in the end becoming used universally. Probably derived from the French Gâchette (Gâche, a hook).

Gaff: A very old common slang term for an Entertainment, Sing-Song or Concert, Social Gathering, etc. Sometimes used in the War for any showy minor event or affair.

Gallants, The: *See* Nicknames of Regiments.

Galloping Lockharts: A name for the mobile Field Kitchens.

"Gangway, Make Way for a Naval Officer!": An expression, heard sometimes among New Army men in the War, anywhere and on any occasion, meaning "Get out of the way", "Stand back", "Clear a passage". "Gangway!" is ordinarily a common warning call on board ship, meaning as above.

Garrison Sports: Washing out quarters. (Old Army.)

Garvies, The: *See* Nicknames of Regiments.

Gas: The use of Poison Gas in war was first proposed some four centuries ago by the famous Florentine, Leonardo da Vinci, primarily for sea warfare, for the purpose of suffocating an enemy by discharging the gas when to windward at close quarters. Leonardo also designed a preventive mask in the event of a shift of wind blowing back the poison-gas on its users. Poison-gas was first used in the War by the Germans at the second Battle of Ypres, on April 22nd, 1915, against the Canadians. We first retaliated in the following September, at the Battle of Loos. Its use in war had been barred by the Hague Convention, to which Germany was a party.

Gas Alert: The term for the customary order in the War, on approaching a danger area, to have anti-gas masks, usually carried slung satchel fashion, caught up and slung round the neck, ready for quick adjustment. Danger areas were marked by notice boards bearing the warning, "Here Gas Masks must be worn at the Alert". The Americans on the Western Front in 1918 widely circulated a printed slip in their trenches by way of a Gas Alert warning bearing these words:—

"In a Gas-Attack
There are only two Crowds;
The Quick and the Dead.
Be Quick and get that Gas Mask on."

Gas Bag: Service slang for an airship.

Gas Guard: The anti-gas night sentry on duty for detecting the first symptoms of a gas attack. The sentry, on the first sniff of poison-gas, had to strike a "gas-gong" (usually an empty shell cartridge-case) and so give warning.

Gas Patrols: The R.A.M.C. parties sent out to locate areas where Mustard Gas (*q.v.*) shells had fallen and warn passing troops.

Gashions: Extra of anything. Navy equivalent of Buckshee (*q.v.*).

Gashly: Steadily, e.g., Go gashly.

Gasper: A cigarette—usually of a cheap, common kind.

Gaspirator: Colloquial for Anti-gas Box-Respirator, a protective appliance introduced in 1916.

Gassed: Drunk.

Gassed at Mons: Whereabouts unknown. An expression by way of jocular reply to anyone asking for an absent man. Poison gas had not of course been introduced as early as The Retreat from Mons in August, 1914.

Gat, A: A revolver. (A Canadian term.)

Gate, On the: Forbidden to leave barracks. (Old Army.)

Gay Gordons, The: *See* Nicknames of Regiments.

Gear: Apparatus generally: appliances: tackle: implements, etc. Also, accoutrements: personal belongings. Also used as a colloquial term for anything giving satisfaction—e.g., "That's it, that's the gear!" [The word in its various applications is centuries old.]

Geddesburg: The Army name on the Western Front for the French town of Montreuil in 1916 when Sir Eric Geddes established his headquarters there as Director General of Transportation, taking over 1,000 clerks and a fleet of 77 motor cars for the use of his staff. According to Colonel Repington, "The First World War", Vol. I., p. 414. (Suggested by the coincidence with the name of the celebrated American city, Gettysburg.)

General: Lieut.-General; Major-General: The order of precedence dates from Cromwell's time, when the three ranks or general officers were styled: "Captain-General" (the Commander-in-Chief); Lieutenant-General (in command of the cavalry and deputy to the Captain-General); Sergeant-Major General (in command of the Infantry). In due course, for convenience, the first and third became shortened to "General" and "Major-General", the original precedence of the three ranks remaining. "General", "Lieut.-General" and "Major-General" became fixed as designations, with the former precedence, after the Restoration, when the modern Army came into being.

General Absolution: The term for the special dispensation, granted in the War by the Pope, dispensing in special circumstances (e.g., when troops were on the eve of going into action) with the otherwise invariable rule of the Roman Communion that individual Confession must precede Absolution. It was confined to men actually about to go under fire. All others, and the survivors after an attack, had to conform to the regular rule as to Confession.

Gentle Annie: A nickname for a certain Turkish gun at the Dardanelles.

George: A colloquial term for an airman, corresponding to "Jack" for bluejacket, and "Tommy" for a soldier. Also used sometimes in the Air Force in addressing any stranger.

Geraniums, The: *See* Nicknames of Regiments.

German Legion: *See* Nicknames of Regiments.

Gerry: A German. (*See* Jerry.)

Get away with it, To: To get off a charge. To get a tale believed. Just to scrape through a difficulty.

Get Down to it: Get on with the job. Also, Go to sleep, lie down on your bed on the floor.

Get it in the Neck, To: To get into trouble.

Get off My Neck: Stop trying to bluff me.

Get off with, To: To make the acquaintance of or "pick up" with anyone, usually some girl, without the formality of an introduction.

Ghost of Joan, A: A colloquialism for a Nursing Sister.

Gibby: A Spoon. (Navy.)

Gin Palace: A nickname for H.M.S. *Agincourt.*

Gippy (or Gyppy): A native Egyptian soldier. The name was apparently originally coined in the British Army of Occupation in Egypt about 1884. The "Gyppie" Army was the common colloquial term for the native force organized by Sir Evelyn Wood and Lord Kitchener and officered by British officers.

Gippy Bint: An Egyptian girl. (*See* Bint.)

Gippo (also Gypo): Gravy. Bacon Fat. Butter. Any greasy sauce.—e.g., "Is there any Gippo?"

Gippoland: Egypt.

Girls are on the Tow-Rope, The: An old Navy expression applied to a ship coming home to pay off.

Give it Best: To stop or finish. To admit defeat—e.g., "That'll do, I've had enough, I'll give it best!"

Glasgow Greys, The: *See* Nicknames of Regiments.

Glass House, The: Detention barracks. An old Army expression, originally particularly applied to the detention barracks for the Aldershot Command at Woking. Later used of any place of military detention. Guard-room, Cells, etc.

Glass House Sailors: One of the nicknames for men of the Royal Naval Division quartered, in the early part of the War, at the depôt in the Crystal Palace, Sydenham.

Glory Hole, A: A colloquial expression for any small billet or dug-out. Also, in particular, the name given to a certain captured German position near Festubert, so called in allusion to the casualties incurred at its capture.

Gnosch, To: To eat (gnash one's teeth on).

Go in, or Go out, To: An everyday expression in the War for the taking over, or being relieved from duty in the trenches.

Go Off, To: To go on board ship. (Navy.)

Go One Better: The motto of the 42nd (East Lancashire) Division of the New Army in the War.

Go Over, To: To attack—go over the Top. Also an Air Force term used of a squadron going out over the enemy's lines.

Gobby, A: A Coastguardsman. The word is said to be derived from the French "Garde de l'eau", through the earlier naval term for a Coastguardsman, "Gobby Loo".

Goffer, A: A Navy term for a man selling soda water or lemonade on board ship. Also, a bottle of aerated water. Suggested by this last, an expression for a man in a passion, bubbling up in a temper. (Navy.)

"Goffer, I'll Draw You off a": A form of challenge to an angry man. If met with the retort "Go on", fisticuffs usually follow.

Gold Stripe, The: The strip of gold braid on a man's sleeve officially indicating that he had been sufficiently seriously wounded to necessitate removal to a hospital, stationary, general, or home. The authorization to wear the gold stripe was not revoked until some time after the War.

Gone Dis: A colloquialism for mentally weak. The term comes from a telegraph or telephone signaller's phrase meaning disconnected ("gone disconnected"), used for a breakdown of the wires.

Gone West: *See* West, To Go.

Gong, A: A medal. (An old Army term suggested by the shape.)

Good Oil: Correct information. A "Straight tip". (An Australian term.)

Goods, The: *See* Nicknames of Regiments.

Goosed: Spoilt.

Gooseberry, A: The name for a wire entanglement device used for stopping gaps. Also for reels of barbed wire, previous to being unwound for use; from their prickly resemblance to the fruit.

Goo-Wallahs, The: A Sanitary Squad.

Gorblimey: "God bless me!" An exclamation or adjective of emphasis. A "Gorblimey" was the common colloquial term for an unwired, floppy, field-service cap worn by a certain type of subaltern in defiance of the Dress Regulations. Lines from a song, popular before the War, ran:—

"My Old Man's a fireman,
An' wot d'yer think o' that,
He wears Gorblimey trousers
An' a little Gorblimey 'at."

Gorgeous Wrecks: A perversion of "George Rex", suggested by the letters "G.R." on the brassards worn by members of the Volunteer Defence Corps in the War. The corps was largely composed of elderly men, mostly of the professional classes, who were over age, or otherwise ineligible for active service, but were desirous of helping in the defence of the country in case of invasion. They spared no pains to make themselves as efficient as possible in drill details, trench digging rifle practice, field ambulance work, etc. One most useful work of theirs, which soldiers returning from the Front gratefully appreciated, was the meeting of leave trains at all hours of the day and night and piloting men across London to various railway centres for their homes in the country. An equally unkind perversion of the letters "G.R." in this connection, often heard, was: "Government Rejects."

Got Me? (Got Me, Steve?): Do you understand? A phrase current in the War from an American film drama in which the "hero" kept producing a revolver to stress his points.

Gotha, A: The generic term for the big German bombing aeroplanes which made raids over London. From the name of the "Gotha Wagen Fabrik", at Gotha, in Germany, the place of manufacture. The Germans got the model from a giant British Handley Page Bombing Machine of exceptional design, with an 80-feet wing span, the first of its kind. Sent across from England the pilot by mistake landed in the enemy's lines with his machine intact, and the raiding Gothas were copied from it. That is the popular story, on which, since the War, some doubt has been thrown. A monument, representing a model Gotha machine, stands in the town of Gotha to commemorate the bombings of London.

Gott Strafe England: (i.e., "God punish England!") The slogan of the Germans in the War. In the German Army, it was heard at parades and displayed on notice boards everywhere in the trenches at the Front. Targets for musketry practice were also inscribed with the words; every barrack room had the words on notice boards, also, barrack squares. "Gott Strafe England" was inscribed on public and other buildings all over Germany, at railway stations, and in places the words were lettered in white pebbles along railway embankments. It was heard everywhere at public meetings, speeches, and addresses, and was a familiar greeting amongst civilians, the usual response being "And He will punish her!" Newspapers, picture postcards, Christmas and New Year cards, ladies' brooches, obituary notices of fallen officers and men, all displayed the words, and they also figured on the walls of hospital wards. At Chemnitz, for instance, in May, 1915, the German Empress, going through the operating room of a hospital, caught sight of the inscription over the door. Turning to those following her she said:—"Kinder (children), that is the one motto for all: 'Gott Strafe England!'"

Grabby: An old Service name for infantrymen of the line, dating from before the Crimean War.

Graft: Work. (An old Army term.)

Grand Fleet, The: The official name for the British Battleship and Battle-cruiser Fleet based on Scapa and Rosyth in the War. Lord Jellicoe is responsible for the name. The Fleet he took over command of early in August, 1914, was officially known as the "Home Fleet". Three weeks later, in his congratulatory message to the Army for its heroism in the retreat from Mons, the Admiral first used the term "Grand Fleet". "The officers and men of the Grand Fleet", ran the message, "wish to express to their comrades of the Army their admiration of their magnificent stand made against great odds, and wish them the brilliant success which the Fleet feels sure awaits their future efforts". The Admiralty did not adopt the term and kept to "Home Fleet" until May, 1916, when "Grand Fleet" was first officially recognized. The term, it may be added, is really an old historic name, first used in William III's War, in the year 1694. "Grand Fleet", after that, was occasionally employed as a name for the Channel Fleet at the end of the 18th Century, but went out of use after that until Lord Jellicoe revived it. The "Grand Fleet" ceased to exist on April 7th, 1916, when Lord Beatty hauled down his flag in the *Queen Elizabeth*. Next day the "Home" and "Atlantic" Fleets were reconstituted and other formations announced.

Granny: A nickname given to one of the first big 15-inch Howitzers sent out to the Western Front; later it was a nickname for other large guns. The original "Granny", or "Grandmother", both nicknames being current, arrived in April, 1915, manned by the Royal Marine Artillery. Its first huge projectiles so surprised the Germans that an aeroplane was at once sent over to locate the monster. A screen of apple-tree branches covered with blossoms was so quickly spread over "Grandmother", whose post was by an orchard, that the Germans could not discover the howitzer. The camouflage was so efficient that our own airmen, coming up to meet the enemy 'plane, also failed to locate "Granny". It was currently reported that "Granny's" first shell (1,413 lbs. weight) fell on a German battalion in column and caused 200 casualties, the rest of the battalion bolting and not being stopped for miles. (*See* Mother.)

Grasshopper, A: A military policeman (as rhyming with the ordinary slang word "Copper".)

Gravel Crusher: An old Cavalry nickname for an infantryman.

Green Cross Society, The: The Women's Reserve Ambulance Society, formed in 1916 for hospital and nursing work (so called from the green cross badge on their khaki uniforms.)

Green Cross Shell: A type of German gas shell, mainly containing Chloropicrin, a poison gas which caused vomiting and had also a lachrymatory effect.

Green Dragoons, The: *See* Nicknames of Regiments.

Green Envelope: The usual name in the War for the ordinary Army envelope, issued to men for writing home (from its colour). The letters in these were liable to censorship, first by an officer of the writer's unit and then also at the Base, and were handed in unfastened. For letters on specially private affairs, which the writer might not wish his officer to see, another kind of Green Envelope was issued periodically, in regard to which the writer had to certify "on honour" that the letter contained no military information. Such letters were liable only to censorship at the Base. These Green Envelopes, being in demand among married men in particular, were often procured illegitimately by others and traded in, "Green Envelope Wallah" being the name for the sellers.

Green Horse, The: *See* Nicknames of Regiments.

Green Howards, The: *See* Nicknames of Regiments.

Green Linnets, The: *See* Nicknames of Regiments.

Greyback: The Army flannel shirt (from its colour).

Greys, The: *See* Nicknames of Regiments.

Gribble, A: The name given by men in certain battalions of the New Army at the Front from Northamptonshire, to the periodical consignments of "comforts", warm gloves, mufflers, chocolate, English cigarettes, etc., provided through the efforts of Mr. Gribble, of Northampton, who maintained a fund for the purpose. In London and elsewhere, all over the country, there were similar organizations, mostly in the form of local committees, who collected subscriptions and held working parties for sending out useful gifts to the men of battalions they were interested in. The Guards' Comforts Fund, an organization of the wives of officers and men for supplying wool mittens and socks, newspapers, tobacco, cigarettes, gramophones, etc., may be taken as a typical organization. Early in the War also, blankets in hundreds were sent to recruiting depôts, on it becoming known that the authorities had not enough to go round, the senders often enclosing money with the blankets for

"The man who is to sleep in this blanket". In like manner, to supply the shortage of sandbags at the Front at the end of 1914, working parties of ladies all over the kingdom turned out hundreds of thousands of them. Among other London Ladies' Associations there was one for making up waistcoats out of long kid gloves, bought or begged from friends, and cut open and pressed, the waistcoats being intended to be worn under the soldier's tunic. Other lady workers also made up and despatched wholesale to military hospitals small lavender bags. Kind messages were often enclosed with the gifts—in one case at least not very graciously welcomed. A soldier did a lengthy march in a new pair of socks sent by an anonymous benefactress. Pain set up in one foot and almost crippled him. When at last he got the socks off, after examining the huge blister that had developed, he turned the socks inside out. He then found that his agony had been caused by a hard lump in the toe of one sock. It proved to be a tight wad of paper, on which loving fingers had inscribed, "God bless the wearer of these socks".

Griffin, The: A private or secret warning. A "tip"—e.g., "I got the griffin about it in time, so I managed all right".

Griffin, The Straight: A trustworthy piece of private information.

Ground Hog Day: An American Army familiar term for November 11th, 1918, Armistice Day, "because on that day every one came out of his underground shelter, or hole".

Ground Stunt, A: An Air Force term for an attack at a low altitude.

Ground Wallah, A: An Air Force term for a member of the R.A.F. whose duties were concerned with administrative, or office and aerodrome technical work, such as Quartermaster, Storekeeper, Mechanic, etc.

Grouse, To: To grumble. (Old Army.)

Grow, I've Seen 'Em: An expression by way of contempt, usually from someone discontented or disgruntled at what appeared the unduly rapid promotion of some junior.

Grub Stake, A: A man's share of rations. The term is an old Western America mining phrase in its origin. To "Grub stake" a prospector meant providing him with outfit and tinned food, etc., on starting out, in return for a share in any "claims" the miner might "stake out" while prospecting.

Gruel Stick, A: A rifle.

Guardian Angel: The name given to the parachute by means of which escape was effected from a "kite" or observation balloon, set on fire by enemy air attacks.

Guards of the Line, The: *See* Nicknames of Regiments.

Guardsman: The official designation for a private in the Brigade of Guards.

Gubbins: Mere stuff. Trash. Anything of no value—e.g., "That's only gubbins, all rot!" Also, personal effects—e.g., "See after my gubbins, will you?"

Gubbins, A: A fool—e.g., "Don't be such a Gubbins".

Guise's Greens: *See* Nicknames of Regiments.

Gull in Night Clothes, A: A Rook. (Navy.)

Gum Boots: Trench Waders. The rubber thigh boots served out to men on going into the trenches. Introduced after the first winter of the War.

Gun-Bus: Air Force slang for a gun-carrying aeroplane. Specifically applied to the first Vickers' "pusher" machine, the first aeroplane specially built to carry a machine-gun.

Gun Fire: The usual term for the early cup of tea served out to troops in the morning before going on first parade, whenever possible. In the War recruits in training always had "Gun Fire" supplied to them, the work before breakfast being found particularly trying. The morning gun in a garrison town suggested the name probably.

Gungoo: Complete. Genuine. (Navy.)

Gunnery Jack (also Guns): The Gunnery Lieutenant on board ship. (Navy.)

Gup: (*Hind.*—Gup). News. Canteen gossip. (Old Army.)

Gut's Horn, The: The dinner bugle-call.

Gutter Crawling: Route marching in the streets.

Gutzer, To Come a: To "crash" or fall badly. (Ordinarily an Air Force term with reference to an aeroplane.) Also used generally. To get into serious trouble, e.g., "He's before a court martial and looks like coming a gutzer". "Gutzer" is pre-war slang, and an old term among Scottish boys for falling flat on the water in diving, instead of making a clean header.

Guyvo, A: A Dandy. Smart fellow. (Navy.)

Guz (Guzzle): A bluejacket's name for Devonport, West Country men having a reputation for being over fond of good feeding.

Gwennie: An anti-aircraft gun mounted on board ship. (Navy— corresponding to "Archie" (*q.v.*) on land.)

Hair-brush Grenade: The name for a type of hand-grenade used in the early part of the War, with a handle, the shape of which suggested a lady's hair-brush.

Hairy, A: Short for "Hairy-heeled". A heavy draught horse, used with medium and heavy artillery; from the hairy fetlocks. The term was used also of any man deficient in manners or breeding, though perhaps good enough in other ways.

Half-Crown Battalion, A: Any "2/6 Battalion", or "Second Sixth". (From the notation entered in official documents.)

Half-inch, To: To steal. (Rhyming slang—pinch.)

Ham Diet, To be for: To have one's name put down on a "charge sheet" for some offence or military "crime". A term used in certain Scottish regiments.

Hammer Blows: A term in the War first employed by the Germans to describe the effect of their "Shock Troops" at Verdun in 1916. Marshal Foch also employed the term in describing the effect of Lord Haig's victorious attacks in August and September, 1918.

Hammer, That's the: Excellent. A good notion.

Hammer, To Swing the: To malinger. To sham illness in order to get off some undesired duty. *Cf.* Lead, To Swing the.

Hand Cart Cavalry: A name sometimes given to Stokes' trench mortar brigades.

Hand-grenade: The Army water-bottle. (Suggested by its shape.)

Handy Billy, A: A bluejacket's name for a small tackle used for a variety of purposes.

Hans Wurst: (*German*—Wurst-sausage). The popular German nickname for a German infantryman corresponding to our "Tommy Atkins". "Hans Wurst" is a derisory term ordinarily, equivalent to "Silly Billy", "Silly Johnny", or the former-day "Jack Pudding".

Happy and Chatty: *See* Nicknames of Regiments.

Hard-lying Money: The extra allowance granted to officers and men for service in destroyers and torpedo boats, and as compensation for wear and tear of uniform and clothing, etc. Extended in the War to the crews of motor launches and other auxiliary small craft. (Abolished in 1923.)

Hard Tack: Biscuit; as contrasted with Soft Tack—bread.

Hard Tails: Mules.

Harkers: Men sent out on "listening patrol" in front of the trenches, specially equipped with appliances to detect indications of enemy activity. At the camps on the East coast of England "Harkers" were similarly employed to listen for sounds of approaching enemy aircraft.

Harry Freeman's, It's: A gift. Something gratis. (Navy.)

Harry Tate's Cavalry: A nickname occasionally applied in jest to Yeomanry. From the name of a well-known comedian whose troupe specialized as caricaturists, displaying comical incapacity in their various rôles.

Harry Tate's Navy: A nickname occasionally used in jest for the Royal Naval Volunteer Reserve. (*See* Harry Tate's Cavalry.)

Hate, the Hymn of: Written by Ernst Lissauer and appearing first in September, 1914, in the Munich Paper *Jugend*. Translated, it ran thus:—
"French and Russian they matter not,
  A blow for a blow and a shot for a shot;
  We love them not, we hate them not,
  We hold the Weichsel and Vosges-gate,
  We have but one and only hate,
  We love as one, we hate as one,
  We have one foe and one alone.

"He is known to you all, he is known to you all,
  He crouches behind the dark grey flood,
  Full of envy, of rage, of craft, of gall,
  Cut off by waves that are thicker than blood,
  Come let us stand at the Judgment place,
  An oath to swear to, face to face,
  An oath of bronze no wind can shake.
  An oath for our sons and their sons to take.
  Come, hear the word, repeat the word,
  Throughout the Fatherland make it heard.
  We will never forego our hate,
  We have all but a single hate,
  We love as one, we hate as one,
  We have one foe, and one alone—
  ENGLAND!
"In the Captain's Mess, in the banquet-hall,
  Sat feasting the officers, one and all,
  Like a sabre-blow, like the swing of a sail,
  One seized his glass held high to hail;
  Sharp-snapped like the stroke of a rudder's play
  Spoke three words only: "To the Day!"
"Whose glass this fate?
  They had all but a single hate.
  Who was thus known?
  They had one foe and one alone—
  ENGLAND!
"Take you the folk of the Earth in pay,
  With bars of gold your ramparts lay,
  Bedeck the ocean with bow on bow,
  Ye reckon well, but not well enough now.
  French and Russian they matter not,
  A blow for a blow, a shot for a shot,
  We fight the battle with bronze and steel,
  And the time that is coming Peace will seal.
  You will we hate with a lasting hate,
  We will never forego our hate,
  Hate by water and hate by land,
  Hate of the head and hate of the hand,
  Hate of the hammer and hate of the crown,
  Hate of seventy millions, choking down.
  We love as one, we hate as one,
  We have one foe, and one alone—
  ENGLAND!"

All Germany went wild over the Hymn of Hate: children learnt it in the nursery; soldiers sang it in the trenches. In England people laughed at it, the Press doing its part in ridiculing it; in particular *Punch*, with an inimitable cartoon, entitled, "A Study of a Prussian Family having its Morning Hate". A Sunday paper which published the words and music, sold out its editions as fast as they appeared. A distinguished musical professor bought up all the copies he could get and taught his classes the "Hymn". Military Bands on recruiting service in Trafalgar Square and elsewhere in London, played the air—a very stirring one—and were enthusiastically applauded and encored. Captured German officers and men were made to sing the "Hymn of Hate" for their captors. The word "Hate" became the war-word of the hour, everywhere with derisive applications. On the Western Front, to take two familiar instances, the German daily trench bombardments, which took place with a curious regularity, often were "Fritz's Evening and Morning Hate". For us, on the other hand, to shell the enemy when he seemed quiet was to "Stir up a little Hate", and so on.

Havercake Lads, The: *See* Nicknames of Regiments.

"Haymaking Drill": An old Army term for bayonet exercise.

Hazy Brook: Army vernacular for the name of the town of Hazebrouck on the Western Front.

Head Worker: A Shirker. A man given to scheming how to evade duty, or danger.

Heavy Stuff: Big shells.

He Kaina No Katoa: A Maori word, meaning "The Home to All". The name given to the New Zealand Hut in the N.Z. camp at Salisbury during the War.

Hectic Show: An Air Force expression for dangerous flying.

Hedge Hopping: An Air Force expression for flying very low.

Heine (or Hiney), A: A German. (A Canadian and U.S. Army term, the name Heine being a common German surname.)

Hell Fire Corner: The name of a specially dangerous place on the Menin Road near Ypres, constantly under shell fire. On a board, a yard long, was painted in white letters on black, "To Hell Fire Corner". It was fixed by Canadian Troops at the Menin Gate of Ypres in October, 1914, and remained there until the end of the War. The name became official and was marked on military maps. In the days of the old Ypres salient, until July, 1917, the board marked the limit for all transport at night, and was the centre of continuous shelling. Said the Town Major of Ypres: "I have repeatedly seen rations and stores drawn with safety two hundred yards away, while this corner itself was a veritable hell". Salvation Corner was a name given to a place in the same neighbourhood, on reaching which troops and transport were comparatively "safe". There were other "Hell Corners" and "Hell Fire Corners" in various sectors on the Western Front.

Herbaceous Borders, The: A popular name in the Navy for a class of single-screw sloops, ordered in 1915, and named after flowers. For convenience, and as a ready means of identifying certain types and classes of special-service and auxiliary vessels designed for special duties in the War, a novel system of nomenclature was adopted by the Admiralty for the various groups. Sloops were all given flower names, H.M.S. *Aster, Begonia, Candytuft, Carnation, Geraniunt, Lobelia, Lupin, Penstemon, Foxglove,* etc. Paddle-wheel mines-weepers were named after Race Courses: H.M.S. *Epsom, Ascot, Sandown, Plumpton, Newbury, Goodwood,* etc. Twin-screw minesweepers were named: some after Hunts (the "Hunt Class"), H.M.S. *Belvoir, Bicester, Cottesmore, Pytchley, Quorn,* etc.; some after Public Schools, H.M.S. *Harrow, Winchester, Sherborne,* etc.; some after Dances (the "Dance Class"), H.M.S. *Cotillon, Gavotte, Minuet, Quardrille, Sir Roger de Coverley,* etc. The Herbaceous Border Class bad their names chosen by the Acting-Librarian at the Admiralty, on being asked to do so. He selected them one morning on his way to Town by walking up and down his front garden and jotting down what took his fancy. The ship-names of the Navy indeed, and the origins of many of them would make an entertaining book. Queen Elizabeth named, for instance, the first *Victory, Dreadnought* and *Revenge* in connection with political events; Cromwell named Commonwealth ships after victories in the Civil War (*Naseby, Marston Moor, Dunbar,* etc.); Charles II named men-of-war after some of his illegitimate children; a First Lord of the Admiralty in William III's reign named ships after towns which returned M.P.'s of his own way of thinking; another First Lord named half the Navy List with mythological and classical names picked out of Lemprière's Classical Dictionary; another fox-hunting First Lord named ships after hounds in his kennels; another went in for Shakespearian names, and another for names such as Beelzebub, Phlegethon, Infernal, etc., scandalizing a colonial bishop who once had to go to his oversea diocese on board one of the diabolically-named ships. And so on to the present time.

Heroine of Loos, The: Mdlle. Emilienne Moreau a girl of seventeen. During the Battle of Loos in September, 1915, she saw some Germans firing on British wounded in a cellar. Going to the rescue she killed three with hand-grenades and a revolver. She was publicly decorated with the British Military Cross by the British Ambassador in Paris.

Herts Guards, The: *See* Nicknames of Regiments.

Hickaboo, A: An Air Force term for an Air Raid.

High Jump, On the: A term used of a man entered on a "Crime sheet", and for trial for a military offence; the suggestion being that the accused would need to jump very high to get over the trouble.

High Stepper: Pepper. (Rhyming slang.)

High-tailing: Bolting off. Running away without looking back. Originally a Canadian backwoodsman's term.

Hipe, A: A rifle. Suggested by the sound of the final executive word "Arms" at drill or on parade. E.g., in giving the order "Slope Arms" or "Order Arms", the first word would be given deliberately and the second sharply and snappily, so seeming to resemble "Hipe". The pronunciation of the word "Arms", also, in such an order as "Slope Arms", might sound like "Slow Pipes". Especially perhaps noticeable among the Guards at drill. It is suggested also that the pronunciation is derived from an ancient Pike Exercise word of command.

Hitchy-Koo: Verminous; lousy. The refrain of a music hall song suggested the name as a synonym for verminous, from the resemblance in sound to "itching" (*See* Chicot.)

Hitting the Roof: Furious. In a temper.

Hob, To be on the: To be a teetotaller. (The reference being, of course, to the tea-kettle on the hob.)

Hobo, A: A cadger. A useless fellow.

Hoick, To: An Air Force term for the action of jerking up an aeroplane rapidly, and making it suddenly climb steeply to a higher level.

Holiday, A: A naval term for a scamped bit of work. A bare space left in painting. A gap on a clothes-line among garments hung to dry.

Holy Boys, The: *See* Nicknames of Regiments.

Holy Joe: A Chaplain. A man affecting piety.

Home and Fried: Safe and correct.

Hommes-Forty, A: A Western Front term for a French railway-van or truck for troop transport. From the marking on it, "40 Hommes, 8 Chevaux". (*See* Ommes and Chevoos.)

Honky Donks: A marine's feet. (Navy.)

Hooch: Spirits of any kind. Originally, liquor from an illicit still.

Hooks, A: A shirker.

Hookey: *See* Nicknames.

Hooks: Spurs.

Hooks, To Catch: To get into trouble.

Hookum: (*Hind.*—Hukam). A regulation. The correct thing, e.g., "That's the hokum". An old Army colloquial term.

Hoop, Through the: Up for punishment.

Hoots in Hell, Two: Nothing, e.g., "I don't care two hoots in hell".

Hop Out: Army vernacular for Hopoutre, a suburb fo Poperinghe.

Hop Out, To: To challenge anyone to fight, e.g., "Say that again and I'll hop you out".

Hop Over: A: An attack, i.e., going "over the Top".

Hop the Bags, To: To attack; go over the Top—over the crest of the sand-bagged parapet.

Horizontal, A: An Air Force term for a bad crash. (*See* Abdominal Crash; also Gutzer.)

Horn, The: The term for the bugle in Light Infantry and Rifle Regiments, e.g., the first Mess Horn for the first Mess Bugle Call in other regiments.

Horse Box, The: The quarters allotted to senior subalterns on board the old Indian troopships.

Horse Marines, The: *See* Nicknames of Regiments.

Horse of Troy, The: One of the nicknames for the collier, *River Clyde*, run aground opposite "V Beach", near Cape Helles, Gallipoli, on the occasion of the landing in April, 1915. The 2,000 men on board swarmed out through exit ports specially cut in the hull, and the name was suggested in allusion to the huge wooden horse by means of which the Greeks captured Troy, as told in the second Book of the Aeneid. "V Beach", says Sir Ian Hamilton, "had we but known it, was next door to impossible as a landing. Our evil genius had planned our ruin there, and yet, at the last hour, good angels came and saved us by sending into the naval minds the thought of how, by the gift of a wooden horse, Troy and all her citadels had fallen." The *River Clyde* lay off "V Beach" all through the fighting on Gallipoli. She was eventually refloated, repaired, and, in spite of protests, sold as a tramp steamer to foreigners, a Spanish firm, in whose employ as the *Angela* she now (1924) is.

Hose of Death, The: An expression for the Lewis gun from the stream of bullets discharged.

Hostility Men: A Navy term for the volunteers who joined the Royal Navy in the War for the "Duration of Hostilities". They comprised men of all professions and callings: architects and artists; school masters; miners; country policemen; potmen; and in one ship "a coffin maker's apprentice". Says "Taffrail", in H.M.S. *Anonymous* (p. 194):—"One cruiser is reported to have steamed into Portland Harbour with a postman at the starboard engine-room telegraph, a baker at the wheel, and the man who hanged Crippen twirling the lead in the chains".

Hot Air: Exaggeration. Lies. Pre-war slang, but a common expression in the Air Force, used often in regard to reports of pilots and observers inclined to report more important enemy movements on the ground than they had actually seen. In use in the Navy long before the War and said to have originated among torpedo men. Earlier still the expression was common in America as a term of contempt meaning "tall talk", lies, etc.

Hot Stuff: Heavy shells.

House: A gambling game permitted in the Service. Played with checks and cards bearing 15 different numbers on each card, which were called out irregularly by the "banker", the first man who had all his numbers called winning. A variety of names was given to the numbers:

e.g., 1 was "Kelly's Eye"; 9 was "Doctor's Shop" (from the No. 9 pill—
q.v.); 10, 20, etc., "Blind Ten", "Blind Twenty", etc.; 11, "Legs Eleven"; 22,
"Dinky Doo"; 33, "Gerty Lee"; and the final 99, "Top of the House". In
the men's conversation "House" names were often used as substitutes
for ordinary numbers, e.g., in reply to a query, "What time is it?" the
answer for, say, 11 o'clock, would be simply "Legs Eleven".

How: The familiar abbreviation for a Howitzer, a short, large-calibre
piece of ordnance, firing with a high angle of elevation and "lobbing"
big shells. The British modem breech loading howitzer was introduced
in 1909. The name is at least four centuries old and was originally
German—Haubitzer. Derived from the Bohemian "hofnice", a catapult.
Both word and weapon were introduced by the famous John Zisca.

Howard's Greens: *See* Nicknames of Regiments.

Huffed, To be: To be killed.

Hum, To: To cadge.

Hump, To: To lift. To carry. (Originally an Australian digger's word,
e.g., to hump one's swag—to carry one's load.)

Hump it, To: To march with full kit. To tramp on foot.

Hun: "Hun" during the War first came in as a generic name for a
German through the newspapers, as an epithet of disgust, expressive of
the universal anger aroused by the accounts of the German outrages in
Belgium and Northern France. The Services, however, did not adopt the
name to any extent; except the Air Force, with whom it was always the
usual name for the enemy. The ex-Kaiser's flamboyant farewell address
to the German Expeditionary Force sent to the Far East in July, 1900, to
co-operate in suppressing the Boxer Rebellion, originated the modern
application of the word "Hun":—"No mercy must be shown. No prisoners must be taken. As the Huns under King Attila made a name for
themselves which is still mighty in tradition and legend to-day, may the
name of German be so fixed in China by your deeds, that no Chinese
shall ever again dare to look a German askance. ... Open the way for
Kultur once for all!" "Hun" was first used in England with reference to
the Germans by Mr. Kipling in "The Rowers", published in the *Times* in
1902, at the time when Germany was working to embroil Great Britain
and the United States over the Venezuela Border question. In the Air
Force in the War the word "Hun", besides being applied to the enemy,
was used as a familiar term for a newly-joined young officer qualifying
for his "wings", in consequence of the destructive effect on the instructional aeroplanes which young officers while learning to fly usually had.
"Hun" was also an old Navy term for a bully on board ship according to
James Anthony Gardner, in use in Nelson's day (Navy Records Society,
Vol. XXXI., p. 55), where the author speaks of a midshipman Shipmate
as "a drunken Hun".

Hun Hunting: An Airman's phrase for going out to look for, or chase, the enemy.

Hun Pinching: Raiding an enemy trench in order to secure prisoners for the benefit of the Intelligence Department.

Hunch, A: A warning. A premonition.

Hungry Hundred: *See* Bob-a-day gunner.

Hunk: To clean.

Hundland: A term generally used in the War by Airmen for the country behind the enemy line, wherever it might be; in Belgium, France, Bulgaria, Turkey, or any other territory where German troops were.

Hunting Flotillas, The: The name given to four patrol-boat flotillas employed in the Channel to search for and destroy enemy submarines. They tracked them under water by means of hydrophones, "fixed" them and then dropped depth-charges on them.

Hurrah Boats: A Navy term for the pleasure steamers of taming tripper that go round the Fleet at Naval Reviews, usually cheering as they pass ships.

Hurrah Kanaille: A Prussian Cavalry derogatory term for German infantrymen, suggested by the Drill Book order that the latter are to give three "Hurrahs" as they charge. (*See* Field Rats.)

Hush Hush Army, The: The special force commanded by General L.C. Dunsterville for service in the Caucasus and at Baku in 1918–19, against the Bolshevik and Pan-Islam combination. (*See* Dunsterforce.) Its composition and objects were kept secret. It was known to exist—that was all. The force owed its name of the "Hush Hush Army" from the fact that officers were asked to volunteer for it, mostly from the Western Front, without details being given them, and on being selected, disappeared. All that was known by their friends was that they had "gone East on some rather desperate enterprise".

Hush Hush Crowd, The: A familiar name for the personnel of the Tank Corps, when first organized in June, 1916, and secretly assembled for training. Officially, they bore the name "Heavy Branch, Machine Gun Corps". When the Tanks, on completion, made their appearance in readiness for taking over, the road to the Camp was guarded by military police, all traffic was kept away, and the blinds in the front rooms of farms and cottages along the route were ordered to be kept drawn and the occupants of the places to keep in their back rooms.

Hush Hush Operation, The: A name given to Lord Fisher's projected beach-landing attack on the Belgian Coast, proposed in the spring of 1916 and again in 1917, special Tank detachments and three Infantry brigades specially trained in climbing a reproduction of a sea-wall being the striking force. Secret trials were made in the Thames with pontoons 600 feet long, lashed together in pairs, and six Monitors to lead the way.

Hush Hush Ships, The: A familiar name in the Navy for certain ships of exceptional design built during the War in conditions of exceptional secrecy. The "freak" ships ("Super Light-Cruisers"), *Courageous, Furious* and *Glorious* were three. The workmen building these are said to have given the ships, from their extraordinary appearance, the nicknames, "Outrageous", "Spurious" and "Uproarious". The *Renown* and *Repulse*, which were building in the last year of the War, were also "Hush Hush" ships, and the expression was also used of the specially designed "M.L.'s" (*q.v.*) ordered by Lord Fisher.

Hutch, The: The guard room. Any place of military detention.

Hypo-helmet: A flannel bag, with eye-pieces of mica soaked in some anti-gas solution, one of the first used being a hypo (sodium thyo-sulphate) solution. The Hypo-helmet superseded the cotton-pad respirator. The first one was made on May 10th, 1915, and is preserved at the Imperial War Museum. (*See* P.H. Helmets.)

I: The Service abbreviation for "Intelligence", i.e., information of military value. The use of the word as a military technical term dates from the 16th Century, but in the War of 1914–18 it was used to denote specially the department of the General Staff dealing with information. A G.S.O. "I" was thus the General Staff Officer of an Army Corps (or lesser formation) dealing with everything to do with Intelligence. Various "I" departments dealt with information, each denoted by a letter. I(a) was concerned with collecting information as to enemy "Orders of Battle", and the identification of enemy divisions, etc., in the battle-area, matters connected with enemy strategy and tactics, equipment, etc., and disseminated the information obtained to subordinate formations. The business of I(b) was to prevent similar information getting to the enemy. I(b) had to do with the checkmating of enemy spies, counter-espionage and also the unobtrusive superintendence of the civilian element in the war area, and especially the "Rapatries" (*q.v.*), who were watched by the "Carnet Section" (so called from the "Carnet" or notebook in which each individual's record was entered). I(b) had also an important function to fulfil in action; the prompt examination of all civilians found in newly captured places. The I(b) police for that purpose followed close after attacking troops. The materials collected by the Secret Service went to I(b), For these and other reasons and the apparently romantic and adventurous nature of the work of this branch, I(b) was more generally known than the others. All sorts and classes found places in I(b): globetrotters and Continental idlers, and men of mixed nationalities; Anglo-Armenians, Levantines, even Arabs. One I(b) man for instance was in private life a travelling showman who had wandered all over Europe from end to end with performing bears. Beginning in France, with counter-espionage, the activities of I(b) spread to Italy, Salonica and the East, and to Russia before the Revolution. I(c) dealt with maps and topography; I(d) with the Press; I(e) with wireless interception, cyphers, etc.

Iddy Umpties, The: A nickname for the 17th Division, whose sign was a dot and dash, painted white on black. Also, for R.E. linemen employed in repairing telegraph and telephone wires at the Front.

Iddy (or Itty) Umpty: An expression first used in India in teaching the dot-and-dash Morse system to native troops. An "Iddy Umpty" in that way came to be used as a term for a signaller.

Identity Disc: Every officer and soldier was supplied with two identity discs, worn round the neck, one suspended from the other, the upper disc, "No. 1", green, and the lower, "No. 2", red. (*See* Cold Meat Ticket and Corpse Ticket.) The green disc was buried with the body; the red disc was removed and retained for record purposes in the dead man's unit.

Idonk: Idea.

Iggry (Iggri): (*Arabic*—Hurry up). A phrase in use in the Egyptian Expeditionary Force. "Iggry Corner" at Bullecourt was so named by Australian troops who had been stationed in Egypt, as being an exceptionally dangerous locality from shell fire, where it was necessary to move rapidly.

Immortals, The: *See* Nicknames of Regiments.

Imperials, The: The name by which British troops were familiarly spoken of by the Canadians and Dominion and Colonial Contingents in the War.

Improperly Dressed: The ordinary Service term for having some detail, or portion, of uniform, not in accordance with regulation; involving official notice and in some cases punishment as a "crime". A sailor, for instance, with his cap not all straight, or a soldier with his boot laces crossed instead of being fastened in straight rows across, or wearing his overcoat with a button unfastened instead of fully buttoned up, would be "improperly dressed" and possibly suffer accordingly.

Imshi: (*Arabic*). Go away. Be off. The word was one of several brought to France during the War by troops who had served in the East, and was often to be heard in the streets of Amiens and elsewhere, used by our men, in ordering off troublesome people, cadgers, newspaper sellers, etc. Similar phrases were Imshi, Iggri, and Imshi Allah, i.e., get away quickly; be off.

In and Out, The: The Naval and Military Club, 94, Piccadilly. So called familiarly from the words "In" and "Out", painted on the pillars of the approach to the courtyard in front.

Indiarubber Man, The: Navy colloquial for the Officer for Physical Instruction R.N. (*See* Bunjee.)

Inky: Tipsy.

Iron Division, The: A name for the 13th Division in the War, coined by London newspapers and adopted as a compliment by the men of the division. Their "sign" was a black horseshoe, points up. (*See* Signs, Divisional.) Every army had its "Iron Division"—so nicknamed. The French 20th Division, and 3rd Brandenburg Division of the German Army, were "Iron Divisions", in the case of the Brandenburgers a prewar nickname, specially given to his pet "Men of the Mark" by the Kaiser.

Iron Ration, The: The Emergency Ration; a sealed supply of concentrated food, issued to troops on service for use only in the last emergency and by special order. Each man carried his own Iron Ration. The term dates from the Thirty Years War, early in the 17th Century; Wallenstein is said to have introduced it. Frederick the Great next had an "Iron Ration" provided for the Prussian Army during the Seven Years War, a reserve biscuit-ration, carried in each soldier's knapsack. Other nations then followed suit, England last of all. "Iron rations" was in the War also a colloquial expression in speaking of a hot shell-fire, e.g., "Jerry is letting them have it, lots of iron rations flying about!"

Iron Ration Day: The day among troops at the Front when a fresh supply of Iron Rations was issued to each man in place of that carried by him since the previous issue. "At fixed intervals", says a writer in the *Morning Post*, "when it was thought that a change in the contents of the little linen bags would be all for the good, the 'last hopes' were collected, and officers and men more or less enjoyed a variation of the daily diet prepared for them. It needed much ingenuity on the part of the cooks, and not a little *camouflage*, to make the resultant dishes welcome."

Issue, An: An official allowance. An "Issue" cigarette, for instance, was a ration cigarette, in contradistinction to one bought at the Canteen. Also, full allowance of anything, e.g., "They've had the issue", i.e., all they are entitled to. In another connection, as meaning all: "Not a soul got back; the whole issue were done in last night".

"It": The nickname of a certain mysterious listening apparatus installed in the trenches, the wires from which extended all along the front lines and into No Man's Land. Designed to "tap" enemy telephone messages, "It" often intentionally tapped our telephone wires and revealed to Headquarters conversations on forbidden subjects among both officers and men, with unpleasant consequences to the delinquents. As no mention of this apparatus was permitted, the nickname "It", as meaning an awe inspiring, mysterious chief spy, so to speak, came into general use.

Ivan: The everyday name in the Russian Army, at any rate down to 1916, for a private soldier, equivalent to our "Tommy Atkins".

Ivory Cross, The: A special organization in the War in connection with the Dental Profession. At the Armistice, numbers of men were passed out of the Service, whose teeth, while not officially "pensionable", had suffered seriously through effects of the War. These were enabled to have their teeth remedied *gratis*, or at reduced charges, through the Ivory Cross. The Ivory Cross now provides dental treatment for all in necessitous circumstances. Since its foundation in 1914 it has dealt with over 100,000 cases involving more than 800,000 dental operations.

Jack Dusty: Ship's Steward's Assistant. (Navy.)

Jack Johnson: The familiar name at the Front for any heavy German shell giving off a dense black smoke in bursting. In allusion to the celebrated negro boxer Jack Johnson. (A name for him in America was "The Big Smoke".) "Eye-witness" introduced the name to the British public in one of his first letters in September, 1914.

Jack Jones: Alone, e.g., "I am going out Jack Jones to-night".

Jack Shilloo, A: A boaster. (Old Navy.)

Jackers: Training Ship boys.

Jacket, To Get the: Colloquial for an appointment to the Royal Horse Artillery. In allusion to the R.H.A. uniform jacket, in contradistinction to the tunic of the Royal Artillery.

Jackies: The U.S. Navy term for seamen.

Jacko, A: A Turk. A Palestine Army term.

Jacks, The: Military Police.

Jag Up, To: To punish.

Jaggers, The: *See* Nicknames of Regiments.

Jam on it: (Old Navy). Something pleasant. Easy, e.g., "You want jam on it", i.e., You expect too much.

Jam Tin Grenade: The crude type of improvised hand-grenade of the earliest stages of the War in the trenches, made at the Front out of old tobacco or jam tins, with fuse or detonator. The detonator was inside; the fuse stuck out. First used in November, 1914.

Jammed Like Jackson: A Navy phrase, used when something goes seriously wrong, or leads to a disaster. (In allusion to John Jackson, Master of the frigate *Leander* in 1787 who refused to listen to the pilot and nearly wrecked his ship in consequence.)

Janc, The: The Junior Army and Navy Club. (From the initials.)

Jankers: Defaulter's punishment. Punishment cells. The defaulters' bugle-call. (*See* Angel's Whisper.)

Jankers King, The: The Provost Sergeant.

Janker's Men: Defaulters.

Japan: (*French*—du pain). Bread. In the War "Japan" eventually superseded "Rooty" (*q.v.*) as the Army word for bread on the Western Front.

Jaunty; Jonty; (also sometimes Jaundy): The Master-at-Arms on board ship. (Navy.) Jaunty, or Jonty apparently originated early in the Nineteenth Century, a little time after the Napoleonic War, being an adaptation from the French war-prisoners' name for the Master-at-Arms on board the English prison hulks—"Le Gendarme". The name was taken up in the Navy and in lower deck parlance became apparently, first "Johndy Damn", shortened then to "Johndy", and finally surviving in the present day form "Jaunty" or "Jonty".

Jericho Jane: The name given by the Australians in Palestine to a long range Turkish gun in the Jordan Valley in July, 1918, which caused considerable trouble till finally destroyed by airmen.

Jerry: A German. In the later stages of the War the universal name for the enemy. In 1914 and 1915 the ordinary term was "Fritz". One rather farfetched suggestion, which has been put forward to account for the adoption of "Jerry", is that "Fritz" became "Fitz" which suggested "Fitzgerald", and that, in turn, became shortened to "Gerald", then "Gerry", or "Jerry".

Jerry Over: "Lights out!" The word passed along the lines at the Front at might on the nearing overhead of an enemy aeroplane.

Jerry, To: To understand, e.g., "Do you Jerry it, man?"

Jerry Up: A warning call on the approach of a German aeroplane.

Jewel of Asia: A name given to a certain heavy Turkish gun at the Dardanelles.

Jewing: Making or mending clothes. Sewing. (Navy.)

Jigger, Up the: In the trenches. Up the line. (Also, *see* Nicknames.)

Jimmy the One: The First Lieutenant on board ship. (Navy.)

Jingling Johnny, The: The celebrated and unique historic trophy of the old 88th, the First Battalion, the Connaught Rangers, captured from the French in 1812 at Salamanca and carried on parade on ceremonial and State occasions at the head of the band and drums. It is a pole, 7 feet, 6 inches high, bearing a crescent and bells and horsehair tails, and is now on view in the Royal United Service Institution, Whitehall. The French took it from the Moors to whom it was both a standard and musical instrument. A somewhat similar "Jingling Johnny", termed a "Chapeau Chinois", used solely as a band instrument, was in use in certain regiments which had black bandsmen (got up in turbans—Oriental fancy uniforms) between 1778 and 1840, when black bandsmen ceased to be employed. Earlier still, Frederick the Great introduced "Jingling Johnnies", known as "Glockenspiel", into the bands of the Prussian Army, after having had sent him as a gift from the Sultan, a set of Turkish Janissary band instruments. "Glockenspiel" are still in use in some "crack" German regimental band. A type of "Jingling Johnny" is also in use at the present time as the standard of French Spahi cavalry regiments.

Jocks: Scotsmen in general. Men of a Highland regiment.

Joey: A Marine. (Navy.) The name is at least a century old; probably a good deal older. Dibdin, in one of his songs has:—

"Poor Joe the marine was in Portsmouth well known,
  His manliness won every heart".

Johnny: A Turk. (As a Service nickname, dating from the Crimean War.) Also, *see* Nicknames.

Jolly, A: A Marine. "'Er Majesty's Jolly—soldier and sailor, too!" (Kipling). The nickname, it has been suggested, is derived from the original composition of the first English marines, raised in 1664, who are traditionally said to have been recruited from men of a regiment of the London Trained Bands, or City Militia. At that period "Tame Jolly" was a current name for a militiaman, and "Royal Jolly" is said to have been given by way of distinction to the Marines. Marryat in "The Poacher" has:—"Jollies, what are they? Why, Marines to be sure".

Jonnick: According to custom, etiquette, etc. (Navy.)

Josephine: The French Army nickname for the 75 mm field gun, the celebrated "soixante-quinze".

Joy Bag: A word at the Front in the War for the bag, usually a sand-bag, in which a man carried "Souvenirs", etc., to take home on leave.

Joy Spot: A familiar colloquial term among officers on the Western Front for certain recognized hotels, *cafés*, and restaurants at various places, Amiens, Arras, Boulogne, Bailleul, Doullens, etc., where good cooking and attendance with properly-laid tables, glass and cutlery, and wash and brush-up facilities, as well as a cocktail bar, were available.

Joy Stick: The airman's popular name for the control lever working the principal controls and controlling the stabilizing mechanism in an aeroplane. The control lever was invented in 1907 by a M. Pelterie, who, in May, 1923, was awarded over seven million francs in a law-suit against the French Government for infringement of his patent during the War.

Joy Waggon: The term for an aeroplane used for practice at a Flying School.

Juice, The: Airman's slang for the petrol supply of an aeroplane. Used generally also for petrol.

Jugged: Arrested. In the cells. ("The Stone Jug" is old thieves' slang for a prison.)

Juggo, To be: To be sick. In the cells. Out of action.

"K" (1): The tabloid title of the "First Hundred Thousand" of Lord Kitchener's "New Army" of 1914.

K.D.G.'s, The: *See* Nicknames of Regiments.

K.G.5.: The Nickname of H.M.S. *King George V.*

K.H.B., A: A King's Hard Bargain. A worthless or incorrigible fellow. (Old Service term.)

Kai: Food. (A Maori word, used among the New Zealand troops in the War.)

Kamerad: (*German*), Comrade. The usual German cry when surrendering: "Kamerad—Pardon!" The word was taken up among our men in jest and used more or less derisively.

Kamerad, To: To yield. To give in. (A common colloquial expression.)

95

Kangaroo, The: The nickname of a type of aeroplane. (*See* Baby.)

Kapai: Very good. Capital. (A Maori word used among the New Zealanders.)

Kaput: (*German*—Kaputt). Finished. No more. Used similarly to "Napoo" (*q.v.*)

Karno: *See* Fred Karno.

Kate Karney: The Army (rhyming slang.)

Kebrock: A Cap (French Canadian.)

Kelly's Eye: No. 1 in the game of "House".

Khaki: The name of a colour—dust colour. First introduced as uniform in 1848, in Lumsden's "Guides" on the Afghan Frontier, and adopted during the Indian Mutiny by some of the British regiments. The Oxford and Bucks Light Infantry (the 1st Battalion, the old 43rd Foot) are said to have been temporarily put into "Khaki" before the Mutiny: when stationed at Peshawar and under orders to go on a punitive expedition against Khyber tribesmen. It was the hot weather and to exchange the white drill uniforms for the regulation thick red tunic was considered out of the question. At the same time, to send men in white against the Afghan marksmen, meant offering targets which could not be missed. To solve the difficulty the Colonel adopted the "Guides'" colour and had the uniforms stained with brown mud. Khaki became the Field-Service uniform of the Indian Army between 1860 and 1870. Its official adoption as the British Army War Uniform dates from the South African War of 1899–1902. (The word is derived from the Persian "Kâk", i.e., dust.)

Khakis, The: The usual enemy name for the British troops, used colloquially among the Germans on the Western Front, in particular during the earlier months off the War.

Kidstakes: Pretence. Flattery (*cf.*, to kid—to deceive.)

Kiel Whale: The name given by our prisoners-of-war in Germany for a nauseous fish-meal, served out to them as a staple dish.

Kiff, All: All right.

Killick, A: An Anchor. A name dating back to the early Seventeenth Century, if not before, and originating apparently as the name of the primitive stone "sinker" used for anchoring vessels, usually a large stone, or stones, held clamped together by crooked timbers frapped round with rope. Also, the lower deck term for the Petty Officers' Anchor arm badge.

King's Birthday, The: Pay Day.

King's Certificate, The: The certificate of having "Served with Honour" presented to men on being discharged from the services. It was designed by Mr. Bernard Partridge.

King's Men, The: *See* Nicknames of Regiments.

King's Message to the Army, The: On the embarkation to France of the British Expeditionary Force on August 19th, 1914, the following message from His Majesty was circulated to all ranks, "You are leaving home to fight for the safety and honour of my Empire. Belgium, whose country we are pledged to defend, has been attacked, and France is about to be invaded by the same powerful foe. I have implicit confidence in you, my soldiers. Duty is your watchword and I know your duty will be nobly done. I shall follow your every movement with deepest interest and mark with great satisfaction your daily progress; indeed, your welfare will never be absent from my thoughts. I pray God to bless you and guard you, and bring you back victorious".

King's Message to the Fleet, The: Immediately on the Declaration of War, on the night of August 4th, 1914, the following message from His Majesty was received by wireless at Scapa, addressed to Admiral Sir John Jellicoe (now Lord Jellicoe) as Commander-in-Chief. "At this grave moment in our National History I send to you and through you to the officers and men of the Fleet of which you have assumed command, the assurance of my confidence that under your direction they will revive and renew the old glories of the Royal Navy and prove once again the Sure Shield of Britain and of her Empire in the hour of trial".

Kingsley's Stand: *See* Nicknames of Regiments.

Kip: A sleep. Rest. A bed. A hammock, e.g., "To do a kip—to have a sleep".

Kitch, A: Colloquial for a recruit in Lord Kitchener's "New Army".

Kitchener's Blue: A name given to the blue serge uniform served out to recruits in the autumn of 1914 in consequence of the shortage of khaki.

Kitchener's Letter to the British Expeditionary Force, Lord: On the B.E.F. starting for France in August, 1914, the following printed message from Lord Kitchener, as Secretary of State for War, was distributed to the troops individually, with instructions that it was to be kept by every soldier in his Active Service Pay Book.:—"You are ordered abroad as a soldier of the King to help our French comrades against the invasion of a common enemy. You have to perform a task which will need your courage your energy, your patience. Remember that the Honour of the British Army depends on your individual conduct. It will be your chief duty, not only to set an example of discipline and perfect steadiness under fire, but also to maintain the most friendly relations with those whom you are helping in this struggle. The operations in which you are engaged will for the most part take place in a friendly country, and you can do your own country no better service than in showing yourself in France and Belgium in the true character of a British soldier. Be invariably courteous, considerate, and kind. Never do anything likely to injure or destroy property, and always look upon looting as a disgraceful act. You are sure to meet a welcome and to be trusted; your conduct must justify that welcome and that trust. Your duty cannot be done unless your health is sound. So keep constantly on your guard against any excesses. In this new experience you may find temptations both in wine and women. You must entirely resist both temptations, and while treating all women with perfect courtesy, you should avoid any intimacy.

Do your duty bravely,

Fear God,

Honour the King".

A somewhat similar order was promulgated in America on July 3rd, 1917, to the first U.S. Division. One of its injunctions ran:—"It is of the gravest importance that the soldiers of the American Army shall at all times treat the people of France, especially the women, with the greatest courtesy".

Kitchener's Mob: The popular name for the men who joined up in response to Lord Kitchener's Appeal, in August, 1914.

Kite Balloon: The general name for the sausage-shaped "Observation Balloon" used for artillery "spotting". It was kept in position by means of a wire cable with winding apparatus, tethered to the ground like a kite. The original Kite Balloons, introduced in 1902–3, comprised a string of box-kites supporting an observer who sat on a cross stick, the kites being tethered to the ground by a wire rope. They were used when the wind was too strong for a captive balloon.

Kiwi, A: Air Force slang for a man on ground duty and not qualified for flying service. (From the name of the flightless bird of New Zealand.)

Knife Rest: The name at the Front for a portable X-shaped wire-entanglement framework, resembling a knife-rest, used for stopping gaps in wire-entanglements in No Man's Land.

Knock the End off, To: To spoil anything.

Knocked up a Catcher: Found out.

Knuts, The: A Dover Patrol familiar term for the personages of importance, Ambassadors, Cabinet Ministers, etc., whose passage to and from France they had specially to safeguard.

Konked (Konked out): An Air Force term used of an aeroplane engine stopped working, failed, or broken down. Also a general expression, meaning "knocked out", dead.

Kosh: A name for a trench club, or knobkerry, used in trench raids. The name is the usual name for the stick, or bludgeon, carried by London roughs when out for mischief.

Krakenhohe: The name of a German town, found awkward to pronounce by our men, who passed it in their advance after the Armistice, and adopted the name as a convenient "Swear word".

Kybosh on, To put the: To finish off, to add the last straw. "To put the Kybosh on the Kaiser" was a familiar expression in the early part of the War.

Laager, To: To camp. The term came into Army use in the South African War, originating from the Cape Dutch word Laager, a camp enclosed by wagons.

Lacedemonians, The: *See* Nicknames of Regiments.

Lackry, or Lackery: (*Hind.*—Lakri). Stick. Piece of wood. (*See also* Nicknames.)

Lad of the Village, A: A cheery companion.

Ladies from Hell: Highland Regiments. Kilted troops. A name coined in the War by the German newspapers and adopted among the German troops on the Western Front.

Lads, The: The Divisional Concert Party of the 47th East Lancashire Division. "Lad" has a distinctive North Country meaning of familiar companionship.

Lambs: Light Armoured Motor Batteries. (From the initials.)

Lambs, The: *See* Nicknames of Regiments.

Lammy Coat: The Navy familiar name for the thick, fleecy, duffle-coat with hood, served out on board ship in wintry weather for men on duty.

Lamps: Eyes.

Lancashire Lads, The: *See* Nicknames of Regiments.

Lancashire Landing: "W" Beach, Gallipoli where the 1st Battalion Lancashire Fusiliers landed on April 25, 1915. The name was given by Sir Jan Hamilton, according to whom, with reference to the special incident, "No finer Feat of Arms has ever been achieved".

Lance-Corporal: The name comes from the Italian "lancia-spezzata" —the term in the Middle Ages for a trooper who had lost his lance or horse in action, and until supplied with a fresh weapon or mount, had to serve with the infantry. Horsemen being considered superior beings, pending his reinstatement, the lancia spezzata ("lance" was also a synonymous term for "trooper") received higher pay than his new infantry comrades, and was employed usually as assistant to the corporals of his company. Thus the title and grade of lance-corporal came in originally. The word "lance" for "acting" was later extended in our service to sergeants as a convenient term.

Lance-Jack: Lance-Corporal. The private soldier's first step upwards; an appointment not a rank. The Lance-Jack is the man of all work in his company and is kept hard at it from reveille to "lights out".

Lancer, A: A term for a shot missing the target.

Land Crabs: Army colloquial for Military Foot Police.

Land Girls: The women and girls who, during the War, came forward as agricultural and farm workers in order to free men for duty at the front.

Landowner: A dead man. From his occupation of his grave. A common colloquialism at the Front in the War for a man killed on the Western Front was, "A landowner in France".

Landship: A Tank. One of the early names occasionally used by war correspondents on the Western Front.

Lash-up, A: A failure. A fiasco. The break-down of anything, e.g., "The attack last night was a regular lash-up". Of naval origin, and in the War a common colloquialism at the Front.

Last Hope, The: An occasional term for the Iron Ration (*q.v.*).

Last Post: *See* Tattoo.

Latrine Rumour, A: A baseless report. An idle tale.

Lawyer, A: A Service term for an argumentative or discontented man: anyone who has a grievance about his "rights" and talks about them.

Lazy Eliza, A: A trench expression for a long distance big shell, passing high overhead and making a slow, rumbling sound in its flight—somewhat resembling the rumble of a late tram returning empty to its terminus.

Lead off, To: To be angry: to lose temper, e.g., "He led off at me".

Lead, To Swing the: To malinger or sham illness. To exaggerate. To evade a duty. To cadge. To impose upon.

Leaf: Leave. A pronunciation universal in the Navy and taken up also in the other Services, e.g., "I am for leaf next month". It has been suggested that the word originated with reference to the leaf, or page, of the Leave Book, the perforated leaf being torn out and given to a man going on leave to serve as his pass.

League of Remembrance, The: The ladies' organization for aiding widows and daughters of officers who fell in the War. The members make surgical dressings, pillow cases, sheets, and garments for sale to hospitals and kindred institutions; and also visit and entertain the wounded of the War still in hospital. The League originated during the War at the instance of Princess Beatrice, who personally supervised its activities. (*See* Not Forgotten Association.)

Lean on Your Chin Straps: An expression sometimes used in going up a steep hill.

Leaning Virgin of Albert, The: The familiar name on the Western Front in the War for the gilded image of the Blessed Virgin Mary, holding the Child in her outstretched arms, on the tower of the Church of "Notre Dame des Brebières", at Albert, a town between Arras and Amiens. The tower was struck by German shells in October, 1914, and the image thenceforward leaned over from its pedestal at right angles, in a horizontal position, apparently about to fall at any moment. It remained like that until March, 1918, when, during the great German "push" on the Western Front, the tower was finally destroyed. During the three and a half years a legend spread widely all over the countryside that the image was supernaturally protected, and would not be permitted to fall until the end of the War; also, that its fall would portend the doom of the Hohenzollern dynasty in Germany. To maintain local confidence the image was, it is said, secretly made secure by British Royal Engineers, which was the real cause of its remaining in position so long.

Leap-frogging: A familiar term in the War for a form of attack, introduced in 1917 for penetrating deeply into the German fortified trench system. Successive lines of objectives, or limits of attack, were appointed to successive "waves", or attack formations of infantry. On the first "wave" capturing its allotted objective, while it consolidated the position, the second passed through beyond it, or "leap-frogged" forward, to capture the second objective ahead, and then in turn the third "wave" passed forward in like manner, following up the artillery barrage as it "lifted" and cleared the way for each advancing "wave".

Leather Bumpers: An infantry colloquial term for cavalrymen.

Leather Neck: A bluejacket's term for a Marine: also for a Soldier. From the leather stock worn at the neck of the coat or tunic in former times.

Leather Necks, The: *See* Nicknames of Regiments.

Leave Train: The term universal in the War for the railway trains on both sides of the Channel carrying officers and men to and fro on leave. Also, for the naval trains North, serving the Grand Fleet.

Lebel Mam'selle: French Army colloquial for the French Rifle. (From the name of its inventor, M. Lebel.)

Left-hand Man of the Line: A name sometimes jestingly used for the sentry on the last post westward of the British line in Flanders. It is related that on one occasion, when the British Commander-in-Chief visited the locality, he asked casually of an astonished soldier if he was aware that he was the left-hand man of the extreme left of the British line. The information left the man quite unimpressed, and after the officers had gone a sergeant took it on himself to explain. "You 'eard wot 'Aig said? Well, it means that if 'e gave the order 'Right wheel!' you'd go on runnin' for the rest of yer blinkin' life!"

Leg, Show a: Wake up. Turn out. The boatswain's mate's call on board ship, rousing out the Lower Deck in the morning. Constantly used in the War also among the soldiers. In the Navy, it dates from long ago, when women, ostensibly as sailors' wives, were allowed to live on board ship. The usual call was, "Show a leg or a purser's stocking!" Everybody had to put a leg outside the hammock, a stockinged leg denoting that its occupant was a woman, who was then allowed to remain until the men had cleared out.

Legs Eleven: An expression for any very tall thin man. From No. 11 in the game of "House".

Lena Ashwell Firing Line Concert Party, The: A celebrated party of five which gave entertainments at places within range of enemy fire—comprising a pianist, violinist, tenor, baritone, and a comic man. Other concert parties arranged by Miss Lena Ashwell and supported by generous donors toured behind the Lines on the Western Front. They were also to be met with elsewhere—at Moascar, for one place, where their performances were much appreciated by officers and men on leave from Palestine.

Let's Hear From You: Hurry up. Get a move on. Look sharp.

Lid, A: A colloquial term for the steel shrapnel helmet.

Lid on, To put the: To finish off. To settle. To have done with.

Lifeboat Party, The: The familiar term in the War for the officers and men usually told off from a unit going into action to remain behind in order to serve as a nucleus in rebuilding the unit in the event of exceptional casualties. *See* Battle Surplus.

Light Bobs, The: *See* Nicknames of Regiments.

Light Duty: Exemption from parade with liability only for easy "fatigue" work. Usually granted in cases marked "M and D" (*q.v.*) by a medical officer. As the notation often carried with it a suggestion of malingering, a "light duty man" was a term used in the ranks as equivalent to a malingerer.

Ligoniers, The: *See* Nicknames of Regiments.

Lilywhites, The: *See* Nicknames of Regiments.

Limo: Bread.

Limmick: (*Hind.*—Namak). Salt.

Limpets: A post-War term, coined by the newspapers and applied in sarcasm to the holders of well-paid Government posts, created primarily for War purposes, who stuck to them although the necessity was not generally apparent. A term during the War, also coined by the newspapers, for civilian "Indispensables", particularly young fellows of military age and fitness retained in Government departments, who were thought to be unfairly sticking to safe stay-at-home jobs, instead of joining up for the front. (*See* Cuthbert.)

Line, The: The firing line—immediately in contact with the enemy.

Line, Down the: At the rear. "Out of the Line", or "Resting".

Line, To Have on the: To be watching someone with a view to future action.

Line, Up the: In the trenches. Also, On long leave (Navy.)

Linseed Lancers, The: *See* Nicknames of Regiments.

Lions, The: *See* Nicknames of Regiments.

Lit Up: Under the influence of drink.

Little Fighting Fours, The: *See* Nicknames of Regiments.

Little Grenadiers, The: *See* Nicknames of Regiments.

Little Willie: *See* Willie, Big and Little.

Live Bait Squadron, The: A name, unhappily of sinister portent, given to the ill-fated *Hogue, Cressy* and *Aboukir* while employed cruising on their exposed "beat" in the North Sea in September, 1914, which resulted in all three being sunk on September 22nd by a German submarine.

Live on the Navy, To: To subsist on service rations without going in for anything beyond.

Liveliness, A Certain: A popular catch-phrase in the War applied indiscriminately among civilians and in the Services. Used colloquially of any exceptional display of activity on the part of anybody. E.g., an over zealous officer would be said by his men to be displaying "a certain liveliness". A newspaper report of a public house brawl might describe it as "a certain liveliness". The expression originated from the Admiralty *communiqué* of August 19th, 1914, issued by Mr. Winston Churchill as First Lord, stating that "a certain liveliness was noticeable in the North Sea".

Lizzie, A: A big gun: also its shell. A term originating at the Dardanelles and suggested by the firing of the big fifteen-inch guns of H.M.S. *Queen Elizabeth.*

Lord of Loose: An expression for the burst on impact of a big shell; from the mass of earth and debris thrown up by the explosion.

Loaf: Head, e.g., "Duck your loaf—i.e., keep your head below the parapet". (Rhyming slang—loaf of bread.)

Lob, To: To arrive.

Lobster, A: A Soldier. A Redcoat. A nickname as old as Queen Anne's time for infantry, and for cavalry (cuirassiers) going back to the Civil War—1642.

Lobster Box or Pot: An old Navy name for a troopship. Applied in particular to the old Indian troopships of forty years ago.

Lock Horns, To: To attack. To come to close quarters with.

Lolly: Anything easy. An easily-tricked person. (Australian term.)

London Thieving Corps: *See* Nicknames of Regiments.

Lone Howitzer, The: A nickname on the Western Front for a certain 4.5-inch Howitzer posted by itself in. an isolated position in a chalk pit near Loos. The piece was in service from August, 1914, to August, 1917, when it was "knocked out", only the gun-barrel remaining intact. It is now at the Imperial War Museum, South Kensington.

Lone Pine, The: The name officially given to a Turkish position on Gallipoli in the neighbourhood of Anzac Cove, captured in August, 1916, by the Australians after long and severe fighting, its final taking being described by Sir Ian Hamilton as "a desperate fine feat". The name was suggested by a solitary dwarf pine tree that formed the principal landmark on the position; and also, possibly, by the title of a song of the hour:—"The Lonesome Pine".

Lone Star: A "one pip" subaltern. (From the single star badge of rank.)

Lone Tree: The name given to a solitary tree that stood in No Man's Land near Loos for upwards of twelve months continually exposed to fire.

Lonely Officers' Dances: The E.E.F. name for the series of dances instituted at Cairo by Lady Allenby for officers on leave.

Lonely Soldier: During the earlier part of the War many kindly-disposed ladies in England advertised in the papers offering to write letters to cheer up any "lonely soldier", any man without relatives. It was a well-intentioned idea, but among men at the Front it only caused amusement, and the term in consequence came to be a stock jest in the army. In the end, as spies were found to be taking advantage of the opportunity, Scotland Yard intervened and stopped the advertisements. In France the rôle of "marraine", or godmother, to soldiers, was authorized, ladies being permitted to interest themselves in friendless soldiers, to write to them, and, in particular, to "shepherd" them about when on leave. A printed card, termed a "Brevet de Marraine", was issued, which had a Cap of Liberty at the top of the card and below it a picture of a lady walking about with a soldier, also, at the foot of the card, a blank space for the man's signature.

Lonely Star: A name given in jest at the Front to the ladies who had advertised their desire to write letters to lonely soldiers.

Long Bertha: A big Krupp gun. (*See* Big Bertha.)

Long-eared Chum: A mule.

Long-faced Chum: A horse.

Long-haired Chum: A girl.

Long Horn: A familiar name for an early type Maurice Farman 70 h.p. two-seater biplane. From its two long projecting buffer-skids in front. (*See* Short Horn.)

Long Jump, The: An Air Force expression for the transferring of an ail squadron from the Home Establishment to active service overseas.

Long Jump, Up for the: For trial by court martial. (Suggesting the need of a long jump to get over the trouble.)

Long Tom: A familiar name for the British 60-pr. "position" gun of the earlier days of the War. Also, colloquially, any big gun. The name became familiarized to the public in the South African War, originating apparently with the name given to a notorious Boer big gun firing from Pepworth Hill at the Siege of Ladysmith.

Look See, A: A telescope. A periscope.

Look Stick: A telescope. A periscope.

Loopy: Silly, daft.

Loos-Wallah: (*Hind.*—Lus: thief; Wala: fellow). Thief, rascal.

Loot: Lieutenant. (Navy—lower deck). Also the usual American pronunciation of Lieutenant.

Lord Adam Gordon's Lifeguards: *See* Nicknames of Regiments.

Lord Wellington's Bodyguard: *See* Nicknames of Regiments.

Lord's Own, The: A nickname for H.M.S. *Vengeance.* ("Vengeance is mine saith the Lord".)

Lorry Hopping (or Jumping): A familiar term at the Front for travelling by begging "lifts" from passing transport vehicles. The main roads at the Front were always thronged with motor transport vehicles going to and fro, full or empty, and though it was against orders to take up or carry passengers, practically every driver would let a man met on the road "hop the lorry" and get a surreptitious ride as far as possible towards his destination. The expression is still in use. A destitute man in a London Police Court in September, 1923, told the magistrate that he could get to his home in Manchester in a day by "lorry hopping".

Lose the Number of One's Mess, To: To die (Navy). (*Cf.* To slip one's wind. To coil up one's ropes.)

Lot's Wife: Salt (Navy.)

Lottie: *See* Nicknames.

Loud One, A: A misfortune.

Louse, To: To search one's clothing for vermin, lice.

Lousy Fellow: A mean man.

Lousy Wood: Army vernacular for Leuze Wood, the scene of hard fighting in the Battle of the Somme in 1916.

Loy Als, The: *See* Nicknames of Regiments.

Lozenges: Revolver or pistol cartridges.

Lump of Lead: Head. (Rhyming slang.)

Lumpers, The: *See* Nicknames of Regiments.

M and D: Medicine and Duty. The letters marked in the Medical Officer's report opposite the name of a man reporting sick, but with really little the matter with him in the Medical Officer's opinion. As the notation consequently often implied a suspicion of malingering, in the ranks at the Front "M and D" was used as an expression applicable to men suspected of malingering, or shamming sickness.

M and V: A familiar expression for the tinned meat and vegetable ration.

M.E.F.: Initials standing for Mediterranean Expeditionary Force. Sent to Egypt in February, 1915, under Sir Ian Hamilton and thence to the attack on Gallipoli.

M.L.: Motor Launch. The Motor Launches of the War were one of the most useful and hard worked classes of small craft, employed on duty of every kind, from carrying messages to sinking enemy submarines.

They were petrol-driven vessels, fast and handy to manoeuvre, and were manned mostly by men of civilian professions and callings. Amateur yachtsmen, stockbrokers, artists and architects, civilians of every sort officered them, with R.N.V.R commissions, while the crews similarly were drawn from promiscuous shore callings and trades, clerks and artisans, etc.

M.M.S.: Military Massage Service. A woman's organization formed in August, 1914, and numbering 2,000 members at the Armistice.

M.T.V.: Motor Transport Volunteers.

Maconochie: A colloquial variant for the M and V ration; from the name of the firm supplying it. Used also generally of any make of tinned rations. The shape of the tin suggested further the expression "Shake up your Maconochie", for "Shake up the telephone receiver". The word was also sometimes used for stomach, e.g., "He got hit in the Maconochie".

Maconochie Cross, The: Colloquial for the M.C. (Military Cross.)

Maconochie, Medal, The: The M.M. (Military Medal.)

Mad Minute, The: A newspaper-coined expression of the autumn of 1914 in accounts of the Retreat from Mons, in allusion to the musketry *feu d'enfer* of our men in action. The rapidity and accuracy of our bursts of rifle fire are said to have so impressed the Germans that they refused to believe that it was not machine-gun fire. The discharge in one minute of fifteen rounds, on the order "Rapid Fire". The *Musketry Regulations,* under which the men of the British Expeditionary Force were trained (1909 Edition), lay down: "With a distinct aiming mark within about 1,000 yards, a well-trained man should be able to fire from 12 to 15 rounds a minute without serious loss of accuracy." One round would be ready to fire in the loaded rifle, four rounds ready in the magazine, and ten rounds instantly at hand to follow, in two clips of five rounds each in buttoned pouches or bandolier. On the executive order "Rapid Fire" being given, in cases where no particular number of rounds is specified, immediately the first minute's fifteen rounds have been discharged, each man continues firing "at his own best rate for combining rapidity with accuracy", loading with clip after clip, until the order "Cease Fire" is given.

Madelon: The famous melody to which the French soldiers marched into battle in the Great War and in particular to the defence of Verdun— with which "Madelon" is now inseparably associated. Madelon is a tune, or song, or dance—all three. The French contingent in the "Victory March" in London, in July, 1919, marched to "Madelon", the men singing the "Victory" version of the chorus:—

"Madelon, emplis mon verre
 Et chante avec les poilus,
 Nous avons gagné la guerre,

Hein, crois—tu qu'on les a eus.
Madelon, ah, verse â boire,
Et surtout n'y mets pas d'eau,
C'est pour fêter la Victoire
Joffre, Foch, et Clemenceau!"

Mafeesh: (*Arabic*). Dead. Done with. Finished. Used colloquially everywhere on Eastern Fronts and much as Napoo (*q.v.*) on the Western Front. It had other meanings: "I can't", "I know", "Get out", "Go to hell", and some meanings that are unprintable.

Maggie: The nickname of H.M.S. *Magnificent.*

Mainga: Water. A Zulu word used among South African troops.

Major, The: The usual name among N.C.O.'s colloquially for the Sergeant Major.

Make, To: To acquire by irregular or doubtful means.

Make and Mend, A: A naval holiday. In old days when bluejackets made their own garments, one afternoon weekly was given for the purpose, usually on a Thursday. Now-a-days the seamen's clothing is usually supplied ready made up, but the weekly half holiday (often transferred to a Saturday) continues to be known as a "Make and Mend".

Makee Learn, A: (Pigeon English). A young officer. One under instruction.

Maknoon: (*Arabic*). Silly. Mad.

Male Tank: A Tank mounting guns, as differentiated from a "female tank" mounting machine-guns. (*See* Female Tank.)

Maleesh: (*Arabic*). Never mind. It doesn't matter. Used colloquially on Eastern Fronts.

Malum: (*Hind.*—Malum). To understand, e.g., "Do you malum it?"

Man and Wife: Knife. (Rhyming slang.)

Mandarin, A: A term sometimes used derisively for any over-pompous official—usually one at a Government Office, e.g., "The Mandarins of the War Office".

Mangle, A: An Air Force colloquial term for a machine gun.

Map, Not on the: Hardly credible. Outside possibility.

Marauders, The: In trench raids a name for the parties of men forming the main group told off to go through an enemy's trench specially to capture prisoners required for Intelligence Department purposes, as distinct from the bombers, whose business was to prevent enemy interference while the marauders were at work. The word "marauder" is usually said to have originated in the Thirty Years War in the 17th Century, from the name of a German Colonel, Count von Merode, whose command acquired notoriety from their plundering habits and brutalities. Other derivations, however, have been suggested. The word became established in England apparently during the wars in Flanders of William III and Marlborough. It occurs in plays of the period and Addison mentions it in the *Spectator*—No. 165 (1711).

Mark, Off the: Quite wrong. Also to start on a thing quickly. (Derivation from the running track.)

Mark One, A: A Nursing Sister. Usually one belonging to Queen Mary's Nursing Service. (Navy.)

Mark Time On, To: To retain or stick to anything. Also, to keep someone under observation.

Mary Anne: No matter (*See* San Fairy Ann.)

Mascot of H.M.S. New Zealand, The: The Maori "Piu-piu", or cloak of black and white strips of flax and feathers, and the carved greenstone amulet figure, ("Tiki") worn round the neck (similar to the old battle insignia of Maori chiefs) presented to the battleship *New Zealand*. They were given by an old Maori Chief in 1913, with the injunction that they must always be worn when the ship was in action, the chief prophesying that they would keep the ship from harm. Both "Piu-piu" and "Tiki" were worn at the Battle of Jutland by the Captain—to the great satisfaction of the crew, who, it is told, before the battle began took special measures to find out that the Captain was actually wearing the ship's mascot. On another occasion, when an action seemed imminent, the *New Zealand* mascot was also worn. On that occasion, word was specially passed round the decks among the men—"It's all right, he's got 'em on!" The *New Zealand* at Jutland escaped with only one shell hit, and had no casualties. Writing home after Jutland an officer said: "This ship bore a charmed life and suffered to the smallest extent though we were right in it the whole time."

Mascots: Before the setting in of the Mascot craze which, during the War possessed everybody in the Services and outside, the usual personal charm, or mascot, among soldiers was in the Infantry a tunic button, and in the Cavalry the tooth of a horse. Long before the War it was usual to adopt some animal or bird as a luck-bringer for the mascot of a unit. In the War, in addition to these, some regiments, particularly in the New Armies while training in England, adopted even boys as mascots. They were generally stray urchins, picked up in the neighbourhood of a camp, who were put into miniature uniforms and marched with the corps, when tired being smuggled into one of the waggons. The Zoo acted as caretaker to hundreds of mascots, many brought by Overseas troops, Canadians, Australians, South Africans and others, and lodged there when the troops crossed to the Front. They included wolves, bears, deer, antelopes, wild boar, and an ostrich. In like manner, most British regiments, with similar mascots, sent theirs to the Zoo. A number of warships also had their mascots: among them were the celebrated "Brindle Boy" dog of the *Lion*, the two black cats of the *Vindictive* at Zeebrugge, the monkey "Jackoo" of the *Loyal* (lost overboard), "Peggy", the bulldog of the *Iron Duke* at Jutland, the black cat of the *Tiger*, etc. Personally worn mascots of every imaginable kind and shape and material were innumerable. On one occasion in Regent's Park, a French actress presented the celebrated "Touchwood" charm— a quaint little cross-legged figure, with a big head and gleaming eyes, wearing a khaki service-cap—as a personal mascot to each of the 1,200 men of a battalion of the City of London Rifles. It was of course the same, in various forms of mascots, among the belligerents of all nations, everything down to bat's wings in certain German regiments serving for the purposes of a charm.

This story is told of one of the Navy mascots at the Battle of Jutland. The *Valiant*, one of the "Super-Dreadnoughts" of the 5th Battle Squadron supporting Lord Beatty's attack before the Grand Fleet joined, had on board, as an officer of the ship describes, "a pedigree cock as her mascot, and he passed through the earlier stages of the battle with an indifference worthy alike of his high breeding and his exalted office. A blast which removed him from the cocks' coop deposited him in a ventilating shaft where he stuck fast all night, but he continued to crow lustily all night until rescued next morning." Three curiously parallel cases, it may be added, are on record in earlier wars: that of the gamecock in battle on board the flagship *Formidable* in Rodney's victory:—

"Through blood and fire,
　Through storm and shock
　Prophet of triumph still crowed on
　Lord Rodney's bantam cock!"

that of the game-cock whose plucky example, perched aloft crowing on the stump of a shattered mast, inspirited the crew of the hard pressed *Montagu* on the "Glorious First of June", and helped to save the ship; that of the game-cock of the *Colossus* at Trafalgar, which likewise flew out of its shattered coop, and then, perching on the captain's shoulder, crowed lustily, its demeanour helping to hearten up the crew (mostly East-end Londoners by the way), at a critical moment when half-a-dozen enemies, attacking at once, had nearly overpowered the ship.

Mat, On the: Up for trial. In trouble.

Maternity Jacket: The name given the double-breasted tunic, worn formerly in the Royal Flying Corps.

Matlo: (*French*—Matelot). A bluejacket. A Service colloquial name.

Mats: Trench "duckboards" (*q.v.*).

Meat Skewer: Bayonet.

Meat Ticket: The Identity Disc (also Cold Meat Ticket *q.v.*).

Mebu: *See* Pill Box. Mebu represents the initials of the long German technicalterm—"Maschinengewehr-Eisenbeton-Unterstand"—Machine-Gun-Iron-Concrete-Emplacement.

Mechanical Cow, The: The name given to the Maurice Farman Long Horn biplane with long skids. (*See* Long Horn.)

Medics, The: R.A.M.C.

Mendinghem: *See* Bandagehem.

Merchant: A fellow. One connected with any special branch of the service. Used with various applications, e.g., "A M.G. merchant"—a Machine gunner; "A paper merchant"—an officer given to worry people with unnecessary written communications.

Mermaid's Visiting Card: A U.S. Army term for the Identity Disc issued to U.S. Troops on embarkation to Europe, in allusion to possibilities of misadventure through German submarines in crossing the Atlantic.

Mesop: Mesopotamia. (*Also* mess-up.)

Mesopolonica: A composite expression for an unknown or doubtful destination on an Eastern Front. Troops in the War, finding themselves issued with equipment for Eastern service would sometimes say that they were for Mesopolonica, either Mesopotamia or Salonica, their actual destination being unknown.

Mess, Out of: Dead.

Mess, To be put out of: To be killed.

Mess, To Lose the Number of One's: To be killed, to die.

Messman's Horror: A Navy term for anyone with an extra large appetite, and so "doing" the Messman out of his prospective profits.

Mespot: Mesopotamia. (*Also* mess pot.)

Meteors: The Meteorological Service at the Front giving weather information by telephone to airmen and others.

Methusilier: A member of the Australian Remount Unit, the personnel of which were mostly men over military age.

Micks, The: The Irish Guards. Any Irish Unit.

Mike, A: Idleness. Slackness.

Mike, To (to do a): To make off. To avoid duty.

Mike and George, The: Colloquial for the Order of St. Michael and St. George decoration, e.g., "Jones got his Mike and George out of that show".

Mill's Spud, A: A Mill's grenade.

Mince Pies: Eyes. (Rhyming slang.)

Minden Boys, The: See Nicknames of Regiments.

Mine Bumping Squadron, The: The name given to the Third Battle Squadron of the Grand Fleet, comprising the eight pre-Dreadnought battleships of the *Kind Edward VII* class. From their being sent ahead of the main Battle-Fleet "super-Dreadnought" squadrons when the Grand Fleet was making a "sweep" in the North Sea, so that, should enemy mines be in the way, the Mine Bumping Squadron, as comprising the less important units, should, by sacrificing themselves, give warning to the ships following and ensure the safety of the all important main fleet. (*See* Uriahites, also Wobbly Eight.)

Minge: Female society (similar to Binge—*q.v.*), e.g., "His failing is Binge and yours Minge".

Mingle, A: A colloquial term for an occasion at an officer's hospital when patients and nurses were officially permitted to meet socially.

Ministering, Angel, A: A Sister of Queen Mary's Nursing Service. (Navy.)

Minnie: The usual colloquial term for the German minenwerfer (trench mortar); also its bomb.

Miracle of the Marne, The: A phrase often used with reference to the "turn of the tide", when in September, 1914, the Allies checked and forced back the German advance.

Mit: Hand.

Mit, The Frozen: The cold shoulder, e.g., "He tried to make up to me but I gave him the frozen mit".

Mizzle, To Do a: To disappear. To slink off.

Moan, To: To complain. To grumble. To be a pessimist. (Navy—equivalent to the Army "grouse".)

Mob: Any collection or body of troops. A very old Army term, without any suggestion of the disorder of a civilian mob. Often used in a semi-humorous sense, e.g., "Kitchener's Mob". "The Mob" was in the War also an occasional name for a North Sea flotilla of destroyers operating in Heligoland Bight and off Zealand in connection with mine-laying operations.

Mob Store: Mobilization Store; where the war equipment of a unit is kept.

Mobile, To Do a: An Egyptian Expeditionary Force expression for going on a route march into the desert.

Moke Train, The: See Nicknames of Regiments.

Molo: Drunk.

Moniker: Name. Signature, e.g., "What's your moniker?"—What's your name.

Monitor: The term officially introduced into the British. Navy by Mr. Winston Churchill in August, 1914, in the first place for three Brazilian shallow-draught, river gun-vessels, taken up by the Admiralty for the War while building, and specially armed and equipped for coast attack purposes, (the *Humber, Mersey* and *Severn*). The name Monitor, for a special type of ship, originated with John Ericsson the celebrated Swedish-American engineer and inventor who gave it to the original ironclad turret-ship of the American War of Secession, the *Monitor,* celebrated for her historic duel with the *Merrimac.* Ericsson announced the name in a letter of January 2nd, 1862, to the Federal naval authorities, in which he said that his new ship was specially designed to "admonish the leaders of the Southern Revolution" and would "prove a severe monitor to them". "On these, and other grounds", added Ericsson, "I propose to name the new battery Monitor". The British monitors of 1914 did notable service off the Belgian Coast, bombarding the German shore batteries, served later in the Mediterranean, destroyed the *Konigsberg* on the East Africa coast, and were useful everywhere. Later monitors the *Lord Clyde*, *General Wolfe*, *General Craufurd*, *Marshal Ney* and others served with the Dover Patrol (*q.v.*), bombarded the Belgian coast, served at Gallipoli and in the Adriatic, and covered the advance of the *Vindictive* at Zeebrugge. Certain of them were also stationed in the Thames to shell Zeppelins making for London with their 12-inch guns. In all 37 Monitors were built, ranging up to 8,000 tons and having speeds varying from 6 to 12 knots. The earliest monitors mounted 6-inch guns, the later, 9.2-inch, 12-inch, 14-inch, 15-inch, up to 18-inch, the biggest gun in the War. The 18-inch gun—only one—was mounted on board the Monitor *Lord Clyde*: two other Monitors, the *General Wolfe* and *Prince Eugene*, were fitted for them.

Monkey Motions: Physical exercises.

Monkey's Island: The small upper-bridge of a warship where the captain and navigating officer ordinarily have their posts at sea. "Monkey", in this connection, is simply a diminutive, with no implication of disrespect.

Mons, On the Wire at: Not present. A colloquial reply in answer to an enquiry for somebody absent. ("Wire" of course had not come into general employment at the time of the Retreat from Mons.)

Moo-Cow Farm: Mouquet Farm. The scene of exceptionally fierce fighting by the Australians in the Battle of the Somme, near Thiepval.

Moonrakers, The: *See* Nicknames of Regiments.

Mopping-up: The term for the work allotted to special parties of men appointed to follow close in the track of advancing "waves" of troops, in order to explore and clear the enemy lines and dug-outs of men remaining behind, or lurking there, to attack the captors of the position in rear. The Mopping-up method was first adopted at the Battle of Arras in February, 1917, as the result of experiences in the Battle of the Somme in the previous autumn, to prevent our infantry as they moved forward, being held up, or interrupted, by attacks in rear. Extract from a Trench Raid Scheme of the 15th Infantry Brigade:—"The 2nd Platoon will mop-up, kill, or otherwise destroy, all parties of the enemy, etc."

Morgenroth: The haunting death-song of the German forlorn-hopes in attacking (written by Wilhelm Hauff):

"Morning bright; morning bright—
Light that lends me to the grave—
Soon shall dawn with summons brazen
Call me to my death to hasten
I, and many a comrade brave!"
(*Professor Blackie's translation.*)

Moss Dog, A: A stingy fellow. A man only interested in saving money.

Mossy Face: An Air Force name for the Bois d'Harincourt on the Western Front.

Mother: The name "Mother" was originally given to a widely celebrated 9.2-inch howitzer, which served on the Western Front from October, 1914, till July, 1916, the first of the type in the service. "Mother" was specially visited by the Prince of Wales at Warneton. While there an infantry guard was specially mounted over "Mother" to keep off inquisitive local civilian visitors, and an anti-aircraft section also was allotted to keep off enemy aeroplanes at night. In November, 1914, "Mother", with eight shots, destroyed an entire German heavy battery. The nickname was given also to other big howitzers at various times. Some of the exploits of one of them, a Naval Brigade howitzer, were commemorated in humorous verse. The concluding lines of one stanza, dealing with the bombardment of a German troop-train (a German being supposed to be the speaker), ran as follows:

"Boom, Mother!

We've picked up several bits,

Of the late lamented Fritz,

But we never saw the blooming trail! Again!"

The end of another verse, on the shelling of a small town where the German Crown Prince was reported to be, ran thus:—

"Boom, Mother!

We found the Kron Prinz braces.

But we can't find any traces

Of the donner vetter blitzen Flemish town!"

The name "Mother" was also given to one of the earliest Tanks experimented with in England. This Tank was also, later, given the name "Big Willie", (*See* Willie, Big and Little.)

Mother's Meeting: An occasional name among bluejackets for the captain's address to a ship's company.

Mouldy: The universal Navy name for a torpedo. (Origin apparently untraceable.)

Mouldy, To Squirt a: To fire a torpedo.

Mournful Maria: A nickname given to the Dunkirk siren, employed to give warning of enemy air attacks and long range shelling.

Mouth Organ: A familiar name for a Stokes' mortar bomb. From the sound made by the air passing through the holes round the base of the shell as it starts.

Movie Man, A: A searchlight operator.

Movies, The: Searchlights.

Muck in With, To: To share, e.g., "Come along and muck in with us".

Muckin: (*Hind.*—Makkhn). Butter.

Muckle Flugga Hussars, The: The name given in the War to the armed merchant ships comprising the Tenth Cruiser Squadron, employed on patrol between Muckle Flugga, the most northerly of the Orkneys, and the edge of the ice-pack fringing the Greenland Coast. The ships were largely Liverpool merchantmen, some twenty-four in number. They carried out blockade work to prevent supplies reaching Germany north-about. Ten of them were sunk by enemy submarines.

Mud: No good. A term expressive of disgust and weariness, e.g., "My name's mud—its all up with me!"

Mud Crawling: Country route marching in wet weather.

Mud Crushers: Infantrymen.

Mud Hook: Anchor. (Navy.) Also the Anchor in tile game of "Crown and Anchor" (*q.v.*).

Mudlarks, The: See Nicknames of Regiments.

Mufti: Civilian clothes as distinguished from uniform. The Infantry term usually, the Cavalry and the Navy term being "Plain Clothes". Hospital nurses, changing into ordinary dress often spoke of "going into mufti". The word was apparently introduced into England by officers of the East India Company at the end of the 18th Century. The universal wearing of mufti by officers off duty came in after 1830, at the instance of the Duke of Wellington it is said, in consequence of the popular prejudice at that period against the army among certain classes of the people. (*See* Civvies.)

Mump, To: To cadge. To borrow.

Mungaree: Bread. Food. Originally a Zulu word, adopted by the old army and carried to Egypt during the Soudan War. The natives picked it up, taking it to be an English word, and from them it became adopted by the men of the New Army serving in Egypt during the War.

Mungy Wallah: A man employed in the Cook House. (Mungy—*French* Manger.)

Mur: Rum (back slang).

Murdering Thieves, The: *See* Nicknames of Regiments.

Murphies, The: The Divisional Concert Party of the 10th (Irish) Division.

Murray's Bucks: *See* Nicknames of Regiments.

Mush: The Guard-room. Cells.

Musical Box: The name of a widely celebrated Whippet Tank in the action at Villers Bretonnaux on August 8th, 1918.

Mustard Gas: Otherwise "Yellow Cross" gas (from the marking on the shells). A vesicant and poison gas, one effect of which was to blister the mouth, armpits and face, and affect the eyes. First used in July, 1917, by the Germans. Nausea was the first symptom, followed by dangerous symptoms and lastly by total collapse. The gas hung long on the ground, often remaining inert till the sun's warmth caused the fumes to rise.

Mutiny: Rum. Grog. (Navy.)

Mystery Port, The: Richborough, on the coast of Kent, transformed during the War into the English terminus and starting point for the Channel Barge Service and Train Ferry, and the depôt for the I.W.T., the Inland Water Transport service on the Western Front. Within twelve months from March, 1916, Richborough was created into a city of ship-yards, wharves, foundries, workshops, and power-plant buildings, with upwards of 80 miles of railway lines. Its establishments supplied over 400 officers and 12,500 men for overseas services, in addition to over 400 officers for technical establishments in various places in Great Britain.

Mystery Ships, The: A name for the "Decoy" or "Q ships" (*q.v.*). The practice of disguising men-of-war for decoy purposes is of course very old, and many instances of its employment are recorded in Naval his-tory, among others for instance Lord Cochrane's famous exploits in the Speedy. It may not be generally known perhaps that a British frigate was specially built in Charles II's reign to serve as a Decoy Ship, being con-structed to have the appearance of a merchantman, but with collapsible bulwarks, detachable figurehead, etc.—the *Kingfisher*. She was specially employed in the Mediterranean to trap Algerine corsairs, and one of her actions, with seven Algerine pirates on her at once, is a notable epi-sode in British Naval History.

Mystery Towers, The: The popular name, which the newspapers originated, for certain structures designed to form part of an anti-submarine device in connection with the Straits of Dover barrage, built at Shoreham in the last year of the War. Seven were proposed, and were to be erected at intervals across the Straits, with electrically fired mines between, to be operated by means of an electric detector. Anti-submarine nets were also to be used between the towers. On a hostile submarine being detected trying to pass between two towers, a knob would be pressed by the operator in one tower and the nearest mines to the submarine would go off, destroying the vessel. Three only had been completed at the Armistice, one of which now serves in place of the Nab lightship at the entrance to Spithead.

Mystery V.C., The: Captain Gordon Campbell R.N., V.C., who won the V.C. in his famous "Q" ship the *Farnborough*. The name was given to him by the newspapers in consequence of the unusual wording of the "London Gazette" notifying the grant of the decoration. It was stated that the V.C. was granted "In recognition of his conspicuous gallantry, consummate coolness and skill in command, of one of His Majesty's ships in action". No further details were given, contrary to the usual practice of setting out in detail how the distinction was won. Carrying out the "Mystery" idea, on Captain Campbell attending one of the King's Investitures at Buckingham Palace to receive his V.C., as he approached His Majesty, the Guards' band in attendance struck up, to the general surprise and amusement, "Hush, here comes the Bogey Man!"

N.A.C.B.: Navy and Army Canteen Board.

N.B.G.: No B— good!

N.E.: A Navy lower-deck contraction of "Not Entitled", i.e., to any pay. Otherwise rendered "A North Easter", e.g., a man on learning that the Paymaster had nothing for him, on coming away would say, "A Nor' Easter (or a N.E.) was blowing for me to-day!"

N.O.: Colloquial for Naval Officer.

Nails: Cigarettes.

Nails in the Coffin of the Kaiser: A U.S. minelayer's expression, used by the men of the mines they laid on the Northern Barrage.

Name (or Number) on, To Have One's: Said of a bullet that hit a man; i.e., that it was destined for him.

Name, To Lose One's: To have one's name taken down on parade; i.e., to be noted for punishment.

Nancy Dawson: The old grog-time tune in the Navy. From the name of a celebrated former-day hornpipe dancer of Covent Garden and Drury Lane Theatres.

Nanny Goats: *See* Nicknames of Regiments.

Napoo (also Nappo Finee): No more; all gone. Finished. Dead. (*French*—Il n'y a pas de plus—fini). A colloquial term, applied universally in the War to anybody or anything. Originally the French shopkeeper's stock reply when asked for anything sold out. A useless, or unsatisfactory man or thing; anything done with or missing; anyone killed—all were "Napoo", or "Napoo'd". E.g., "That fellow's napoo"; i.e., a rotter. "This strap is napoo"; i.e., won't hold. "That trench was full of water and we had to napoo it", i.e., abandon it. "You're too late, breakfast napoo", i.e., finished, "Smith and Jones napoo'd the lot". "Half the platoon got napoo'd last night", i.e., killed. Napoo, used to French shopkeepers, had a meaning they quite understood. A cottager, with eggs for sale, for instance, who had been previously sold out, on being asked for two napoos would at once know what was wanted. Similarly, at a village estaminet, a request for a glass of napoo would at once produce the required beer or spirits.

Napper: Head. (Old common slang.)

Nark: A bad-tempered man. A spoil-sport. (Originally thieves' slang for an informer or police agent.) Also, a man eager to curry favour by running about and doing odd jobs for a superior.

Nark It: Be quiet. Shut up.

Narky: A nickname for H.M.S. *Narcissus*.

National Guard, The: The City of London Volunteer Corps, formed during the War and composed of business men. Two battalions were formed and the Lord Mayor was, *ex officio*, the Colonel.

Naval Battle Rig in the Great War: In Nelson's time and before that seamen fought their guns, stripped to the waist and bare-headed, or with neckerchiefs, or handkerchiefs, tied round the forehead to keep the sweat out of their eyes. At the outset of the Great War each man in the Grand Fleet had served out to him to wear in action a suit of white working dress, which had been specially disinfected. How far it was worn in Grand Fleet actions is, however, not clear. At Jutland, for instance, in several ships the men wore ("No. 4" Dress (night clothing), and in a few ships, "No. 5" Dress (white working jumper and duck trousers). The wearing of boots was optional usually. In some of the bigger ships they were worn by most of the men. Before the action the men's lanyards were removed, so as not to catch in moving parts of the gun machinery. Caps were not worn in turrets. In the magazine shell-rooms, where the work was hot and heavy, jumpers were thrown off, the men mostly being stripped to the waist, as of old. In the batteries, men mostly wore storm-caps or Balaclava helmets. The stokers wore flannels, "fearnought" trousers and stokehold boots. Ordinarily in the North Sea the everyday wear was "No. 4"; blue jumpers without collars, blue trousers; with flannels in summer, and in winter, jerseys. The officers at Jutland wore their ordinary everyday rig; monkey jackets and sea gear. At Jutland also, as being after May 1st, white cap-covers were worn almost universally. Earl Beatty wore a white cap-cover on all occasions in the war, winter and summer, apparently, so that, when on deck with other officers, or on the bridge, he should be readily "spotted" by anyone needing to find him. Swords were not worn in action at Jutland, but most officers kept their revolvers, etc., in some handy place in case of emergency, going off in boats for boarding, etc. Officers in exposed positions on board ship carried respirators of the pad-type and anti-gas goggles. Before the Battle of the Falklands, Sir Doveton Sturdee specially ordered clean flannels to be put on. All in the squadron were in coaling rig at first that morning, as the ships were coaling when the enemy were first reported. Otherwise all wore ordinary day-time blue serges in the action. The officers and men of the *Sydney*, when they fought the *Emden*, were in white "No. 5" working rig.

Navy, Thank God We've Got a: An expression often heard in the Army during the War when things went wrong. Really an old phrase of years ago, said to have originated in a soldier's sarcastic comment when standing and watching a party of the old Volunteers marching by one Saturday night.

Neaters: Rum. (Navy.)

Nellie: The nickname of H.M.S. *Lord Nelson*.

Nelson's Blood: Rum. Old Navy, and probably derived from the old story of the sailors on board the Victory tapping the cask in which Nelson's body was brought home and drinking the spirits. A Portsmouth newspaper first gave it currency in January, 1806, the story being possibly suggested by the fact that during the voyage from Gibraltar to St. Helens there was rather an exceptional number of floggings for drunkenness on board. Extra liquor had probably been smuggled on board at Gibraltar. The cask with the body was kept in the open on the main deck, under sentry, and surreptitious approach to it was impossible.

Nichevo: No more. Finished. Dead. A Russian word, used colloquially in the North Russia Expeditionary Force in the War much as "napoo" on the Western Front.

Nick, The: The Guard-room. Cells.

Nicknames (Personal): These are among the most widely used adaptations of surnames customary in the Services.

Nickname	For a man named
Betsy:	Gay. Old Navy, originally from a song with the refrain: "That charming Betsy Gay".
Blanco:	White.
Bodger:	Lees.
Bogey:	Harris.
Buck:	Taylor.
Bunty:	For any short man.
Busky	Smith.
Charts:	Harris.
Chats:	Peace (from the notorious burglar).
Chippy:	Carpenter.
Darky:	Smith.
Dinghy:	Reed.
Dodger:	Green.
Doughy:	Baker.
Dusty:	Jordan; Miller; Rhodes; Smith.
Edna:	May (from the celebrated actress).
Fanny:	Fields (from "Happy" Fanny Fields, the Music Hall Actress).
Ginger:	Jones.
Granny:	Henderson.
Gunboat:	Smith (from the well-known boxer).
Hooky:	Walker.
Jigger:	Lees.
Jimmy:	Green.
Johnny:	Walker (from the well-known brand of whisky).
Jumper:	Collins; Cross.
Knocker:	White; Walker.

Lackery:	Wood (*See* Lakry.)
Lottie:	Collins (from the celebrated Music Hall actress).
Mouchy:	Reeves.
Nobby:	Clarke; Ewart; also Hewett or Hewart. A nickname of naval origin. From Admiral Charles Ewart (Captain of H.M.S. *Melpomene*, 1859–62) an officer noted for his personal neatness of dress, and, when a Captain, for his insistence on the spick and span appearance of everything on board his ship. According to one story, objecting one day to the appearance of a goose in its coop, he had the goose's bill and feet blacked and its body whitewashed, so as to be in keeping with Navy regulation as to colouring. The story went the round of the Fleet, and on at least one occasion caused the gallant officer some embarrassment. At the Opera at Malta one night, it is told, on Captain Ewart taking his seat in the stalls, a crowd of bluejackets in the gallery at one side broke out in chorus with "Who whitewashed the Goose!" Those opposite responded with "Why, Nobby Ewart", and they kept it up alternately till the harassed captain got up and walked out.
Nocky:	Knight.
Nutty:	Cox.
Pincher:	Martin. The nickname is of naval origin, and was given first to Admiral Sir William Martin, who commanded in the Mediterranean between 1860 and 1863; a very noteworthy character in his day.
Pony:	Moore (after the name of a former day well-known sporting character).
Rattler:	Morgan.
Shinner:	Bright; Black; Bryant; Green; White; Wright.
Shoey:	Smith.
Shorty:	Wright.
Smoky:	Holmes.
Smudger:	Smith.
Snip:	Parsons; Taylor.
Spiky:	Sullivan (from the celebrated prize fighter).
Spokey:	Wheeler; Wheelwright.
Spud:	Murphy.
Taffy:	Jones; Owen, etc., or any Welshman.
Tich:	Any small man (from the name of the popular comedian "Little Tich").
Timber:	Wood.
Topper:	Brown.
Tottie:	Bell.

Tug: Wilson. "Tug", as a nickname for all Wilsons is of naval origin. It was given in the first place to the late Admiral of the Fleet, Sir A.K. Wilson, V.C., when a lieutenant sixty years ago, as a variant of an earlier nickname which blue-jacket swerving with him had for him, "Chug, or Choog".

Wheeler: Johnson.

Wiggy: Bennett.

Nicknames, Sobriquets, and Titles of Regiments: These are some of the better known, with their origins in most cases, as far as these can be traced. A complete list would require a volume to itself, the great majority of Army nicknames being temporary and casual, and constantly changing.

Agamemnons, The Old: The Welch Regiment. Through the 2nd Battalion, as the 69th Foot. From their service with Nelson on board H.M.S. *Agamemnon,* 1793–5.

Aiglers, The: The Royal Irish Fusiliers. Through the 1st Battalion, as the 87th Foot. From their capture of the Eagle of a French regiment at Barrosa in 1811.

All Very Cushy: The Royal Army Veterinary Corps. A War nickname, suggested by the initials A.V.C.

Ally Sloper's Cavalry: The Royal Army Service Corps. A humorous perversion of the initials of the Army Service Corps (now "Royal"). Ally Sloper being the name of a buffoon whose fooleries constituted the attraction of a comic paper. "Army Safety Corps" was a variant, also from the initials.

Artists, The: The title adopted for themselves by the original two nucleus companies of the old 38th Middlesex Rifle Volunteers of 1859, which after being renumbered the 20th Middlesex Rifle Volunteer Corps, developed later into the celebrated 28th Battalion The London Regiment (Artists' Rifles) of to-day. A 2nd and 3rd Battalion were formed during the War. The 2nd Battalion was an O.T.C. unit in England throughout the war. It and the 3rd Battalion have since been demobilized. In December, 1914, shortly after the 1st Battalion had had its first experience of the trenches, Lord French one day came down the Street at Bailleul where the battalion was billeting, and had a hurried talk with Colonel May, asking him to supply 50 men of pre-war experience from the ranks to go into the trenches on the following day as Second-Lieutenants. Fifty men thereupon volunteered, and in privates' tunics, with one "pip" on the shoulder, they took up their duties in the line. From that time, in addition to other duties, the battalion supplied from 70 to 100 officers a month, until 1917, when the Artists went into the line again as a fighting unit, and remained as such till the end of the war. They have continued as a Territorial battalion to the present time, and continue to bear their pre-war number and designation. The original members of 1859, who comprised artists, sculptors, architects, engravers, musicians, and actors, adopted as a badge the heads of Mars and Minerva and the motto "Cum Marte Monerva", a combination that inspired the following lines by a member of the Corps:—

"Mars he was the god of war,
And didn't stick at trifles,
Minerva said she didn't mind—
And so the Artists' Rifles!"

Assayes, The: The Highland Light Infantry. Through the 2nd Battalion, as the 74th Foot. From their distinguished part at the Battle of Assaye in 1803.

Back Numbers, The: The Gloucestershire Regiment. Through the 1st Battalion, as the 28th Foot. From the badge, a Sphynx, worn on both the front and back of the helmet, which took the place of the regimental number, so worn previous to 1881. Granted as a distinction for service at the Battle of Alexandria in 1801, where, on the battalion being attacked in front and rear at once, the rear rank was faced about, and fighting back to back, the men beat off the enemy. In the Great War, in January, 1916, during a violent German attack near Givenchy, the Gloucesters, attacked in front and rear at once, again faced the rear rank about and forced the enemy off.

Baker's Dozen, The: The 13th Hussars.

Bangers, The: The 1st Life Guards.

Barrell's Blues: The King's Own Royal Regiment (Lancaster). Through the 1st Battalion, as the 4th Foot. From the royal blue colour of their facings and the name of a celebrated officer, General William Barrell, of George II's Reign, Colonel from 1734 to 1749.

Battle-Axe Company, The: "J" Coast Battery, R.A. From the French battle-axe specially awarded to the predecessors of the battery, the 43rd Company, 7th Battalion, R.A., as a special trophy for services at the capture of Martinique in 1809.

Bays, The: The 2nd Dragoon Guards. Dating from 1767 when the regiment was first mounted on bay horses. "Blacks" were the regulation at the period in all other Cavalry regiments.

Bingham's Dandies: The 17th Lancers. From the name of their Colonel (1826–37) Lord Bingham, afterwards the Earl of Lucan of Balaclava fame, and the exceptional smartness of turn-out insisted on during his command.

Birdcatchers, The: A nickname common to the 1st Royal Dragoons, the Scots Greys, and the Royal Irish Fusiliers. From their each having captured French Eagles in action; the Royals and Greys at Waterloo, and the Royal Irish Fusiliers at Barrosa.

Black Cuffs, The: The Northamptonshire Regiment. Through the 2nd Battalion as the 58th Foot. From the original black facings.

Black Horse, The: The 7th Dragoon Guards. From the black facings:—
A nickname dating from the early 18th Century.

Black Watch, The: The Black Watch (Royal Highlanders). Through
the 1st Battalion, as the 42nd Highlanders. From the dark tartan worn
by the battalion on its organization in George II's reign—1739. "The
Watch" (i.e., police), or "Highland Watch", a semi-military border force
to keep the King's peace in the North of Scotland, was the original
title of a force supplied by certain clans during the 17th Century. Each
company wore its own clan tartan. When reorganized in 1725 in six
Independent Companies, they were uniformed in kilts of one pattern, a dark tartan, a combination in black, green, and blue, known
as the "Government tartan". From that they were popularly called in
the Highlands "The Black Watch", in Gaelic "Am Frieceadan Dubh".
When, in 1739, the companies were brought together into a regiment of
Highlanders, renumbered a little later as the "42nd" the popular *sobriquet* was transferred to the new corps. All other infantry regiments at
the time wore red coats, waistcoats and breeches, and were spoken of in
Scotland as the "Seidaran dearag" or "Red Soldiers". "The Black Watch"
is now the official title of the regiment.

Blayney's Bloodhounds: The Royal Irish Fusiliers. Through the 1st
Battalion, as the 87th Foot. From their relentless hunting down of Irish
rebels in 1798, Lord Blayney being their commanding officer.

Blind Half Hundred, The: The Royal West Kent. Through the 1st
Battalion as the 50th Foot. Originating on its return from Egypt in
1801, in allusion to the large proportion of men suffering from
opthalmia contracted on service. An earlier nickname of the 50th was
"Mediterranean Greys", given when at Gibraltar in 1793, from the elderly look of all ranks. "From being so long on the station (ten years) the
locks of the men and officers had assumed a grisly hue", according to
Captain Paterson of the regiment, in his "Adventures" (p. 9).

Bloodsuckers, The: The Manchester Regiment. Through the 1st
Battalion, as the 63rd Foot. According to one story the nickname originated from a fancied resemblance to mosquitoes of the *fleur de lys* badge,
as carved very small on tombstones in America of men who fell in the
American War, and on other tombstones of men who died while serving
in the West Indies, where the regiment was quartered for several years,
at various periods.

Bloody Eleventh, The: The Devonshire Regiment. Through the 1st
Battalion, as the 11th Foot. Dating from the Battle of Salamanca in 1812.
Out of a total strength of 412 officers and men, 341 were casualties.

Blue Caps, The: The Royal Dublin Fusiliers, From the 1st Battalion,
as the 1st Madras Fusiliers. Given during the Indian Mutiny, from the
blue gauze puggarees worn round their caps. Also "Neill's Blue Caps",

from the name of their heroic colonel, killed at Lucknow. (*See* Lambs, the earlier nickname of the 1st Battalion.)

Blue Horse, The: The 4th Dragoon Guards. Dating from early in the 18th Century, From the colour of the facings, and the original designation of the regiment as "Horse", i.e., heavy cavalry as distinguished from dragoons.

Blue Marines, The: The Royal Marine Artillery, From their blue uniform, in contrast to the "Red Marines", The Royal Marine Light Infantry.

Blues. The: The Royal Horse Guards. Dating as a nickname from 1690, just before the Battle of the Boyne, when the name, in the form "Oxford Blues", was first given the regiment, on the occasion of their joining William III's camp; from the name of their Colonel, the Earl of Oxford, and the colour of the uniform, to distinguish them from the King's Dutch Regiment of Blue Guards, also in the camp.

Body Snatchers, The: The Royal Army Medical Corps.

Bold Fifteenth, The: The 15th Hussars. An old nickname, as recorded in a regimental song. The two last lines of two of its verses ran:—

"And when forward's the watchword for Venus and Mars,
  Oh shew me the boys like The bold King's Hussars!"—
and again,

"Then damn those old Heavies and Lumping Lifeguards,
  And pledge me success to the bold King's Hussars!"

Bomb Proofs, The: The Prince of Wales' Own West Yorkshire Regiment, Through the 1st Battalion, as the 14th Foot. A Crimean War nickname, from the immunity from casualties when in the trenches before Sebastopol.

Braggs, The: The Gloucestershire Regiment. Through the 1st Battalion as the 28th Foot. (*See* Old Braggs.)

Brass Before and Brass Behind: The Gloucestershire Regiment. (*See* Back Numbers.)

Brass Heads, The: The Leinster Regiment, Through the 2nd Battalion, as the 3rd Bombay European Regiment, An Indian Mutiny nickname, from the way the men stood the sun in Sir Hugh Rose's Central India campaign of 1858.

Brave Fifteenth, The: The 15th Hussars. From an old regimental song— "The Brave Fifteenth".

Brickdusts, The: The King's Shropshire Light Infantry. From the 1st Battalion, as the 53rd Foot. (*See* Old Brickdusts.)

Bubbly Jocks, The: The Scots Greys. (A Bubbly Jock is a Scots name for a turkey cock.)

Buff Howards, The: The Buffs. (East Kent) Regiment. Through the 1st Battalion, as the 3rd Foot. A nickname dating from George II's reign, when regiments were known by the name of their colonels, from the name of the Colonel, Thomas Howard (1738–49), to distinguish the regiment from the "Green Howards", then commanded by Colonel the Hon. Charles Howard. Also, from the facings. (*See* Old Buffs.)

Calvert's Entire: The Prince of Wales' Own West Yorkshire Regiment. Through the 1st Battalion, as the 14th Foot. From the name of the Colonel Sir Harry Calvert (1806–26) and the fact that the 14th at that time (1804–16) had the unusual establishment of three battalions. "Calvert's Entire" was a familiar inscription outside taverns at that day, being the name of a celebrated brewer.

Camarhas, The: The Queen's Own Cameron Highlanders. Through the 1st Battalion, as the 79th Highlanders whose original nickname it was. From the nickname "Old Cia Ma tha" (Gaelic for "How are you") of its first Colonel, Sir Alan Cameron; in allusion to his habit of responding to salutes with the phrase "Cia Ma tha".

Canaries, The Old: The Third Dragoon Guards, from their yellow facings.

Cast Iron Sixth, The: The 6th City of London Rifles. Said to have originated some years ago, from the endurance shown by the corps while training on Salisbury Plain.

Castor Oil Dragoons, The: The Royal Army Medical Corps.

Cauliflowers, The: The Loyal Regiment (North Lancashire). Through the 1st Battalion, as the 47th Foot. From the white facings.

Celestials, The: The Queen's Own Royal West Kent Regiment. Through the 2nd Battalion, as the 97th Foot. From the original sky blue facings, the colour of the ribbon of the Order of St. Patrick, the 97th bearing the title of "The Earl of Ulster's" when first raised in 1824. "Earl of Ulster" was one of the titles of George III's second son, the Duke of York, Commander-in-Chief of the British Army for many years down to his death in 1827, who is commemorated by the monument off the Mall. There being various "Duke of York's Own" regiments in 1824, the title "Earl of Ulster's" was given to the newly raised 97th specially to distinguish it from the others.

Chainy Tenth, The: The 10th Hussars. From the chain pattern belt of the officer's uniform introduced in 1820.

Charles O'Malley's Own: The 14th Hussars. A former-day occasional nickname, in allusion to Lever's novel in which the hero figures as an officer of the regiment.

Cheeses (also Cheesemongers), The: The Life Guards. A nickname dating from 1788, when the "Horse Troops" of the Household Cavalry were remodelled and styled "Life Guards". The members of the former "Horse Troops" professed to look down on their successors and sneered at them, saying they were not "Gentlemen", but Cheesemongers, "Gentlemen" being the official form of address to the men on parade. At Waterloo, it is related, the commanding officer called to the men as he led a charge "Come on, Cheesemongers!"

Cherry Pickers, The: The 11th Hussars. A nickname said to have originated from a camp legend of Peninsular War Days to the effect that on some occasion in Spain during the war some men of a picquet of the regiment were surprised by the French while stripping a cherry orchard. *Cf.* also *Cherubims, The.*

Cherubims, The: The 11th Hussars. Said to have originated (with a certain *arrière pensée*) from the crimson overalls introduced by the Prince Consort in 1841, on becoming Colonel-in-Chief.

Chestnut Troop, The: "A" Battery, Royal Horse Artillery. From the colour of the horses when the battery was formed in 1793, as the first horse artillery troop in the British Army. (Originally a nickname—now the official title.)

China Tenth, The: The 10th Hussars. A nickname dating from about 1810 when the Prince Regent was Colonel, it being popularly said that "the regiment was so precious that it required to be taken care of like valuable china as it moved from station to station".

Coalheavers (Coalies), The: A nickname of the Grenadier Guards, dating from the 18th century when Guards' officers were permitted, as a privilege, to hire out, or "let" a percentage of the men to civilian employers the profits going to maintain the officers' mess of the St. James's Palace guard. More than once in the War the Grenadier Guards went "over the Top" to the cry "Forward the Coalies!"

Cookies, The: An Indian Army nickname of the 55th (Coke's) Rifles.

Cross Belts, The: The 8th Hussars. Dating back to Queen Anne's time, when the privilege was granted to the 8th Dragoons of wearing the sword suspended by a cross belt over the right shoulder, as in regiments of "Horse" or heavy cavalry, instead of from the waistbelt as in other dragoon regiments, to commemorate the capture of a regiment of Spanish Horse in the War of the Spanish Succession.

Dandies, The: The London Rifle Brigade (5th Battalion City of London Regiment). A nickname, traditionally dating from about 1862, from the smartness of appearance of the men at the Hyde Park reviews.

Dandy Ninth, The: The 9th (Service) Battalion Royal Scots. A Great War nickname.

Death or Glory Boys, The: The 17th Lancers. From their badge, a death's head with the words "Or Glory". Adopted in memory of Wolfe by Colonel Hale, Wolfe's A.D.C. at Quebec, who raised the regiment in 1760.

Delhi Spearmen, The: The 9th Lancers. Dating from the Indian Mutiny.

Devil's Own, The: The Connaught Rangers. Through the 1st Battalion as the 88th Foot. Dating from the Peninsular War, in allusion to their reckless daring in action. Also the Inns of Court Territorials (now O.T.C.). Given by George III to the original Inns of Court Volunteers at the Hyde Park review of 1803 on the King being told that the regiment consisted of lawyers. "Who are these?" asked His Majesty. "All Lawyers, Sire", was the reply. "What, what, Lawyers! Call 'em Devil's Own!"

Devil's Royals, The: The Queen's Own Royal West Kent Regiment. Through the 1st Battalion as the 50th Foot. A Peninsular war nickname, originating from their celebrated charge at the Battle of Vimiera in 1809, when they charged a French column of five regiments with seven guns and routed it single-handed.

Die Hards, The: The Middlesex Regiment. Through the 1st Battalion, as the 57th Foot. Originating at Albuera in 1811. In allusion to their Colonel's call to the battalion when hard pressed: "Die Hard men, Die Hard!" "Albuera Day" (May 16th) is always kept with special observance in the regiment, and at mess the time-honoured toast, drunk in solemn silence "To the memory of those who fought and fell at Albuera." At Albuera 570 officers and men of the 57th went into action; 160, all told, came out alive after it, many severely wounded. Of the rest:—

"Even as they fought, in files they lay.
Like the mower's grass at the close of day,
When his work is o'er on the levelled plain—
Such was the fall of the foremost slain!"

Dirty Half Hundred, The: The Queen's Own Royal West Kent Regiment. Through the 1st Battalion, as the 50th Foot. Dating from Vimiera in 1809, in allusion to their appearance on the battle-field with faces, according to tradition, begrimed by the dye off their black cuffs, made use of in the heat of the fighting as handkerchiefs to wipe the sweat out of their eyes. Napier describes them as charging "with faces begrimed with powder, as black as their own lapels".

Dirty Shirts, The: The Royal Munster Fusiliers. Through the 1st Battalion as the Bengal European Regiment. The nickname was given by General Lord Lake, then Commander-in-Chief in India, when visiting the Battalion in the trenches at the Siege of Bhurtpore in 1805.

Docs, The: The Duke of Cornwall's Light Infantry. From the initials. Also, D.C.L.I.

Double X's, The: The Lancashire Fusiliers. Through the 1st Battalion, as the 20th Foot. From the "XX" representing the regimental number.

Dozen, The Old: The Suffolk Regiment. From its former number as the 12th Foot.

Drogheda Light Horse, The: The 18th Hussars. From the name of its first Colonel, Lord Drogheda (1760–1819).

Dubs, The: The Royal Dublin Fusiliers.

Duke's, The: The Duke of Wellington's (West Riding Regiment). The title "Duke of Wellington's Regiment" dates from June 18th (Waterloo Day), 1853, the year after Wellington' death, when Queen Victoria specially granted the distinction to the then 33rd West Riding Regiment. Wellington commanded the 33rd from 1798 to 1805 as lieut.-colonel, in the Flanders campaign of 1794 (where Wellington, at the head of the regiment, was under fire for the first time), and in India during the Seringapatam campaign of 1799 and the Mahratta War. He was colonel of the 33rd from 1806 to 1813. It had been proposed more than once to give the regiment the title "Duke of Wellington's" during the Duke's lifetime, but Wellington would not hear of it. "Wait till I am dead!" he repeatedly said.

Dumpies, The: The 19th Hussars. A nickname dating from the formation of the regiment in 1859, in allusion to the size and build of the recruits, who were mostly men volunteering from disbanded East India Company's cavalry regiments. Also, a nickname of the 20th Hussars and 21st Lancers, for similar reasons.

Eagle Takers, The: The Royal Irish Fusiliers. Through the 1st Battalion, as the 87th foot. (*See* Aiglers.)

Eagle Troop, The: "N" Battery Royal Horse Artillery. From the Eagle badge, conferred on the then 1st Troop, Bombay Horse Artillery, the predecessors of the present battery, by the Governor General of India in 1848, to be worn on the appointments in recognition of distinguished service in the Afghan and Scinde wars. Now embroidered on the trumpet banner and painted on the limbers. (Not a nickname: the recognized *sobriquet* in the service.)

Earl of Mar's Greybreeks, The: The Royal Scots Fusiliers. Through the 1st Battalion. From the name of the first colonel, the Earl of Mar, who raised the regiment in 1678.

Elegant Extracts, The: The Shropshire Light Infantry. Through the 2nd Battalion, as the 85th Foot. Dating from 1813, when, owing to dissensions among the officers, all were drafted to other regiments and their places filled with officers from twenty-two different corps, to whom the nickname "Elegant Extracts" was given. The Royal Fusiliers are also said to have had the same nickname.

Emperor's Chambermaids, The: The 24th Hussars. Dating from the Battle of Vittoria in 1813. From a silver utensil, spoil from Joseph Bonaparte's carriage, captured in the rout of the French Army. The trophy figures, filled with champagne, as a Loving Cup at mess on guest nights.

Ever Sworded, The: The Worcestershire Regiment. Through the 1st Battalion, as the 29th Foot. From the former regimental custom of all the officers wearing their swords at mess, now confined to the Captain and Subaltern of the Day. The custom is traditionally stated to have originated in consequence of the surprise and massacre by Indians of a detachment, landed to forage on the Island of St. John's, Cape Breton, in 1746. The regimental Standing Orders of 1792 lay down:—"Officers are to accustom themselves always to wear their swords when in regimentals, except in their own room."

Evergreens, The: The 13th Hussars. Suggested by the motto of the regiment "Viret in aeternum", in allusion to the former green facings when dragoons.

Excellers, The: The Prince of Wales' Own South Lancashire Regiment. Through the first battalion, as the 40th Foot. From the Roman numerals "XL" of the number. Also an occasional *sobriquet* of the 12th Battalion, The London Regiment (The Rangers), whose motto is "Excel", an allusion to the letters "XL" of former days, representing the old number of the corps as the 40th Middlesex Rifle Volunteers.

Eyes, The Old: The Grenadier Guards. An old nickname. An "Eye" was adopted as the Divisional Sign of the Guards Division in the War.

F.S.R., The: The 21st Battalion, The London Regiment (First Surrey Rifles). From the Original title, "1st Surrey Rifles", on the raising of the battalion in 1859. Their predecessors of the Napoleonic period were known as the "1st Surrey Volunteers".

Faithful Durhams, The: The Durham Light Infantry. Through the 1st Battalion, as the 68th Foot. Traditionally said to date from the Carib War in the Island of St. Vincent in 1772, and to have been given in recognition of special service then rendered.

Fancy Greens, The: The Worcestershire Regiment. Through the 2nd Battalion, as the 36th Foot. From the pea-green facings formerly worn.

Faugh a Ballagh Boys, The: The Royal Irish Fusiliers. Through the 1st Battalion as the 87th Foot. From the war-cry "Faugh-a-Ballagh", Clear the Way), with which the 87th charged at the Battle of Barrosa in 1811, when they captured a French Eagle. (*See* Aiglers.) "Barrosa Day" (March 5th) is observed in regiment with special ceremonies and festivities every year and kept as a holiday, and a special reunion of officers, wherever possible, takes place at the "Barrosa Dinner" on that day.

Fighting Fifteenth, The: The 15th Hussars. Dating from the exploits of the regiment in Germany at Emsdorff in the Seven Years War as the 15th Light Dragoons. The regiment was authorized in 1763 to bear this inscription on its Light Dragoon helmets: "Five Battalions of French defeated and taken by this regiment, with their colours and nine pieces of cannon, on the Plains of Emsdorff, July the sixteenth, 1760."

Fighting Fifth, The: The Northumberland Fusiliers. Through the 1st Battalion. A Peninsular War nickname of the 5th Foot.

Fighting Fortieth, The: The Prince of Wales's Volunteers (South Lancashire Regiment). Through the 1st Battalion, as the 40th Foot. Dating from the Sikh wars of 1843 and 1848, and in allusion to the regimental number.

Fighting Ninth, The: The Norfolk Regiment. Through the 1st Battalion, as the 9th Foot. From the number, and traditionally with special reference to the services of the regiment in the War of the Spanish Succession in Queen Anne's Reign.

First Tangerines, The: The Queen's Royal West Surrey Regiment. Through the 1st Battalion. The original title of the regiment when raised in 1661 for garrison service in defence of Tangier, on Tangier becoming a British possession, as part of the dowry of Queen Catherine of Braganza.

Fitch's Grenadiers: The Royal Irish Rifles. Through the 1st Battalion, as the 83rd Foot. A nickname given in Dublin when raised by Major William Fitch in 1793, by way of jest at the diminutive size of the recruits.

Five and Threepennies, The: The Shropshire Light Infantry. Through the 1st Battalion, as the 53rd Foot. From the "5" and "3" figures of the number. Secondarily, in allusion to five and three pence, an ensign's pay *per diem.*

Flamers, The: The Dorsetshire Regiment. Through the 2nd Battalion, as the 54th Foot. In allusion to the part taken by the regiment at the burning of New London in 1781 during the American War.

Fore and Afts, The: The Gloucestershire Regiment. A nickname apparently coined by Kipling in his story "The Drums of the Fore and Aft", referring to the badge worn on both back and front of the helmet. (*See* Back Numbers, *also* Brass Before and Brass Behind.)

Forty Thieves, The: The 40th Pathans of the Indian Army. From the regimental number, and in allusion to certain bad habits credited to the Pathans of the Afghan border in general.

Gallants, The: The 9th (Service) Battalion of the Royal West Surrey. A Great War nickname.

Garvies, The: An old nickname of the 2nd Battalion Connaught Rangers, when raised as the 94th Foot in Glasgow in 1823. From the lean appearance of the men, garvie being a West of Scotland name for a sprat.

Gay Gordons, The: The Gordon Highlanders. In particular the 2nd Battalion, the 92nd Highlanders.

"Rising, roaring, rushing like the tide,
 Gay goes the Gordon to the fight!"

Geraniums, The: The 13th Hussars. From the former green facings of their predecessors, the 13th Dragoons.

German Legion, The: The Leinster Regiment. Through the 2nd Battalion, as the 109th Foot. Dating from about 1860, when the battalion, formerly the East India Company's 3rd Bombay European Regiment, on being then taken over into British Service, was brought up to strength with men of the disbanded German Legion which had been raised for the Crimean War.

Glasgow Greys, The: The East Surrey Regiment. Through the 2nd Battalion, as the 70th Foot. From its place of raising in 1756, and the grey facings of the uniform.

Goods, The: The Gordon Highlanders.

Green Dragoons, The: The 13th Hussars. From their former facings when dragoons.

Green Horse, The: The 5th Dragoon Guards. The original popular name of the predecessors of the regiment, the old 5th Horse (converted into Dragoon Guards in 1788). From the colour of the facings.

Green Howards, The: The Green Howards (Alexandra Princess of Wales's Own Yorkshire Regiment). Through the 1st Battalion, as the 19th Foot. A nickname now adopted officially as the title of the regiment. From the name of the Colonel (the Han. Charles Howard) 1738–48, and the colour of the facings, to distinguish the regiment from the "Buff Howards", commanded during the same period by Colonel Thomas Howard (*see* Buff Howards). The nickname is said to have first come in during the War of the Austrian Succession, in 1744, when the two regiments were together in camp in Germany, in order to distinguish between them.

Green Linnets, The: The Dorsetshire Regiment. Through the 1st Battalion, as the 39th Foot. From the green facings.

Greys, The: The Scots Greys. The regiment, when first raised in Scotland in 1781 as the "Royal Regiment of Scots Dragoons", was uniformed in stone-grey coats, there being, an official document states, not enough red cloth procurable in Scotland for all the men. The mounting of the regiment on grey horses dates from about 1700. The *sobriquet* "Greys" was well established before 1750, as contemporary letters and documents show.

Guards of the Line, The: The Worcestershire Regiment. Through the 1st Battalion, as the 29th Foot. The origin of the old nickname seems now untraceable. A Horse Guards' letter of August 7th, 1877, makes a reference to the traditional association of the 29th with the Guards: "His Royal Highness with a view to the assimilation as much as possible of the pouches of the 29th to those of the Guards has approved of white ammunition pouches being issued in lieu of black." (*See* Star of the Line.)

Guise's Greens: The Royal Warwickshire Regiment. Through the 1st Battalion, as the 6th Foot. From the name of a Colonel in George II's reign, John Guise (pronounced Geeze), 1738–5; and the colour of the then facings.

Havercake Lads: The Duke of Wellington's Regiment (West Riding). Through the 1st Battalion, as the 33rd Foot. Originated in 1782 in the American War, from the practice of the recruiting sergeants, during a period of dearth in Yorkshire owing to a bad harvest, carrying an oatcake, locally called a Havercake, stuck on the points of their swords to attract hungry lads as recruits in the villages.

Herts Guards, The: A Great War nickname of the Hertfordshire Territorials of the Bedfordshire Regiment. In allusion to their having served during the Great War from October, 1914, to August, 1915 in the 4th Guards Brigade with the 2nd Grenadiers, 2nd Coldstream and 1st Irish Guards. The name seems to have been first suggested when the Hertfordshires landed at Havre where the enthusiastic French crowd greeted them with shouts of "Voila la Garde!", to which some of the men called back amid laughter "Yes, the Herts Guards!" Their inclusion in the 4th Guards Brigade after that, recalled the incident and led to the adoption of the *sobriquet* in the corps.

Holy Boys, The: The Norfolk Regiment. Through the 1st Battalion, as the 9th Foot. There are two traditional origins suggested for the nickname, both dating from the Peninsular War. (1) That it was given by the Spanish peasants, who mistook the regimental badge of Britannia for a medallion of the Virgin Mary. (2) That it originated with a camp story to the effect that the men of the regiment on some occasion had sold their bibles to buy drink.

Horse Marines, The: The 17th Lancers. An occasional nickname from the regiment having temporarily done duty as marines on board a British frigate, H.M.S. *Hermione*, while on passage to the West Indies in 1796.

Howard's Greens: The South Wales Borderers. Through the 1st Battalion, as the 24th Foot. An 18th century nickname from the name of the Colonel, Thomas Howard (1717–37). (*See* Buff Howards and Green Howards.)

Immortals, The: A nickname of the 2nd Battalion, the Duke of Wellington's Regiment, going back to when it was the 76th Foot. Dating from the Mahratta War of 1803–4, and originating from a story current among the enemy and other natives, in consequence of the number of men wounded in action recovering and reappearing in the ranks, that the soldiers of the regiment were immortal.

Jaggers, The: Kings Royal Rifle Corps. Originating with the 5th (Jäger or Yäger) Battalion of the 60th Rifles, which served in the Peninsular War as a sharpshooter, or skirmisher, battalion, and after the war was absorbed into the present 1st Battalion K.R.R. The 5th Battalion, when raised in 1798, was largely composed of German Jäger (riflemen, gamekeepers and marksmen) from foreign corps in British pay, then disbanded, who re-enlisted as British regulars and formed the Battalion.

K.D.G's., The: The King's Dragoon Guards.

King's Men, The: The Seaforth Highlanders. Through the 2nd Battalion, as the 78th Highlanders. In allusion to one of the Gaelic mottos of the regiment, "Cuidich 'n righ" (Help the King), the motto of the Mackenzie Clan, adopted to commemorate the rescue of a Scottish king, attacked by a stag at bay when hunting, by an ancestor of the Earl of Seaforth, hereditary chief of the Mackenzies, who raised the regiment in 1793.

Kingsley's Stand: The Lancashire Fusiliers. Through the 1st Battalion, as the 20th Foot. From the name of their colonel, William Kingsley (1754–69), who commanded them at Minden. Also, from their distinguished part in the battle and their volunteering for guard-duty the next day, although they had been specially exempted on account of their very severe casualties.

Kosbs, The: An occasional nickname of the King's Own Scottish Borderers. (From the initials.)

Koylis, The: An occasional nickname of the King's Own Yorkshire Light Infantry. (From the initials.)

L.R.B: The London Rifle Brigade (5th Battalion City of London Regiment).

Lacedemonians, The: The Duke of Cornwall's Light Infantry. Through the 1st Battalion, as the 32nd Foot. Dating from 1777, in the American War, In allusion to the then colonel (Markham), on One occasion Just before an action, making the men a long address on the military discipline of the Spartans, the Lacedemonians.

Lambs, The: The Queen's Royal West Surrey Regiment. Through the 1st Battalion. In allusion to the historic "Lamb" badge dating from 1661, through which, and the name of the first colonel, the nickname, originally "Kirke's Lambs", attained widespread fame.

Lambs (Sweet Lambs), The: The Royal Dublin Fusiliers. Through the 1st Battalion, as the 1st Madras European Regiment. Dating from Clive's time, in the middle of the 18th century and the regimental nickname down to the Indian Mutiny when "Blue Caps" (*q.v.*) took its place. Two origins have been suggested: (1) That the nickname came in through a Captain Kirke commanding the grenadier company, which was nicknamed by way of jest "Kirke's Lambs", the nickname becoming later applied to the whole battalion. (2) That the nickname was given in consequence of the regiment being at one time largely recruited with drafts from the Queen's the original "Lambs".

Lancashire Lads, The: The Loyal Regiment (North Lancashire). Through the 1st Battalion, as the 47th Foot. Dating from 1782, when Lancashire was first appointed officially as the territorial designation. According to a tradition, the authorities allotted the battalion, which had been originally raised in the West of Scotland, to "Lanarkshire", and the error of a War Office clerk in writing "Lancashire" instead, in making out the *London Gazette* notification, caused it to be re-allotted, the authorities not troubling, to correct the *Gazette* announcement. Also, a nickname of the Lancashire Fusiliers.

Leather Hats, The: The King's Regiment (Liverpool). Dating from old times when the regiment was the 8th Foot.

Light Bobs, The: The Somerset Light Infantry.

Ligoniers, The: The 7th Dragoon Guards. From the name of their colonel in George II's reign, the famous Earl Ligonier (1720–49).

Lilywhiles, The: The East Lancashire Regiment Through the 2nd Battalion, as the 59th Foot From the white facings. Also the former nickname of the Leicestershire Regiment for the same reason.

Linseed Lancers, The: The Royal Army Medical Corps.

Lions, The: The King's Own Royal Regiment (Lancaster). Through the 1st Battalion, as the 4th King's Own. From the "Lion" badge, traditionally said to have been granted by William III to the regiment, as being the first English regiment to join him in 1688 after his landing in Torbay.

Little Fighting Fours, The: The Essex Regiment. Through the 1st Battalion, as the 44th Foot. Dating from the Peninsular War, in allusion to the small stature of most of the men.

Little Grenadiers, The: The Royal Marines. Dating from 1761, and given by the French at the capture of Belleisle in that year. The tall mitre-shaped grenadier caps that the Marines then wore apparently suggested the name; also, in allusion to the men being smaller than the average big grenadier of the period.

London Thieving Corps, The: The Royal Army Service Corps. A Crimean War nickname suggested by the initials of the "Land Transport Corps", which, after various changes of name and organization, developed eventually into the present R.A.S.C.

Lord Adam Gordon's Lifeguards: The 3rd Hussars. A nickname dating from the 18th century, traditionally said to be derived from the regiment being kept in Scotland for a considerable period to supply escorts for Lord Adam Gordon, Commanding the Forces in Scotland.

Lord Wellington's Bodyguard: The Northumberland Fusiliers. Through the 2nd Battalion 5th Foot, dating from the Peninsular War, from their having, during the winter of 1811, furnished the guard at Wellington's headquarters.

Loyals, The: The Loyal Regiment (North Lancashire). Through the 2nd Battalion, as the 81st Foot, "Loyal Lincolnshire Volunteers". The "Loyal" was adopted Cram the family motto, "Loyauté m'oblige", of General Albemarle Bertie (9th Earl of Lindsay), who raised the 81st in 1793, at Lincoln and became its first colonel. The Territorial organization of 1881 transferred the battalion from Lincolnshire to Lancashire.

Lumpers, The: The Lifeguards. (An old nickname. *See* "Bold Fifteenth".)

Minden Boys, The: The Lancashire Fusiliers. Through the 1st Battalion, as the 20th Foot. In allusion to their part at the Battle of Minden. (*See* Kingsley's Stand). In common with the others of the "unsurpassable six" British infantry regiments who made the historic charge on the French cavalry at Minden, August 1st is always specially observed. A rose is worn by all ranks at the special parade, the colours and drums being also decked with roses; a reminder of the Minden rose gardens through which the six regiments moved to the attack, many of the men plucking roses as they passed through. The "Minden Yell", the shout with which the 20th charged is historic. It was repeated at Inkerman, as an eyewitness describes, adding, "to the consternation of the Russians who had never before heard such a frightful noise".

Moke Train, The: The Royal Army Service Corps. A nickname suggested by one of the former titles of the R.A.S.C., the "Military Train" (1857–70), originating when mules were substituted for horses during part of the period. A variant was "Muck Train".

Moonrakers, The: The Wiltshire Regiment. Through the 1st Battalion, as the 62nd Foot. In allusion to the popular story of Wiltshire rustics being seen dragging a pond with rakes one bright moonlight night and saying they were raking for the moon. On the occasion, actually, they were raking with hay-rakes for some tubs of brandy which a party of smugglers, chased by preventive men, had dropped in the pond. At Mons, in 1914, an officer of the Wiltshires fell with the call on his lips: "Come on, Moonrakers!"

Mudlarks: The Royal Engineers. (An old nickname.)

Murdering Thieves, The: The R.A.S.C. Another nickname given to the former Military Train. Suggested in jest by the initials M.T. (*See* Moke Train.)

Murray's Bucks: The Duke of Cornwall's Light Infantry. Through the 2nd Battalion, as the 46th Foot. Dating from the middle of the 18th century, from the name of the then colonel, the Hon. Thomas Murray (1743–64). Said to have originated when the battalion was stationed in Edinburgh as "A tribute to its gay appearance in the Scottish Royal Livery"—i.e., red coats with bright yellow facings.

Nanny Goats, The: The Royal Welch Fusiliers. In allusion to the historic regimental goat. Also, "Royal Goats".

Nobody's Own: The 13th Hussars, and also the 20th Hussars. As not being allotted in their title to any Royal personage or other person of distinction, as with other cavalry regiments outside the Household Brigade. The following verses from "The Yellow Plume", the magazine of the 20th Hussars, explains the meaning of the name, with special reference to that regiment.

There are fine gallant regiments passing all praise,
Should you ask by what name they are known—
Well, say "King" or "Duke So-and-So's" Browns, Blacks, or Bays;
But one answers, "Nobody's Own."
These no painting possess of their Colonel-in-Chief,
With gift sword, golden casque, jewelled throne;
Nor bear they his badge, "The Red Strawberry leaf",

For are they net" Nobody's Own"
Vimiera bebeld them, the Cape and old Nile;
By Marne, Somme, and Lys have they shown
How in trench or in saddle to meet with a smile
Each challenge to "Nobody's Own."
Should shirt on the polo ground puzzle your eye—
Striped yellow, 'twixt blue and maroon,
That team has won trophies, and always will try
For the honour of "Nobody's Own."
They fought like the rest in good Chetwode's Brigade:
With their dead are wide battlefields strown,
And at the last roll-call they'll not feel afraid
To answer. "Here! 'Nobody's Own'!"

Nottingham Hosiers, The: A nickname of former days of the 45th Foot, the 1st Battalion, The Sherwood Foresters (Nottinghamshire and Derbyshire Regiment). For long they had striven with red-tape officialism in high places for sanction for their present dearly-prized title. The strong feeling over the subject led to this incident at a big review. "Prince's Irish—Attention!" called the C.O. of the regiment on one side. "Connaught Rangers—Attention!", called the C.O. of the regiment on the other side. It was exasperating. The C.O. of the 45th (who were then known only by the number) turned to his men, and in a voice that resounded all over the review ground, called out "Nottingham Hosiers—Attention!"

Nut Crackers, The: The Buffs. Through the 1st Battalion. Dating from the Peninsular War and, according to tradition, with special reference to the Buffs at Albuera.

Old and Bold, The: The Prince of Wales's Own West Yorkshire Regiment. Through the 1st Battalion, as the 14th Foot. An old Peninsular War nickname.

Old Bold Fifth, The: The Northumberland Fusiliers. An old nickname of the 5th Foot.

Old Braggs, The: The Gloucestershire Regiment. Through the 1st Battalion, as the 28th Foot. From the name of its colonel, Philip Bragg, a celebrated officer of George II's time, who commanded the regiment from 1734 to 1759. At a brigade parade some years ago the officer in command of the 28th, getting irritated at hearing other C.O's calling out the special titles of their regiments, gave, it is related, this as his word of command. "Neither King's nor Queen's nor Royal Marines, only 28th Old Braggs, Brass before and Behind—Shoulder Arms!"

Old Brickdusts, The: The King's Shropshire Light Infantry. Through the 1st Battalion, as the 53rd Foot. From the distinctive "brickdust" shade of their facings.

Old Bucks, The: The Bedfordshire. Regiment. A former title of the Bedfordshire Regiment, through the 1st Battalion, as the 16th Foot. Originally styled the Buckinghamshire Regiment, in 1809 it was ordered to exchange county titles with the then Bedfordshire Regiment, the 14th Foot, and for years afterwards was known as the "Old Bucks", the 14th being known as the "Young Bucks". The exchange, it was said, was made to suit the convenience of the Colonel of the 14th, Sir Harry Calvert, the Adjutant General, who had large estates in Buckinghamshire.

Old Buffs, The: The Buffs. The East Kent Regiment. Through the 1st Battalion. The name "Buffs" originated, according to one account, from the regiment being the first corps to wear buff, or buffalo, leather accoutrements; and when the wearing of similar leather accoutrements was extended to other regiments, the nickname "Old" *Buffs*, for the first wearers, came into being.

Old Eyes, The: The Grenadier Guards. (*See* Eyes, The.)

Old Fighting Tenth, The: The Lincolnshire Regiment. Through the 1st Battalion the 10th Foot. In allusion to the former number of the regiment.

Old Fogs, The: The Royal Irish Fusiliers. (*See* Faugh-a-Ballagh Boys.)

Old Jocks, The: The Scots Greys.

Old Loyals, The: The 23rd Battalion of the London. Regiment (Territorial). From the old motto, "Loyalty Unites Us" of the former Volunteer regiment of the Napoleonic war period from which the 23rd London traces its origin.

Old Toughs, The: The Royal Dublin Fusiliers. Through the 2nd Battalion, as the East India Company's European Regiment. Dating from the 18th century. Also, "Bombay Toughs".

One and All, The: The Duke of Cornwall's Light Infantry. (In allusion to the County motto.)

Orange Lilies, The: The Royal Sussex Regiment. Through the 1st Battalion, as the 35th Foot. From its historic orange-coloured facings, worn from 1700 to 1832, and said to have been granted as a distinction to the corps, as the "Belfast Regiment", by William III, (William of Orange) for war service in Ireland in 1690–1.

Paget's Irregular Horse: The 4th Hussars. The nickname, given on their return from India in 1842 after twenty-six years service abroad, arose from their "loose" drill as compared with regiments on the Home establishment.

Pals, The: The familiar name of the four "City" (Service) Battalions of the Liverpool and Manchester Regiments, raised in 1914.

Patent Safeties, The: The Life Guards. (In allusion to their cuirasses.)

Peacemakers, The: The Bedfordshire Regiment. Through the 1st Battalion, as the 16th Foot. Three origins have been suggested for the nickname. (1) From there being no battle honours on the Colours previous to 1881, when Marlborough's victories were first authorized to be recorded. In the interval, the 16th, though constantly employed and engaged in many minor actions and affairs in several wars, were never present, apparently, at any general engagement for which a "Battle Honour" was granted, and so the Regimental Colour remained blank a white flag. The nickname seems to have been given in chaff by other regiments, and led to many rows in garrison town public-houses when soldiers were drinking together. (2) Another tradition is that the nickname originated in Marlborough's time, and was a tribute to the fighting enthusiasm of the regiment and its effect on the enemy in battle. (3) According to a third tradition the nickname originated in 1815 in consequence of the 16th forming part of the Army of Occupation to keep the peace in France after Waterloo.

Perthshire Greybreeks, The: The Scottish Rifles. Through the 2nd Battalion, as the 90th Light Infantry. From the grey breeches worn by the men when the battalion was raised in Perthshire in 1793, white breeches being the usual regulation wear.

Piccadilly Butchers, The: An old nickname of the Life Guards, dating from over a hundred years ago, in allusion to their having charged a mob during the "Burdett Riots" in April, 1810. On the occasion, however, as a fact only one of the rioters was killed.

Pig and Whistle Light Infantry, The: The Highland Light Infantry. Through the 1st Battalion, as the 71st Foot. In allusion to the Elephant and Hunting Horn badges. The 71st, in the Peninsular War, had the nickname of the "Glesca' Keelies" from the number of Glasgow men in the ranks.

Pigs, The: A nickname of the 2nd Battalion Black Watch as the 76th Foot, in jocular allusion to the Elephant Badge granted by the East India Company in recognition of the battalion's brilliant service in 1803–5, in the Mahratta War.

Poachers, The: The Lincolnshire Regiment. In allusion to the regimental march "The Lincolnshire Poacher".

Pompadours, The: The Essex Regiment. Through the 1st Battalion as the 54th Foot. From the colour of the original facings, crimson or puce, called "Pompadour", as being the favourite colour of Madame de Pompadour, the mistress of Louis XV of France. On the raising of the regiment in 1756, at the beginning of the Seven Years War, the first colonel, it is said, adopted the colour as being specially associated with the arch-enemy of England out of pique, to score off the authorities, who had refused to allow Royal Blue facings for his regiment.

Pontius Pilate's Body Guards: The Royal Scots. According to tradition, the nickname was given to the Royal Scots upwards of three hundred years ago, when they formed part of the French Army under the name of "Hepburn's Regiment", owing to a dispute as to seniority with the oldest of the French regiments, the "Regiment of Picardy", who mockingly gave them the name. According to a well-known story, on one occasion two officers, one of Hepburn's and one of the Picardy Regiment, were disputing the point as usual and the Frenchman referred to the night after the Saviour's Crucifixion. "We had the guard that night", said the French Officer. "We were not on duty", replied the Scottish Captain; "*we should not have slept at our post*"!

Pothooks, The: A nickname of the 2nd Battalion Middlesex Regiment, as the 77th Foot. Suggested by the figures of the number.

Poultice Wallopers (also Poultice Wallahs), The: The Royal Army Medical Corps.

Pump and Tortoise, The: The South Staffordshire Regiment. Through the 1st Battalion, as the 38th Foot. Dating traditionally from the 18th century, when for fifty-eight years (1707–65), the battalion was kept in the West Indies, apparently forgotten by the Home authorities, and existing practically for most of the time ragged and shoeless. The officers, as a fact, received no pay for seven years on end, and their consequent enforced teetotalism, coupled with the incapacity of the half starved and enfeebled men to exert themselves on the drill ground, apparently suggested the nickname.

Q.V.R.: The Queen Victoria Rifles (9th Battalion London Regiment). Sometimes also "Queen Vics".

Ragged Brigade, The: The 13th Hussars. A Peninsular War nickname, given originally to both the 13th and 14th Hussars, from the tattered and patched state of their uniforms, worn out as the result of protracted hard service. Only the 13th Hussars, however, now retain the nickname.

Rammugger Boys, The: The 14th Hussars. From their brilliant exploits at the Battle of Ramnugger in the Sikh War of 1848.

Rangers, The: The Connaught Rangers. Also the 12th Battalion, The London Regiment. The title "Rangers" was a very popular one in the latter half of the 18th century with provincial battalions raised to reinforce the Army during the Seven Years War and the American War. Many corps also adopted it during the war with the French Revolution, and among these The Connaught Rangers, whose official title it was from the first. The 12th Londons when raised as the 40th Middlesex in 1859 had the subsidiary title of "Central London Rangers", which was shortened to "The Rangers" in 1908 when the battalion became Territorials. The Sherwood Rangers were one of the Territorial Yeomanry Corps (Nottinghamshire) of 1908. They had a distinguished career, and for the Great War were awarded fourteen Battle Honours won in Macedonia, on Gallipoli, and in Palestine.

Raspberries, The: The King's Royal Rifle Corps. An allusion to the colour of their facings.

Red Feathers, The: The Duke of Cornwall's Light Infantry. Through the 2nd Battalion, as the 46th Foot. From the feathers design on the regimental badge. The "Light Company" of the 46th, with the light companies of other regiments forming a Light Battalion, during the American War surprised the enemy at Brandywine Creek on September 20th, 1777. The enemy, in revenge, vowed to give no quarter when next they met the Light Battalion. On hearing that, the British stained their green cap-feathers red and sent word to the Americans, telling them what they had done, in order that, as they said, on future occasions the Americans should know them and make good their threat, if they dared.

Red Knights, The: The Cheshire Regiment, through the 1st Battalion, as the 22nd Foot. In allusion to the red breeches supplied to the regiment in 1795, at a time when these had been obsolete for thirty years. The wearing of them gave the battalion a unique appearance until the authorities replaced the breeches with the ordinary regulation white ones.

Red Marines, The: The Royal Marine Light Infantry. From their scarlet uniform as contrasted with the uniform of the R.M.A. (The Blue Marines.)

Redbreasts, The: The 5th Lancers. From the scarlet plastrons of their jackets.

Resurrectionists, The: The Buffs. Through the 1st Battalion. Dating from Albuera in 1811. In allusion to the unexpected turning up, towards the close of the battle, of a large number of the men after the regiment had apparently been annihilated by the Polish Lancers, who had charged into them under cover of a thick rain squall.

Right Abouts, The: The Gloucestershire Regiment. Through the 1st Battalion, as the 28th Foot. Dating from the Battle of Alexandria in 1801. (*See* Back Numbers.)

Rob all my Comrades: A Great War nickname for the R.A.M.C. (from the initials).

Robin Hoods, The: The 7th (Territorial) Battalion of the Sherwood Foresters (the Nottinghamshire and Derbyshire Regiment).

Rocket Troop, The: "O" Battery, Royal Horse Artillery, as representing the Rocket Troops R.H.A. which served at Leipzig in 1813 and at Waterloo in 1815. There were two Rocket Troops in the British Army at that time, and the present battery represents both. (Not actually a nickname.)

Rollickers, The: The Royal Irish Fusiliers. Through the 2nd Battalion, as the 89th Foot. An old nickname.

Rorys, The: The Argyll and Sutherland Highlanders. Through the 2nd Battalion, as the 93rd Highlanders. An old nickname.

Royals, The: The 1st Royal Dragoons.

Royal Goats, The: A nickname of the Royal Welch Fusiliers. From the historic regimental goat.

Royal Tigers, The: The York and Lancaster Regiment. Through the 1st Battalion as the 65th Foot. From the "Royal Tiger" badge, granted for distinguished service in India between 1802 and 1822.

"Run Away, Matron's Coming!": An occasional nickname in jest for the R.A.M.C. (From the initials.)

Rusty Buckles, The: The Bays (2nd Dragoon Guards.)

Sandbags, The: The Grenadier Guards.

Sankey's Horse: The Dorsetshire Regiment. Through the 1st Battalion, as the 39th Foot. Dating from the War of the Spanish Succession. From the name of the then Colonel, and in allusion to a tradition that the battalion was mounted on mules for special service.

Sappers, The: The Royal Engineers. (The Corps of "Royal Sappers and Miners", formed in 1812, was amalgamated with the officers' staff corps of "Royal Engineers" as the Corps of Royal Engineers in 1856.)

Saucy Greens, The: The Worcestershire Regiment. Through the 2nd Battalion, as the 36th Foot. From the colour of the facings.

Saucy Pompeys, The: The Essex Regiment. Through the 2nd Battalion as the 56th Foot, the Pompadours (*q.v.*).

Saucy Seventh, The: The 7th Hussars.

Saucy Sixth, The: The Royal Warwickshire Regiment. From the number previous to 1881.

Scarlet Lancers, The: The 16th Lancers. From their scarlet jackets. (The only British lancer regiment wearing scarlet.)

Seven and Sixpennies, The: A nickname of the 2nd Battalion Duke of Wellington's, as the 76th Foot. From the figures of the number, and in allusion to seven and sixpence, a lieutenant's pay *per diem*.

Shiners, The: The Northumberland Fusiliers. Through the 1st Battalion, as the 5th Foot. Dating from the middle of the 18th century when Hugh Earl Percy (later the second Duke of Northumberland), was Colonel (1767–84). From the exceptionally smart appearance always presented by the regiment on parade.

Shiny Seventh, The: The 7th Battalion: City of London Regiment. Originally given, it is said, because of the always brightly polished brass buttons of their tunics, in contrast to the dark metal buttons worn by the three other battalions with which they were brigaded under the Territorial System.

Six and Two's, The: The Wiltshire Regiment. Through the 1st Battalion as the 62nd Foot. From the figures of the number previous to 1881.

Slashers, The: The Gloucestershire Regiment. Through the 1st Battalion as the 28th. Foot. Dating from the Battle of White Plains, in November, 1776, in the American War, when, according to tradition, on ammunition running short, the men drew the short swords which

Infantry carried at that period and attacked and routed the enemy. Another tradition derives the nickname from a different incident during the American War, when it is said, a number of persons, officers and civilians, disguised as Indians, cut off the ears of a Mr. Walker, a magistrate who had refused to provide shelter for the soldiers' wives and children during very severe wintry weather. The subsequent Court of Inquiry, however, did not connect any officer of the 28th with the affair. The nickname "Slashers" is immortalized also on the Admiralty charts. In 1842 a transport, sailing from Australia to India with the 28th Regiment on board, ran on an unknown reef in, Torres Strait, and the reef has been marked as "Slashers' Reef" ever since.

Snappers, The: The East Yorkshire Regiment. Through the 1st Battalion, as the 15th Foot. Dating from 1777 in the American War. While fighting a much superior force of the enemy in a wood, on ammunition running short, those men who had used up their cartridges were ordered to skirmish among the trees, snapping off their musket locks, while the men who had ammunition left kept up firing. The proceeding puzzled the Americans the men dodging among the trees making the enemy think that our numbers were larger than they really were. The Americans, in consequence, stopped advancing, and the delay give time for reinforcements with fresh supplies of ammunition to arrive, after which the enemy were driven back.

Springers, The: The Wiltshire Regiment. Through the 1st Battalion as the 62nd Foot. Dating from 1776–7 in the American War when the battalion was acting as light infantry. After one action General Burgoyne, the Commander-in-Chief, rode up to the 62nd and greeted them with "Well done, my brave Springers!" Spring-up was a Light Infantry word of command, and "Springers" was a name that Light Infantry battalions affected for themselves by way of swagger over ordinary linesmen.

Staffordshire Knots, The: The South Staffordshire Regiment. Through the 2nd Battalion as the 80th Foot. From the badge adopted in 1793 when the battalion was raised as the Staffordshire Volunteers.

Star of the Line: The Worcestershire Regiment. Through the 1st Battalion as the 29th Foot. From the eight-pointed "Garter Star", worn as a special distinction on the great coat straps and formerly on the valises. The Star of the Order of the Garter is a Guards' badge. It is officially stated to have been originally granted to the 29th for "distinguished service in the field", but when, or for what service, does not seem to be known. (*See* Guards of the Line.) During the reign of William IV, the War Office, pressed by the Treasury to economize in Army expenditure, ordered the removal of the Star from the ammunition pouches worn by the regiment. On that officers and men offered to pay for the Star and provide it for themselves. In the end, the War Office withdrew the order.

Steelbacks, The: The Northamptonshire Regiment. Through the 1st Battalion, as the 48th Foot. In allusion to the stoical way in which, according to tradition, the men bore their punishment when flogged. (An 18th century nickname.)

Strawboots, The: The 7th Hussars. Dating from the Seven Years War. According to a tradition, the men wore out their boots in hard service in Germany and had to wrap straw round their feet in cold weather.

Also a nickname of the 7th Dragoon Guards. Dating from about 1820, and said to have been given originally in consequence of the regiment being employed in dealing with rick-burning outrages in the Midlands.

Stubborns (also Old Stubborns), The: The Sherwood Foresters. Through the 1st Battalion, as the 45th Foot. Derived from a passage in Napier's "History of the Peninsular War" (Book VIII, Chapter 2), referring to the regiment at Talavera, as a "stubborn regiment".

Supple Twelfth, The: The 12th Lancers. Dating from the Peninsular War.

Surprisers, The: The Duke of Cornwall's Light Infantry. Through the 2nd Battalion as the 46th Foot. Dating from the American War, with special reference to the surprise of the enemy at White Plains in September, 1777. (See Red Feathers.)

Sweeps, The: The Rifle Brigade. In allusion to their dark-coloured uniform.

Thin Red Line, The: The Argyll and Sutherland Highlanders. Through the 2nd Battalion, as the 93rd Highlanders. First suggested by a phrase in the letter of the celebrated *Times* correspondent in the Crimean War, Dr. Russell, describing the formation of the battalion to stop the massed Russian cavalry attack at Balaclava on October 25th, 1854. The 93rd in pre-Territorial days was the only infantry regiment entitled to bear "Balaclava" on its Colours. During that action, when the Turks had bolted, Sir Colin Campbell addressed the line of the 93rd before they began to fire and as the Russians were nearing them. "There is no retreat, men, from here! You must die where you stand!" The answer came back in a shout: "Aye, Aye, Sir Colin, and need's be we'll do that!" Their commanding officer refused to form square. His words were: "We can beat them off without that!" He kept them in the ordinary two-deep formation, and their fire stopped the Russian horse and rolled them back in disorder. "The gallant and splendid 93rd" was what Queen Victoria called the regiment.

Three Tens, The: The East Lancashire Regiment. A nickname of the 1st Battalion as the "XXX" (30th) Foot.

Tichborne's Own: The 6th Dragoon Guards (Carabiniers). A temporary nickname, originating in 1873 in allusion to the notorious Tichborne trial, the "Real Sir Roger" having been an officer of the regiment. Another nickname of the time was "The Wagga-Wagga Guards", Wagga-Wagga in Australia being constantly mentioned during the long trial.

Tigers, The: The Leicestershire Regiment. Through the 1st Battalion, as the 17th Foot. From the "Royal Tiger" badge, granted in 1825 for distinguished service in India between 1804 and 1823. Former occasional nicknames were "Bengal Tigers" and "Green Tigers", the latter from the colour of the tiger as displayed on the Colours. Whether the green tiger was originally a Herald's College fancy, or commemorates some Indian battle trophy, is not clear.

Also the Hampshire Regiment. Through the 2nd Battalion, as the 67th Foot. From the "Royal Tiger" badge granted in 1827 for distinguished service in India.

Tin Bellies, The: The Life Guards. Dating from 1821, when George IV, for purposes of display at his coronation, converted the regiment into cuirassiers, as at present. "The Tins" was the nickname given in the War to the "Composite Regiment of Household Cavalry" which served on the Western Front.

Toughs, The: See Old Toughs.

Trades Union, The: The King's Dragoon Guards. A nickname originating about 1830 from the K.D.G's being constantly employed in suppressing Trades Union disturbances in Lancashire and the Midlands between 1825–34. Trades Unions were at that period illegal organisations.

Triple X's, The: The East Lancashire Regiment. From the letters "XXX" of the number of the 1st Battalion, as the 30th Foot.

Two and a Hook, The: An old nickname of the 1st Battalion Worcestershire Regiment, as the 29th Foot: Suggested by the numerical figures.

Two Fives, The: The Border Regiment. Through the 2nd Battalion, as the 55th Foot. From the figures of the number.

Two Fours, The: The Essex Regiment. Through the 1st Battalion, as the 44th Foot. From the figures of the number.

Two Red Feathers, The: The Duke of Cornwall's Light Infantry. (*See* Red Feathers.)

Two Tens, The: The Lancashire Fusiliers. From the figures "XX" of the number, as the 20th Foot.

Two Twos, The: The Cheshire Regiment. From the figures of the number of the 22nd Foot.

Ups and Downs, The: The Welch Regiment. Through the 2nd Battalion, as the 69th Foot. In allusion to the appearance of the numerical figures.

Vein Openers, The: The Worcestershire Regiment. Through the 1st Battalion, as the 29th Foot. Originally given by the townsfolk of Boston in Massachusetts, from the regiment being the first to draw blood in the struggle between Great Britain and the American Colonists, by firing on a violent Boston mob on March 5th, 1770, the so-called "Boston Massacre".

Vics, The: The Queen Victoria Rifles (9th Battalion City of London Regiment). Also known as the Q.V.R. and "Queen Vics".

Virgin Mary's Bodyguard, The: The 7th Dragoon Guards. A nickname dating traditionally from 1743, during the War of the Austrian Succession. The regiment had been for thirty years stationed in Ireland, and a large number of Roman Catholics were in its ranks—whence the nickname. The regiment was then officially known as the "4th Horse".

Warwickshire Lads, The: The Royal Warwickshire Regiment. Dating from 1782, on the 6th Foot being given the Territorial title. Also, with reference to the regimental march, "Warwickshire Lads and Lassies". The song, "Ye Warwickshire Lads and Lasses" dates from 1769, when it was introduced at the Garrick Jubilee Celebration at Stratford-on-Avon. Its popularity led to its being adopted as the County Song, and when the 6th became the "Royal Warwickshire" it was adopted as the regimental tune:—

"Ye Warwickshire lads and lasses,
 See what at Our Jubilee passes,
 Come revel away and rejoice and be glad
 For the lad of all lads is a Warwickshire Lad!"

ran the first verse, attributed to Garrick.

Whitewashers, The: The Gloucestershire Regiment. Through the 2nd Battalion, as the 61st Foot. Dating from the Indian Mutiny, in allusion to the white facings of the uniform and the care bestowed in keeping them clean. An older nickname was (for the officers) the "Silver Tailed Dandies", a Peninsular War nickname, in allusion to the elaborate silver embroidery on the tails of their coats.

Wild Macraes, The: The Seaforth Highlanders. Through the 1st Battalion, as the 72nd Highlanders. The Clan Macrae provided a large proportion of the recruits when the regiment was raised in 1777 and the nickname seems to have originated on the newly raised battalion arriving in Edinburgh, when "the sober people of the Scottish capital" we are told, "taken aback at the frolics of the Highlanders in the streets gave them the name of the 'Wild Macraes' ".

Wolfe's Own: The Loyal Regiment (North Lancashire). Through the 1st Battalion, as the 47th Foot. Dating from the Battle of Quebec in 1759. An occasional variant was "The Wolves".

Young Bucks, The: The Prince of Wales's Own West Yorkshire Regiment. Through the 1st Battalion, as the 14th Foot. Dating from 1809, when the battalion, till then known as the Bedfordshire Regiment, exchanged County titles and depots with the 16th Foot, the hitherto Buckinghamshire Regiment. (*See* Old Bucks.)

Young Buffs, The: The East Surrey Regiment. Through the 1st Battalion, as the 31st Foot. Originating from an incident at the Battle of Dettingen; from King George II's special commendation on the occasion. The King mistook the regiment for the Buffs and called out to them, "Bravo, Old Buffs!" On learning of his mistake the King called out "Bravo, Young Buffs", and the regiment adopted the *sobriquet* thenceforward.

Young Fusiliers, The: A Peninsular War nickname of the Lancashire Fusiliers, as the 20th Foot.

Nicky, A: The saved end of a cigarette, nipped out for smoking later.

Niet Dobra: No good. A Russian word used colloquially in the North Russia Expeditionary Force in the War, much as Nichevo (*q.v.*), and usually with an intermediate English expletive, e.g., "Niet blanky dobra".

Niffy, A: A strong, nasty smell.

Niffy Jane: A nickname of H.M.S. *Iphigenia.* (Probably suggested in pronouncing the name.)

Niggers in a Snow Storm: Boiled rice and curry. (Navy.)

Nip, To: To cadge.

Nipped, Before You: Before you joined up. An expression used contemptuously by an older man to a younger.

Nissen Hut: Named after the inventor, Lieut.-Col. P.N. Nissen, D.S.O., a Canadian Mining Engineer. Corrugated iron and wood structures, semi-cylindrical in form, used for general and hospital purposes. Enormous numbers were used in the War. Their weather-resisting qualities and the ease with which they could be taken down, shifted, and re-erected rendered them invaluable.

Nit, A: A Military Policeman.

Noah's Doves: Men, or reinforcements, at sea when the Armistice was signed. (An Australian Army expression.)

Nobby: *See* Nicknames.

No Compree: (*French*—non compris). "No thanks! I don't want any." "I don't understand."

No Man's Land: The strip of open ground, strewn with war wreckage, broken wire, dead bodies, fragments of shells, etc., dividing the opposing trenches which extended all along the front and on the Western Front varying in width, in places, from a few yards to a quarter of a mile. (The name was coined apparently by "Eyewitness", and first appeared in print in his official "Narrative" of September 15th, 1914.)

Nocky: *See* Nicknames.

Nonstop, A: A trench expression used of a long range shell passing high overhead.

Norperforce: The contracted term for the name of a special force operating at the end of the war in Northern Persia.

Nose Well Down: In a great hurry.

Nosebag, Straight from the: Authoritative. Trustworthy, e.g., "I got it straight from the nosebag, so you can rely upon it." Probably of racing stable origin.

Not Forgotten Association, The: Formed at the conclusion of the war to help and insure the comfort of all disabled soldiers and sailors, detained temporarily or permanently in hospitals all over the Kingdom, by visiting them and making them gifts, providing entertainments of every kind for them, and doing everything possible to show interest in them and alleviate their lot. Upwards of 30,000 disabled men were in the hospitals of Great Britain at the end of 1923: about a quarter of the total housed in London. Princess Mary, Viscountess Lascelles, is Patroness of the Society, and the King and Queen, in addition to showing constant interest in the sufferers, periodically have all who can attend specially entertained at Buckingham Palace.

Nugget, A: A short man. (An Australian expression.)

Number Nine, A: The popular name for the Service aperient dose or pill. From its listed number, No. 9, in the Field Hospital Case of drugs. Being the Medical Officer's stock remedy in case of doubtful ailments, or suspected malingering, in the war the expression "A No. 9" came to be used with all kinds of applications, more or less in jest.

Number not Dry, Your: A sarcastic expression from an older soldier to a cheeky raw recruit. In allusion to the number stencilled in blacking on a soldier's kit.

Number One: The 1st Lieutenant on board ship. (Navy.) Also, a general Army term for the close crop of hair, cut short according to Service regulation. At an inspection, for instance, an officer would tell a man, whose hair seemed too long, to "Get a Number One before next Parade".

Number Up, To Have One's: To be in trouble. Dead.

Nut, To Do One's: To get flurried. To lose one's head. To desert.

Nutty: *See* Nicknames.

Nut: The latter-day descendant of the "Fop", through the "Dandy", the "Heavy Swell", the" Masher", the "Chappy" and the "Johnny". The derived adjective was in use a century and more ago:—

"Who on a lark. with black-eyed sal (his blowing)
  So prime, so swell, so nutty and so knowing?"

Byron: Don Juan, Canto xi., stanza 19.

In general use before 1914, "Nut" was further popularized in a song, the chorus of which began:—

"I'm Gilbert the Filbert, the Colonel of the Nuts",
first sung by Basil Hallam, afterwards killed while serving as an officer in the Royal Flying Corps. A crude parody of the song was much used as a marching song. The word was sometimes written and pronounced "K'nut", to form a species of superlative. (*See* Knuts, The.)

Nut Out, To: "To think over. Consider. To use one's head., e.g., "I've got to nut it out".

Nutcrackers, The: *See* Nicknames of Regiments.

Nutworker, A: A Shirker. A man given to contriving methods of evading duty.

O.C. Swills: A familiar colloquialism for the Controller of Salvage, the Officer in charge of the Salvage Corps, or of any detachment on salvage work.

O.P. or O. Pip.: Observation Post. (Pip being the Signallers' vernacular for the letter "P".)

Oath, Miss Weston, My: On my word of honour. An expression originating in the lifetime of Dame Agnes Weston, the widely known and honoured foundress of hostels for bluejackets at the naval ports, in connection with temperance pledges. From the frequency of repetition, the expression passed into current speech among bluejackets as equivalent to "On my honour".

Oatmeal Party: Scotsmen. (Navy.)

Obbo: Observation balloon.

OBOF: Old Buffer over Forty. A jocular war-time term from the initials, for certain elderly recruits under the Conscription Act.

OCAC, also Okak: Officer Commanding Administrative Centre. (A word coined from the initials.) Administrative Centres were established for the, New Army and Territorials in 1915; later termed depôts.

Ocakery: Depot where records were kept.

Ocean Villas: Army vernacular for the name of the town of Auchonvillers near Arras.

Odds, To Shout the: To talk too much; too loudly. To brag.

Office, The: An airman's term for the cockpit of an aeroplane, the pilot's compartment, with speaking tubes, writing pad, etc.

Oil Can: A name for a German 10-inch diameter trench-mortar shell filled with high-explosive, often in the earlier months of the War fired from wooden trench mortars. (From its shape.)

Oiled: Drunk.

Oily Wads: A Navy nickname for a class of oil-burning torpedo boat destroyers.

Old and Bold, The: *See* Nicknames of Regiments.

Old Bill, An: A veteran. Any old Soldier; in particular one with a heavy, drooping moustache. (From Captain Bairnsfather's celebrated creation "Old Bill".) Used sometimes colloquially by older men in "setting down" a young soldier giving himself airs, e.g., "You think yourself an Old Bill; you haven't joined up six months!" Also, the nickname of a celebrated London General Omnibus Company's motor bus which served on the Western Front; employed throughout the War on transport service. It is now preserved as an honoured veteran, with a brass tablet on it, bearing inscribed the name "Ole Bill" (*sic.*) and these "Battle Honours":—"1914, Antwerp"; "1915, Ypres"; "1916, Somme"; "1917, Ancre"; "1918, Amiens". Below the dates are the words "Lest we Forget". "Ole Bill" was inspected by the King at Buckingham Palace after the Armistice and has figured, decked with Flanders poppies, in Armistice Day processions to the Cenotaph.

Old Braggs, The: *See* Nicknames of Regiments.

Old Brickdusts, The: *See* Nicknames of Regiments.

Old Bucks, The: *See* Nicknames of Regiments.

Old Buffs, The: *See* Nicknames of Regiments.

Old China: Friend. Pal. (Rhyming slang. China Plate—Mate.)

Old Contemptibles, The: *See* Contemptibles.

Old Eyes, The: *See* Nicknames of Regiments.

Old Fighting Tenth, The: *See* Nicknames of Regiments.

Old Fogs, The: *See* Nicknames of Regiments.

"Old Gents", The: (*See* Gorgeous Wrecks.) One of the names for the elderly Volunteers of the War.

Old Jocks, The: *See* Nicknames of Regiments.

Old Loyals, The: *See* Nicknames of Regiments.

Old Man, The: A Captain R.N. on board his ship. Also, a Commanding Officer of an Army unit.

Old One Eye: A Nickname for H.M.S. *Cyclops*.

Old Sweat, An: Old Soldier. Veteran. (Old Army.)

Old Toughs, The: *See* Nicknames of Regiments.

Olive Branch: A jesting name for a reinforcement arriving after the Armistice of November, 1918.

Omms and Chevoos: Army vernacular for the French railway vans and trucks of troop-trains on the Western Front, which were marked "Hommes 37–40. Chevaux en long 8", Wrote a soldier to his sweetheart from France:—"here was trucks for Omms and Chevoos, which means men and horses in French. I went in one, and we were packed so close we hadn't even room to change our minds."

On the Pegs: An expression used of a N.C.O. awaiting trial by Court Martial.

One the Tapes: Ready to commence. In allusion to the white tapes marking the "lie out" positions before an attack, where the attacking infantry formed up while waiting for the Artillery barrage to open. (*See* Tape.)

On the Toot: At once. Quickly.

Once a Week: Cheek. (Rhyming slang.)

One and All, The: *See* Nicknames of Regiments.

One Gun Salute, To Get a: To be court martialled. (Navy.) A ship in which a court martial is to be held fires one gun at 8 a.m. on the day, as an intimation to members of the court and witnesses to attend.

One Pip, A: A Second Lieutenant. (From the one star rank-badge.)

One Up: A step in rank. In allusion to the addition of a fresh star, or stripe, rank badge on promotion.

Onion: A naval expression meaning a fraction of a knot, e.g., "We got sixteen and an onion out of her".

Onks: Francs.

Oofs: (*French*—Oeufs). Universal Army vernacular for Eggs.

Oojah (also Ooja-ka-pivi): A substitute expression for anything the name of which a speaker cannot momentarily think of, e.g., "Pass me that h—m, h—m, oojah-ka-pivi, will you?"

Oojiboo: Much the same as Oojah.

Oper, No: No chance, e.g., "We've no oper this time".

Opera House: Guard Room. Cells. Detention quarters.

Operations B: Training for actual operations, the planning and carrying out of which came under "Operations A". The rehearsals for attacks were often of a very elaborate nature. In the case of important raids full size replicas of the enemy trenches were often made in some convenient back-area. Cases occurred where German attacks were forestalled through the appearance of a replica of some of our trenches. On an air-photograph taken for other purposes, miles behind the front line.

Opposite Number: An expression used of individuals performing similar functions in different ships (Navy) or units (Army) concerned in joint operations.

Ops: Operations.

Optimists, The: The Concert Party of the 89th "Pals" Brigade.

Orange Lilies, The: *See* Nicknames of Regiments.

Ord: A bluejacket's familiar contraction for the rating of "Ordinary Seamen".

Orderly Buff: Orderly Sergeant.

Orderly Dog: Orderly Corporal.

Orders, Up for: Directed to attend at the Orderly Room, for examination or punishment by the Commanding Officer.

Organ, To Want the: To be trying to borrow money.

Oscar: Money.

Other Ranks: The usual official designation for N.C.O.'s and privates in orders, etc., as distinguished from Commissioned Officers, e.g., "2 Officers and 37 Other Ranks will proceed, etc."

Otter, The: The name of a device for safeguarding vessels against mines, used in the Mercantile Marine in the War. Similar to the Paravane (*q.v.*).

"Our Home": The name given to the building erected at Göttingen in Germany by the American Branch of the Y.M.C.A. for Prisoners of

149

War; used for concerts, lectures, and religious services. It was completely equipped with a library and everything for recreation.

Out There: A colloquialism for on the Western Front.

Outed: Killed.

Outfit, An: Air Force colloquial for an aeroplane squadron.

Over the Bags: Leaving the trenches to attack—going over the sandbags of the trench parapet. "Over the Bags and the best of luck!" was a common phrase in this connection.

Over the Side: Absent without leave. (Navy.)

Over There: In France. (A U.S. Army expression.) An American marching song in the Great War. The refrain and title of a popular song, with something of the lilt of the old Civil War songs.

Over to Gilbert: Something askew; awry; irregular. (Navy.)

Overseas Men: A term for the British subjects who, on the outbreak of the War, made their way from foreign countries all over the world to enlist in the British Army. Also, a depôt term for men sent from the Front to a hospital in England and on discharge returned to their depôts; given to distinguish them from Home Service men and others stationed at the depôt.

Owl, The: A warning device employed in the War to enjoin discretion in conversation among men in the Services, particularly against talking on naval and military topics before strangers. At Etaples and other French railway stations, these lines were to be seen painted on boards:

"A wise old Owl lived up in an oak,
  The more he saw the less he Spoke,
  The less he spoke, the more he heard,
  Soldiers should imitate that old bird."

The Owl lines were also displayed in England for the benefit of people in Government services, the last line being rendered, "Try to copy that wise old bird".

Owner, The: A Captain R.N. on board his Ship. (Navy.) Also, a bluejacket's name for a visitor from shore, coming to look round on board. According to one story the term arises from an incident that happened at Birkenhead some years ago. A new battleship was on the point of leaving there when a man walked aboard and asked for the captain. "Who shall I say wants him?" said the quartermaster. "Oh", replied the man nonchalantly, "just tell him that one of the owners wants to have a look round the ship." This answer so tickled the bluejacket's sense of humour that he told the story everywhere and a visitor has been an "owner" ever since.

P: Pronounced "Pip" by Signallers for clearness of expression and to prevent misunderstanding.

P.B.I.: Poor B—y Infantry. The customary phrase, applied more or less humorously to themselves, by British infantrymen in general in the

War, in comparing their lot as "men-of-all-work" with that of men of other arms. Also, the name of the Concert Party of the 72nd Brigade.

P.D.Q.: A colloquial contraction for "Pretty d—n quickly".

P.G.: Nickname of H.M.S. *Prince George.*

P.H. Helmet, The: A type of anti-gas helmet with glass eyepieces and breathing tube introduced at the end of 1915. Superseded by the box respirator. The P. and P.H. helmet was issued as an improvement on the hypo-helmet (*q.v.*) to meet the German use of phosgene-chlorine gas mixtures in 1915. The helmets were made of flannelette soaked at first in a solution containing sodium phenolate, and later with hexamethylene-tramine added to the solution.

P.O.Q.: Colloquial contraction for "Push off quickly", i.e., "Be quick about it".

P,P., also P.P.C.L.I.: Princess Pat's. The initials of the famous Canadian Corps, Princes Patricia of Connaught's Light Infantry, of which Princess Patricia (Lady Patricia Ramsay) was, and is, Colonel-in-Chief.

P.R., The: H.M.S. *Princess Royal.*

P.T.: The universal colloquial contraction for Physical Training.

P.U.O.: From the initials of "Pyorrhea of Unknown Origin", the notation adopted by medical officers for various ailments. It also meant "Placed under observation whilst symptoms are developing".

P.V.: The initials for Paravane, the mine-deflecting device attached at the bows of a warship, enabling a passage to be made through a mine-field. (Invented by Commander Burney, R.N.) The Paravane sweeps the mine aside and cuts through its moorings, bringing it to the surface where it can be destroyed.

P.Z.: The naval equivalent for an Army field-day, fleet tactical exercise by opposed squadrons, as in action. From the code letters, P.Z., of the two signal flags hoisted as the order for the exercise.

Pack: The infantry knapsack.

Pack Up (Pack One's Hand), To: To stop (as opposed to "carry on"). To give up. To finish. To die.

Packet: A bullet wound, e.g., it would be said of a wounded man:— He "stopped a packet" or "bought a packet"—i.e., got hit by a bullet. Also, any trouble or unexpected bad luck.

Packing: Rations. Food in general, e.g., a train-load of packing.

Paddy Doyle, To Do: To undergo confinement in Cells. To do "time".

Padre, A: A Chaplain. As an English word, apparently originating with the English in India in the days of the East India Company more than two hundred years ago, and adopted in the first place from the Portuguese Roman Catholics of the Portuguese settlements in India. British troops serving in India took the word up and thus "Padre" came to be a general Service term. As a curiosity, by way of comparison, this is the German Army slang word for a Padre: "Sündenabwehrkanone" (Anti-sin-gun).

Padre's Flag, The: The historic Union Flag, used all over the Western Front at celebrations of Holy Communion, other religious services, at the funerals of hundreds of soldiers, and as the pall at the burial of the "Unknown Warrior", now hanging permanently in Westminster Abbey. The flag, which now hangs by a pillar at the side of the grave, was given to a Church of England Chaplain early in the War for use in France, where it did duty both in and behind the lines: at Vimy Ridge, in the Ypres Salient, on the Somme, at Messines, at Cambrai, and elsewhere. After the Armistice it was brought home and hung in an English Parish Church until offered for the funeral of tile Unknown Warrior. The Rev. David Railton, afterwards Vicar of Margate, was the clergyman to whom the flag was originally given; on his appointment as a Chaplain in the 47th (London) Division in 1915. The flag was solemnly dedicated in Westminster Abbey and placed in position by selected representatives of the 47th Division on "Remembrance Day", 1921.

Paget's Irregular Horse: *See* Nicknames of Regiments.

Paint: Jam.

Pakaru: Broken; smashed. A Maori word, in use among the New Zealand Troops.

Palestine Pops, The: The Divisional Concert Party of the 74th (Yeomanry) Division.

Pals, The: *See* Nicknames of Regiments.

Pancake, To: An Air Force term. To descend with the wings of an aeroplane at a very large angle of incident and land flat, the aeroplane under-carriage collapsing and spreading itself like a pancake on the ground, as in a forced landing on rough ground.

Pandemonium: The subalterns' quarters on board the old Indian troopships.

Panic, A: The culminating phase of a "Flap" on board a ship when getting ready for sea, etc., at top speed in an emergency. (See Buzz and Flap.)

Panic, To: To lose one's head. To be unnecessarily anxious. To get flurried.

Panic Party: *See* Decoy Ships.

Panicker, A: A man showing needless anxiety beforehand over anything by word or act.

Parasol: The colloquial name for a type of monoplane, largely employed in the War, the wings of which were raised above the fuselage and over the pilot's head, giving a clear view of the ground below.

Pass Out, To: To die.

Patent Safeties, The: *See* Nicknames of Regiments.

Pay (also Paybob): Paymaster R.N. Also a familiar term for the Army Pay Department.

Peacemakers, The: *See* Nicknames of Regiments.

Peas in the Pot: Hot. (Rhyming slang.)

Peckham Rye: Tie. (Rhyming slang.)

Pedlars, The: The Divisional Concert Party of the 31st Division.

Peechy: (*Hind.*—Pichhe). Presently. Soon, e.g., "Come peechy".

Peek, To: To give in.

Peg, On the: Under arrest. Awaiting trial.

Pelicans: The Divisional Concert Party of the 62nd Lancashire Division, whose "sign" was a Pelican with its right foot raised. In this connexion the men of the Division had a popular saying: "When the b—y Dook puts its b—y foot down, the b—y war will be b—y well over".

Penguins, The: A nickname for the "Wrafs" (*q.v.*) the Women's Section of the Royal Air Force organised in the War, the members being employed in various auxiliary capacities to free men for service at the Front. The nickname was of course suggested by the inability of the penguin to fly, Penguin was also a name for a type of low-powered aeroplane with small planes or wings, used for instructional purposes.

Pepper Box: Lighthouse. (Navy.) (Suggested by the shape.)

Perisher: Periscope.

Perked: Drunk.

Persuader: A nickname for the club, or knob-kerry, carried by trench raiders. Also, bayonet.

Perthshire Greybreeks, The: *See* Nicknames of Regiments.

Pervyse, The Two of: Two ladies, Mrs. Knocker (now Baroness T'serclaes) and Miss Mairi Chisholm, a young Scottish lady. They went out in September, 1914, with Dr. Munro's Ambulance and worked for months for the Belgian Red Cross under fire, succouring and nursing wounded, living by themselves in a small cellar under a shattered house in the continuously shelled village of Pervyse, between Nieuport and Dixmude. Both were specially permitted to remain and both were specially decorated by King Albert. Their marvellous and romantic adventure is one of the most heroic episodes of the War.

Petrol Hussars, The: The Armoured-Car force sent to Egypt in 1916 and serving under the Duke of Westminster. So named originally by the sailors who conveyed the force to Egypt, the reason for the name being that before the war, as it happened, most of the official's had served in Hussar regiments.

Pharaoh's Foot: A nickname given to the companies of Volunteers raised among European civilians in Egypt in 1915.

Phosgene: An anti-gas Instructor. Foolish talk. Profanity.

Physical Jerks (also Physical Torture): Physical drill.

Piccadilly Butchers, The: *See* Nicknames of Regiments.

Pictures, The: Colloquial for the operating-theatre of a hospital, e.g., "Brown is for the pictures to-morrow", i.e., to undergo an operation.

Pig and Whistle Light Infantry, The: *See* Nicknames of Regiments.

Pigeon, The V.C.: A name sometimes given to a certain messenger pigeon in the War, No. 2709, belonging to the Sixth Corps, credited with a heroic feat of endurance. During the action on the Menin Road on October 3rd, 1917, it was despatched at 1.30 p.m. with a message from the front line to Divisional headquarters. While in flight the bird was hit by a bullet which broke one of its legs, drove the message-cylinder into its body, and passed out through its back. The bird lay out all night in the wet, but next day, in spite of its wounds, it struggled home to its loft and delivered the message at 10.53 a.m. Two hour later it died. The pigeon, stuffed, is now one of the exhibits at the Royal United Service Institution, Whitehall.

Pigs, The: *See* Nicknames of Regiments.

Pijaw: Admonition; Censure: serious talk.

Pile up One's Bus, To: An airman's expression for coming a "crash".

Pill Box: The name, from the shape (often circular in plan and roughly suggesting a ship's conning tower) for the German ferro-concrete small battlefield-redoubts or forts, employed from the autumn of 1917 onwards to defend sections of the line in Flanders. Some of the larger were quadrangular in shape they were garrisoned by small detachment of infantry with machine guns and were proof against anything except a direct hit by a big gun. Their capture was often effected by infantry with hand grenades flung into the entrance at the rear or through the loopholes, while other infantry kept down the German rifle fire by shooting at the loopholes.

Pills: Colloquial for shells or bombs. Also, a nickname for a Medical Officer's orderly.

Pilot: The Navigating Officer, R.N. Also, the aviator in charge of an aeroplane, as distinct from other occupants, the Observer, Gunner, etc.

Pimple: A common slang term for any hill. "The Pimple" was a name given to certain noted hills on various fronts. On the Western Front, in particular, the name of an elevation on Vimy Ridge, the scene of heavy fighting. Another notable "Pimple" was on Gallipoli, a hill near Suvla Bay, adjoining the Lone Pine plateau, round which fierce fighting took place in August, 1916. There was also a "Pimple" well known to the Salonika troops, on the Bulgarian Front. The "Pimples" at Havre and Boulogne were two steep hills with camps and training schools on top, the march up which was often very trying to troops just disembarked or arrived for embarkation.

Pincher: *See* Nicknames.

Pineapple: A name, suggested by its form for a type of German grenade weighing 4lbs., fired by means of a special device called a "granatwerfer", a rocket on the grenade fitting on a rod on the thrower. Also one of the various kinds of lachyrmatory gases used by the Germans, the being suggested by the smell.

Pink: Secret. An expression in some Government Offices during the war for secret telegrams. From the colour of the paper, e.g., "That matter must be kept pink".

Pink, In the: In good health. An abbreviation of the old sporting phrase "In the pink of condition". The usual valediction of a soldier's letter—"Hoping this finds you in the pink, as it leaves me"

Pinko: Drunk.

Piou-Piou: The pre-war nickname for the French infantryman, equivalent to our Tommy Atkins.

Pip: The letter "P" in the Signaller' vernacular. The star indicative of an official rank, e.g., "He is putting up three pips!" (i.e., is now a captain).

Pip Emma: P.M. From the Signallers' pronunciation of the two letters. (P—Pip; M—Emma.)

Pip Squeak: A type of German shell fired from a small trench gun. From the sound of its discharge and flight. The word was often used by young officers in semi-official and official documents until an order was issued condemning its employment. Also a small man, or one objectionable in some way, was often contemptuously termed a "Pip Squeak".

Pipped, To be: To be hit by a bullet.

Pirates, The: The German U-boats. Also a nickname for one of our Auxiliary Patrol squadrons in the North Sea on anti-submarine service.

Pish: Whiskey. Any spirits.

Piso: A mean or miserly fellow.

Plain Clothes: The equivalent expression in the Navy and in the Cavalry for Mufti (*q.v.*).

Plaster, To: To shell heavily, e.g., "The village was plastered badly last night".

Plonk, To: To shell. Suggested by the sound of the impact and burst.

Plug Street: Army vernacular for the Flemish village of Ploegsteert near Armentières.

Plum and Apple: Jam of any kind. The familiar term at the Front for the ration issue of tinned jam. Officially, the ration included jam of every kind,—strawberry, raspberry, etc., but actually only the commoner sort, almost invariably "Plum and Apple", reached the rank and file, the better kinds, according to popular opinion, being intercepted for the benefit of the N.C.O.s.

Plum Pudding: The name for a type of trench mortar shell; suggested by its shape and size.

Plush: Surplus grog. A Navy (lower deck) term for the extra rum which became the perquisite of the Petty Officer issuing the grog; sometimes, it is said, obtained by a trick, by inserting the thumb into the half-pint measure.

Poachers, The: *See* Nicknames of Regiments.

Poggle (also Puggle): (*Hind.*—Pagal). Mad. An idiot. An old Army term.

Poilu: The universal name for the French soldier in the War, familiar all over the world. It ousted the prewar name Piou-Piou early in the War. The term Poilu came in first apparently as being descriptive of the bearded, unkempt, hairy appearance of the majority of the elderly reservists as they arrived to join their regiments. Soon Poilu became extended to include all soldiers at the front, suggested also by their facial appearance in most cases, the exigencies of life in the trenches, necessitating a disregard of non-essentials such as shaving. Poilu thus became a generic name for a French soldier and was largely adopted for them among our men and the Americans. The word is really an old word and was current in French Army slang, meaning any private, not necessarily bearded or hairy, for years before the war. Apparently, it made its first appearance in Balzac's "Le Médécin de Campagne", published in 1833, and there had the meaning of "intrepid", being used with reference to the French pioneers at the Passage of the Beresina in Napoleon's Moscow Retreat in 1812. A tall pointed stone, bearing the words, in French, "Here triumphed the tenacity of the poilu", has been placed at Haudroy, at the exact spot where the German plenipotentiaries crossed the French line on November 7, 1918, to negotiate for the armistice.

Point Blank: (*French*—Vin Blanc). White Wine.

"Poisoned Arrows from the Air": The German General Ludendorff's phrase for the British propaganda leaflets dropped on the German lines and in districts behind the Front by airmen and balloons.

Policeman's Truncheon, A: A type of hand-grenade, exploding on impact. So called from its handle and shape. It had streamers of tape attached, to steady its flight.

Polite Pirate, The: A name sometimes given to the German U-boat commander, Lieutenant Otto Weddingen, who sank the *Hogue, Cressy* and *Aboukir* in 1914. He sank several merchant ships in Home waters, but always gave the crews opportunity of making their escape, supplying them with cigars sometimes, on occasion towing their boats towards land for some distance, and in one case asking a skipper to "Give my compliments to Lord Churchill!" He and his submarine were sent to the bottom in making an attack on the Grand Fleet off the coast of Scotland, the ram of the *Dreadnought* crashing into the German submarine as it tried to escape.

Polling On: Taking advantage of. Assuming. Reckoning on.

Pompadours, The: *See* Nicknames of Regiments.

Pompey: Portsmouth. (Navy.)

Pond, The: The Sea. (Navy.)

Pong: A stink.

Pongelow: Beer. (Old Army.)

Pongo: A soldier. (Navy.)

Ponkey Land, In: Weak minded. Daft. Silly.

Pontius Pilate: Provost Sergeant.

Pontius Pilate's Bodyguard: *See* Nicknames of Regiments.

Pontoon: A popular card game, a form of Vingt et Un.

Pony: *See* Nicknames.

Poodle Faker: A ladies' man. (Navy.)

Poodle Faking: Paying afternoon calls. (Navy.)

Poop (or Poop Off): To fire (of artillery), e.g., "They pooped off heavily last night".

Pop: The familiar contraction for Poperinghe, seven miles from Ypres, a British staff centre and rendezvous in that portion of the Western Front for concert parties, etc. "Toc H" (*q.v.*) and "Skindles" were at Poperinghe. When opportunity offered and short leave could be obtained, a visit to "Pop" always offered a much appreciated "break" in the life of soldiers at the Front. Also. Lemonade or any other "soft" drink.

Pop Wallah, A: A Teetotaller.

Poppy Day: Armistice Day, November 11th, known widely by that name through the sale everywhere of artificial red Flanders Poppies, made during the year at the British Legion Poppy Factory in South London by the two hundred disabled ex-Service men employed there, in aid of Lord Haig's British Legion Appeal Fund. The numbers of poppies made runs into millions and the Poppy Day Collection by means of the sale of them, realized, on November 11th, 1923, over £250,000. The money is utilized in aid of the work of the Benevolent Department of the British Legion to assist distressed ex-Service men and their families. The world-famous poem, written after the Second Battle of Ypres, in the summer of 1915 by a heroic Canadian Officer, who died in the War, Lieut.-Colonel John McCrae, M.D., and published in *Punch* on December 8th, 1915, inspired and originated the idea of "Poppy Day". "The Army poem of the War" it has been called. The first lines run:

"In Flanders' fields the poppies blow
  Between the crosses, row on row."

No verses were better known and more widely quoted at the Front and all over the Empire during the War. The blood-red poppy has always had associations with battlefields, particularly in Flanders, the historic "cockpit of Europe". So indeed contemporary letters of old times describe, mentioning the amazing profusion in the years following, to name four battles, Ramillies, Malplaquet, Fontenoy and Waterloo. Lord

Macaulay, in Chapter XX of his "History of England", in his account of William III's defeat in the battle of Landen in 1693, after describing the fearful carnage on the battlefield, says this:—"The next summer the soil fertilised by 20,000 corpses, broke forth into millions of poppies. The traveller who on the road from Saint Tron to Tirlemont, saw that vast sheet of rich scarlet spreading from Landen to Neerwinden, could hardly help from fancying that the figurative prediction of the Hebrew was literally accomplished, that the earth was disclosing her blood and refusing to cover the slain."

Pork and Beans, The: A nickname for the Portuguese troops serving on the Western Front. According to one story, when the Portuguese first arrived the military authorities happened to have on hand a large surplus of tinned rations of pork and beans, of which our own men had long been heartily sick, and the opportunity was taken to pass them on to the Portuguese. To the general surprise, the newcomers took to the pork and beans with avidity, and the ration established itself as their favourite food. Their fondness for it highly amused everybody, and then a song came out at a Divisional Concert Party performance with the refrain, "Pork and Beans for the Portuguese!" Apparently, however, someone in authority became anxious lest the nickname, which, through the Concert Party song, had become widespread, should give offence to the Portuguese, and issued the following order:—"In future the forces on our left will be referred to by all ranks as 'Our Oldest Allies', and not as heretofore as the 'Pork and Beans'." The order was intended to be confidential, but an indiscreet adjutant reproduced it in battalion orders, with the result that the order became a general jest. Another story, told of our "Oldest Ally" at the Front may incidentally be mentioned. In March, 1918, to assist the Portuguese in establishing a pigeon-messenger service, the Signal Staff of the 42nd (East Lancashire) Division sent two pairs of pigeons to the Portuguese headquarters, with instructions. They awaited results, but no birds returned to the loft. Then, on the third day, a Portuguese Staff Officer arrived with a letter: "We thank our comrades the British Officers for their hospitality, which we have much enjoyed!"

Porpoising: An Airman's term for the movement of an aeroplane when an imperfect "get off", or landing, is made.

Port Holes in your Coffin, You Want: An expression used to a man hard to please. (Navy.)

Posh: Smart. Spruce.

Possy (or Pozzy): A position. Dug-out. Also jam (pozzy).

Potato-masher Grenade: The name given a species of German handgrenade, resembling in form a domestic potato-masher.

Pouch: Always pronounced "Pooch" in the Army. (*Cf.* Route.)

Pothooks, The: *See* Nicknames of Regiments.

Potty: Half-witted. Silly.

Poultice Wallopers: *See* Nicknames of Regiments.

Pow-Wow, A: A senior officers' conference as, for instance of a General with the Commanding Officers of units after a field-day or an operation.

Prat one's Frame in, To: To intrude. To join others uninvited.

Pretty Pretties: A naval expression for the polished ornamental brass work on board ship.

Pretty Royal: H.M.S. *Princess Royal.* (An old Navy nickname.)

Prick for a Plank, To: To look for a comfortable place to lie down and have a sleep, i.e., on deck. (A bluejacket's expression.)

Princess Mary's Gift Box: In October, 1914, Princess Mary appealed for funds to send a Christmas present from the Nation to "every Sailor afloat and every Soldier at the Front". £131,000 was subscribed, and a brass box of cigarettes or tobacco with pipe and tinder was sent; and others distributed to men at home. It is on record that at least thirty lives were saved directly by the boxes deflecting bullets, they being usually carried in the tunic breast pocket.

Problems, The: The Divisional Concert Party of the 14th Division. In allusion to the Divisional Sign, which bore a design resembling the figure in a problem of Euclid (I. 4, 14).

Promenade, A: An old universal Army expression for a walk.

Pronto: (*Spanish*—Pronto). Hurry up. Be quick. Adopted from the U.S. troops, who themselves originally adopted the word from the Spaniards in one of the Mexican Wars.

Propaganda: Tall Talk. Meaningless information.

Proverbial, The: A fall. A smash. Coming to grief. A colloquial contraction of the much used phrase "A proverbial gutzer", e.g., "I knew how it would be; pride goes before a fall; he's come the proverbial". (*See* Gutzer.)

Pucka (or Pukka): (*Hind.*—Pakkha). Genuine. True. Real. Permanent. Used both of things and people, e.g., a Pukka building; a Pukka major, i.e., one holding substantive, not honorary or temporary rank. A pukka billet—a permanent job.

Puckerow: (*Hind.*—Pakrao). Catch hold; take a grip of.

Pudding Basin: The British steel shrapnel helmet. (From its shape.)

Puggle Pawnee: (*Hind.*—Pagal-pani). "Mad water". Rum. Alcohol—*cf.*, the "Fire Water" of the North American Indians.

Puggled: (*Hind.*—Pagal). Insane. Mad-drunk.

Pull Through, A: The cord, with a weight at one end and an oiled rag at the other, used to clean a rifle barrel by being pulled through. A tall, thin man. (Suggested by the foregoing.)

Pulpit, A: Artillery Observation Ladder.

Pump and Tortoise, The: *See* Nicknames of Regiments.

Pung, A: A signaller's word for a surreptitious doze while on telephone duty, though ready to wake up at any call.

Punk: Food.

Pup, A: A nickname for the small, fast Sopwith single-seater 80 H.P. aeroplane, used both for war and for instructional purposes. (*See* Baby.)

Pup Tent: The U.S. Army name for the small field-service *tente d'abri* or shelter tent.

Purge, To: To swear. Grumble. Worry. e.g., "The Captain purged no end about it".

Push, A: An attack in force, e.g., the Somme Push.

Push Off, To: To go; to leave.

Push the Boat Out, To: To stand treat.

Pusher, A: An aeroplane with the propellor in rear. A young woman friend:—The soldier's perambulator-pushing nursemaid companion in garrison towns when walking out, first probably suggested the name.

Pushing Daisies: Dead and buried, e.g., "Old Jack's been pushing daisies these last six months".

Puss in Boots, A: A swaggerer.

Pusser: (Purser). A Paymaster R.N.

Pusser's Crabs: Seamen's boots. (Navy—lower-deck.)

Pusser's Dip: A candle—the usual illuminant of messes previous to the introduction of electric light on board ship.

Pusser's Dirk: A knife. (Navy—lower-deck.)

Pusser's Yellow: Soap. (Navy—lower-deck.)

Put a Sock in it: Leave off making a noise. Stop talking. (Suggested by the handiest method of gagging a gramophone.)

Put it Across (or Over), To: To punish someone. To beat; defeat. Also, to deceive.

Put the Acid on, To: To test a statement, or a man. To put a stop to.

Put up, To: To charge with a military "crime". Also, to do anything, e.g., To put up a stunt.

Put up a Stall, To: To mislead.

Putty: A ship's painter. (Navy.)

Putty Medal, A: A derogatory colloquialism, suggesting that a decoration has been earned cheaply.

Q.A.I.M.N.S.: Queen Alexandra's Imperial Military Nursing Service.

Q.A.M.F.N.S.: Queen Alexandra's Military Families Nursing Service.

Q.A.R.N.N.S.: Queen Alexandra's Royal Naval Nursing Service.

Q.E.: H.M.S. *Queen Elizabeth.*

Q.F.: Quick-firing. In the British Services a gun in which the charge is in a brass case.

Q.M., The: The Quarter-Master.

Q.M.A.A.C.: Queen Mary's Army Auxiliary Corps. (*See* W.A.A.C.)

Q Ships: *See* "Decoy Ships", also "Mystery Ships". These verses from *Punch* of September 4th, 1918, may be added:—

"She's the plaything of the Navy, she's the nightmare of the Hun,
She's the wonder and the terror of the Seas:
She's a super-censored secret that eludes the prying sun,
And the unofficial wireless of the breeze:
She can come and go unseen,
By the fore-doomed submarine:
She's the Mystery Ship, the 'Q-boat' if you please!"

Q.V.R.: *See* Nicknames of Regiments.

Quakers: A colloquial name for Conscientious Objectors. Also, a very old name for dummy guns.

Quarter, The (also, Quarters): Quarter Master Sergeant.

Quarter Bloke, The: The Quarter Master; also, the Quarter Master Sergeant.

Quarter Master's Erasmic: Soap issued for scrubbing floors.

Quarter to one Feet, A: Used of a man who turns his feet out more than usual. (Navy.)

Quash: Good; nice. An Arabic word (Khwush) in use colloquially on Eastern Fronts.

Quash Kateer: Very good. (*Arabic*—Khwush Kethir—similarly used.)

Queenstown Navy, The: A familiar name for the U.S. Destroyer flotilla, based on Queenstown in 1917, under the command of Admiral Sir Lewis Bayley—familiarly called by the Americans "Uncle Lewis".

Queer: The usual service term for feeling unwell.

Quick Dick: The nickname of one of our guns on the Western Front.

Quiff, A: Any specially ingenious smart, tricky, or novel or improvised way of doing anything. (Navy.) In the Army used of any drill method peculiar to a battalion, and not usually done in others. Where the wording of the Drill Book is vague, units often read different meanings into the phraseology and invent their own "Quiffs", As a colloquial term—smartly got up. e.g., of a man carefully dressed for some special occasion—"He looks very quiff". Also, the Soldiers' name for the forelock of hair worn long—the rest of the poll being cropped close—and then oiled and brushed back over the forehead. The fashion came in years ago when the old "muffin" or "pill-box" and Glengarry forage caps were worn, the word itself being East-End slang.

Quiff Tack: Materials for cleaning harness equipment.

Quimp: Slack. Unsoldierly.

Quirk, A: A term applied to Air Force Officers while under instruction qualifying for their "wings". A name for a "B.E." type of aeroplane; very stable, but very slow. Also any freak type, or unusually designed aeroplane.

R.A.C.D.: Royal Army Clothing Department.

R.A.Ch.D.: Royal Army Chaplains' Department. Made "Royal" by Army Orders of February 22nd, 1919, for "splendid work in the War".

R.A.M.C.: Royal Army Medical Corps. (*See also* Nicknames of Regiments.)

R.A.S.C.: Royal Army Service Corps. (*See also* Nicknames of Regiments.)

R.A.V.C.: Royal Army Veterinary Corps. (*See also* Nicknames of Regiments.)

R.N.D.: The Royal Naval Division. Originally a prewar organization, devised to absorb men, surplus to the Navy, on mobilisation. It was formed, on the outbreak of the war, in three Brigades—2 Naval, 1 of Marines. The Division comprised eight battalions, named after Admirals: Drake, Benbow, Anson, Hawke, Hood, Howe, Nelson and Collingwood. The men, were drawn from the Royal Naval Reserve, Royal Fleet Reserve, Royal Naval Volunteers and Royal Marines. The headquarters were at Deal, and the depôt at the Crystal Palace. The R.N.D. served at Antwerp and the Dardanelles, and then was transferred to the Army in Flanders in 1916, as the "63rd (Royal Naval) Division". As these last they considered themselves throughout as sailors, in spite of repeated efforts by the authorities in Flanders to militarize them. Men returning from leave, for instance, always "came aboard"; they regulated their time by bells; their N.C.O.'s were "Petty Officers" or "Leading Seamen". To go on leave was always to "go ashore"; to be absent without leave, to be "adrift". Hospital was "sick bay"; the cookhouse was the "galley"; the officers' mess, the "wardroom"; and the officers themselves also invariably followed the naval usage of drinking the King's health seated. On the outbreak of war the London Division mobilized 40 officers and 804 ratings by the morning of August 5, 1914; 11 officers and 216 ratings rejoined and 312 recruits were obtained, bringing the war strength to an aggregate of 1,383. Of these 179 were killed, 518 received commissions, 129 were awarded decorations and medals, including one Victoria Cross; 38 were mentioned in despatches, and, as a result of the Antwerp Expedition, 457 were interned.

Race Card, The: The morning Sick Report.

Raffish: Air Force slang for anybody or anything connected with the R.A.F. or Royal Aircraft Factory; not belonging to the Royal Air Force. Not usually intended as a complimentary expression.

Rag, The: The Army and Navy Club. An old nickname dating back nearly a hundred years and referred to by Thackeray and humorous writers of early Victorian times as "The Rag and Famish", in the days when many hard-up half-pay veterans of the Peninsular War and Waterloo were members.

Rag Fair: Kit Inspection. (An old Army word.)

Rag Pickers, The: U.S. Army occasional slang for their Army Field Salvage Corps.

Rags and Bones: A familiar colloquialism for the Officer in charge of the Salvage Corps, Also the Salvage Corps itself, and any member of it.

Ragged Brigade, The: *See* Nicknames of Regiments.

Raggie: A bluejacket's term for his confidential friend or mate on board ship with whom he shares "brass rags" (*q.v.*). In the Old Navy of Nelson's time "Tie-Mate" was a word in use equivalent to Raggie; one of two special chums who, among other acts of mutual help, dressed and tied each other's pigtail.

Rainbow, A: A post-Armistice reinforcement, or recruit. As arriving after the storm was over.

Rainbow Division, The: A name given to the American 42nd Division, one of the first to cross to Europe, because it was composed of men of all colours from twenty-seven States. It was also called the "All America Division".

Ramnugger Boys, The: *See* Nicknames of Regiments.

Rangers, The: *See* Nicknames of Regiments.

Rapatrie, A: A Great War term for a native of a district under enemy occupation allowed to return to unoccupied territory. As the war of 1914–18 progressed and the naval blockade was tightened considerable numbers of civilians, usually women and children and men well over military age, were returned by the Germans to France. Though every effort had been made to prevent their seeing or hearing anything of military importance in the occupied territory, they were able frequently to supply information of great military value to the Allies. There being no equivalent in English, the French word was in general use in the British Army.

Rat, To: To steal. To search a dead body. To betray or act the informer.

"Rat Catcher Churchill": A German newspaper term of abuse for Mr. Winston Churchill, in allusion to a passage in one of his speeches as first Lord of the Admiralty about the German Fleet in Wilhelmshaven and Kiel: "If they do not come out to fight, they will be dug out like rats in a hole!"

Rations: "Dry" rations: bread; cheese; butter; jam; uncooked food. "Wet" rations; tea; porridge; any cooked food; stew, etc. (Also, *see* Iron Rations.)

Rats After Mouldy Cheese: The Royal Army Medical Corps. (From the initials.)

Rats, In the: Muddled with drink.

Rats in the Garret: Of weak intellect. Mad. (*See* Bats in the Belfry.)

Rattle, In the: A defaulter. (Navy.)

Rattle, To: To irritate. To scare.

Razors: Bad quality liquor. (Old Army.)

Razzle, Going on the: Going on the spree. (Navy.)

Read a Shirt, To: To search it for lice.

Really not a Sailor: The Royal Naval Air Service. (A chaffing expression coined from the initials, R.N.A.S.)

Rear Up, A: A row. Quarrel. Noisy argument.

Red Cap, A: A Military Policeman. (From the red cap cover.)

Red Capes: The Sisters of Queen Alexandra's Imperial Military Nursing Service (in allusion to their uniform.)

Red Coats: A name in the War given to Women Inspectors of the Anti-poison gas department, from the red uniform worn indoors. Upwards of 12,000 women were employed making respirators, etc., with 1,000 trained educated women as inspectors over them. The ordinary workers wore nigger brown uniforms.

Red Duster, The: The Red Ensign of the Mercantile Marine.

Red Feathers, The: *See* Nicknames of Regiments.

Red Hat: A Staff Officer.

Red Hussar: A special Government brand of cigarettes introduced in the War to obviate difficulties with the Trade, resulting from the adoption of any special popular brand, on account of trade rivalries. (*See also* Ruby Queen.)

Red Ink: Red Wine.

Red Ink, In: No money forthcoming. A bluejacket's term, from the notation made in the ledger by the paymaster when a bluejacket is in debt to the Crown.

Red Knights, The: See Nickname of Regiments.

Red Lamp, A: The common term on the Western Front for a French "Maison toléree". In use also on other Fronts.

Red Lamp Corner: The name of a notoriously dangerous point near Festubert on the Western Front; so called from the red lamp set up there as a warning to troops after dark.

Red Marines, The: The Royal Marine Light Infantry (now amalgamated with the Royal Marine Artillery—Blue Marines). From their uniform in prewar days.

Red Tabs: The Staff Officer's gorget patches.

Red Triangle Man, A: A nickname at the Front for a member of the Y.M.C.A. (From the badge of the Association.)

Red Wings: A Staff Officer.

Redbreasts, The: *See* Nicknames of Regiments.

Regimental: Smart. Soldierly. Strictly according to regulation.

Regimental, The: The Regimental Sergeant Major, as differentiated from a Company Sergeant Major.

Regimental, To Come a: (Smash implied). Used of a N.C.O. and meaning to be courtmartialled and reduced to the ranks. Also, a downfall or "crash".

Regimental Journals: The following is a list, approximately complete, of Journals and Magazines published by units, monthly or quarterly. In the majority of cases the titles have reference to the regimental badge, or a distinctive name or *sobriquet* of the Corps.

The Guards and Household Cavalry: "The Household Brigade Magazine".

The Royal Scots: "The Thistle".

The Buffs: "The Dragon".

The King's Own Royal Regt. (Lancaster): "The Lion and The Rose".

The Northumberland Fusiliers: "St. George's Gazette".

The Royal Warwickshire Regt.: "The Antelope".

The Royal Fusiliers: "Royal Fusiliers Chronicle".

The Lincolnshire Regt., 1st Bn.: "The Imps Magazine".

The Suffolk Regt.: "The Suffolk Regimental Gazette".

The Somerset Light Infantry: "The Light Bob Gazette".

The East Yorkshire Regt.: "The Snapper".

The Bedfordshire and Hertfordshire Regt.: "The Wasp".

The Leicestershire Regt.: "The Green Tiger".

The Green Howards: "Green Howards' Gazette".

The Lancashire Fusiliers: "The Minden Magazine".

The Cheshire Regt.: "The Oak Tree".

The Cameronians (Scottish Rifles), 1st Bn.: "The Covenanter".

The Royal Irish Fusiliers: "Sprig of Shillelagh".

The Worcestershire Regt.: "The Green 'Un".

The East Lancashire Regt., 1st Bn.: "The XXX".

The East Lancashire Regt., 2nd Bn.: "The Lilywhite Gazette".

The East Surrey Regt.: "Regimental News".

The Duke of Cornwall's Light Infantry: "One and All".

The Duke of Wellington's Regt., 1st Bn.: "Battalion Notes" and "The Havercake Lad".

The Royal Sussex Regt.: "The Roussilon Gazette"

The Hampshire Regiment: "Hampshire Regimental Journal".

The South Staffordshire Regiment: "The Staffordshire Knot".

The Dorsetshire Regiment: "Dorset Regimental Journal".

The Welch Regiment: "The Men of Harlech".

The Black Watch: "The Red Hackle".

The Oxfordshire and Buckinghamshire Light Infantry: "The Oxfordshire and Buckinghamshire Light Infantry Chronicle" (annual).

The Essex Regt.: "The Essex Regiment Gazette".

The Sherwood Foresters, 1st Bn.: "The Sherwood Foresters' Regimental Annual".

The Sherwood Foresters, 2nd Bn.: "I'm Ninety-Five".

The Loyal Regt. (North Lancashire): "The Lancashire Lad".

The Royal Berkshire Regt.: "The China Dragon".

The Queen's Own Royal West Kent Regt.: "The Queen's Own Gazette".

The King's Own Yorkshire Light Infantry: "The Bugle".

The Middlesex Regiment: "The Diehards".

The King's Royal Rifles: "The King's Royal Rifle Corps Chronicle" (annual).

The Wiltshire Regiment: "The Nines".

The Manchester Regiment: "The Manchester Regiment Gazette".

The North Staffordshire Regt.: "China Dragon".

The York and Lancaster Regt.: "The Tiger and Rose".

The Highland Light Infantry: "The H.L.I. Chronicle".

The Seaforth Highlanders: "Cabar Feidh".

The Queen's Own Cameron Highlanders: "The 79th News".

The Gordon Highlanders: "The Tiger and Sphynx".

The Royal Irish Fusiliers: "Faugh-a-ballach".

The Connaught Rangers: "The Ranger" (now quarterly).

The Argyll and Sutherland Highlanders, 2nd Bn.: "The Thin Red Line".

The Leinster Regiment (Royal Canadians): "The Maple Leaf" (ceased on disbandment).

The Royal Munster Fusiliers: "The Bengal Tiger" (ceased on disbandment).

The Royal Dublin Fusiliers: "The Blue Caps" (ceased on disbandment).

The Rifle Brigade: "The Rifle Brigade Chronicle" (annual).

The Royal Marines: "The Globe and Laurel".

The Royal Artillery: "Journal of the Royal Artillery".

The Royal Artillery: "The Gunner".

The Royal Engineers: "The Royal Engineers' Journal" and "The Sapper".

All Cavalry Regiments: "The Cavalry Journal".

1st Royal Dragoons: "The Eagle" (pre-War).

The 3rd Hussars: "The Third Hussars 'Old Comrades' Journal".

The 17th Lancers: "The White Lancer".

The 20th Hussars: "The Yellow Plume".

The 21st Hussars: "Vedette".

Royal Corps of Signals: "The Wire".

The Royal Tank Corps: "The Royal Tank Corps Journal".

The Royal Army Service Corps: "The Royal Army Service Corps Quarterly" and "The Royal Army Service Corps Journal".

The Royal Army Medical Corps: "Journal of the Royal Army Medical Corps".

The Royal Army Ordnance Corps: "The Royal Army Ordnance Corps Gazette".

The Royal Army Chaplains' Department: "Quarterly Journal of the Royal Army Chaplains' Department".

The Corps of Military Accountants: "The Balance".

The Honourable Artillery Company: "Journal of the Honourable Artillery Company".

The London Rifle Brigade (5th City of London Regt.): "L.R.B. Record".

The London Scottish (14th Bn. The London Regiment): "London Scottish Regimental Gazette".

19th Bn. The London Regiment (St. Pancras): "Memories".

The Artists Rifles (28th Bn. The London Regiment): "Artist's Rifles Journal".

Regimental Sports: Coal carrying fatigue. (Old Army.)

Remembrance Day: The Armistice anniversary day—November 11th.

Render, To: Used of anything mechanical. To act. To work properly. (*See* Function.)

Rent: Money: cash.

Rest: In the War to go "into Rest" meant for Divisions, Units, etc., to be temporarily withdrawn to a back-area away from the fighting line, in order to reform and be reinforced. The term implied really the antithesis of rest or repose, the interval, while it lasted, being used for intensive training in preparation to return to the fire-trenches, reorganization, the distribution of reinforcing drafts, etc.

Rest Camp: In the War, a term for a place where worn out men were sent for restoration to fighting efficiency; usually some town a short distance in the rear, where duty was of a light description and there were opportunities for recreation. Also, the Camp, formed at the ports in France, to which all men had to go on their return from leave, usually spending one night there.

Resurrectionists, The: *See* Nicknames of Regiments.

Reveille: The name for the early morning bugle call; the first bugle call of the day. The name is as old as the Army itself. An old drill book of 1701 (*see* Tattoo) says this: "The Revally takes as is most likely, its denomination from the French word *Reveiller*, which signifies as much as to arise up or awake from Sleep; for this is beaten in the Morning to give notice to the People that they may goe abroad, at which time the Out-centinels are taken off."

Revving: An airman's term for circling round rapidly in the air. Also of machinery, referring to the "revs" or engine revolutions per minute.

Rhino: Cheese. Money.

Richard (or Ripe Richard), To Get the: To be openly snubbed: hooted: ragged.

Rifting: Cleaning gear, harness, etc.

Rifleman: The official designation of a private in a Rifle Regiment.

Rigging, To Climb the: To get angry. (Navy.)

Right Abouts, The: *See* Nicknames of Regiments.

Ring, A: A Good Conduct Stripe.

Ring It, To: To show cowardice. To cheat. To introduce something surreptitiously.

Rise and Shine: Turn out. Get up. A barrack-room orderly corporal's call on reveille sounding for the men to rouse out.

River Clyde, The: The now historic transport from which the landing of part of the 29th Division at "V Beach", Gallipoli, was made on April 25th, 1915. (*See* Horse of Troy.)

"Road of Remembrance", The: The name now borne by the road in Folkestone leading down from the Leas promenade to Folkestone Harbour, where hundreds of thousands of troops from all parts of the Empire embarked en route for the battlefields of France and Flanders. The road has been planted with hundreds of rosemary bushes "For Remembrance". A memorial tablet has now been affixed there by the Folkestone Town Council bearing the following inscription:—

"The Road of Remembrance, 1914–1918 'Not once or twice in our rough island story, the path of duty was the way to glory.' During the Great War tens of thousands of British soldiers passed along this road on their way to and from the battlefields of Europe. 'At the going down of the sun and in the morning we will remember them.'"

Roar Up, To: To abuse.

Rob All My Comrades: *See* Nicknames of regiment.

Robin Hoods, The: *See* Nicknames of Regiments

Rocket, Off One's: Mad.

Rocket Troop, The: *See* Nicknames of Regiments.

Roger: Rum. A slang word derived from an old American coon ditty with the refrain "O Rogerum!" Toc H. has adopted a version as its own special song. These are four of the many verses:—

Now there was a rich man and he lived in Jernsal-e-um, Glory alley belurium. O Rogerum.

And he used to live on the fat of the land-e-um, Glory alley belurium. O Rogerum.

Chorus—

O Rogerum, O Rogerum O-o-o, sling-ammy, ling-ammy oreum. O Rogerum.

Now there was a poor man and he lived in Jerusal-e-um. Glory, etc.

And he used to live on the crumbs from the rich man's tabl-e-um. Glory, etc.

Chorus.

Now the poor man he died and he went up to heaven-e-um, Glory, etc.

And he sat down on the starboard side of Abraham Glory, etc.
Chorus.
Now the rich man he died; but he didn't fare so well-e-um, Glory, etc.
For the devil he came and he popped him down to hell-e-um. Glory, etc.
Chorus.

Also a term for a poison-gas cylinder. From the code-term, in use on the Western Front for gas cylinders, introduced in June, 1916, before the Battle of the Somme. The code was changed later, but the word "Roger" continued to be used in current speech.

Rogue's Salute, The: The gun fired on board ship on the morning of a court martial to warn all whose duty it is to attend, to come on board the ship in which the trial is to be held.

Rogue's Tarn The: The old name for the coloured strand running through lengths of cordage made for the Navy, among other reasons to mark it as Government property in case of theft.

Roll Me in the Gutter: Butter. (Rhyming slang.)

Rollickers, The: *See* Nicknames of Regiments.

Roody Boys: Army vernacular for Rue du Bois in Flanders, near Neuve Chapelle.

Roof, The: The highest point to which an aeroplane can climb. (*See* Ceiling.)

Roof, To Hit the: To get into a temper.

Rooky, A: Recruit.

Roosters, The: Divisional Concert Party of the 60th Division.

Rooty: (*Hind.*—Roti)—Bread. An old Army term in use at the Front in the earlier part of the war; giving place later to "Japan" (*q.v.*). Also, food generally, anything to eat.

Rooty Gong: Long service Medal. (Old Army.)

Ropeyarn Sunday, A: A Navy name for Thursday. The afternoon devoted to "make and mend" clothes. Practically a half holiday, when the ship's company can occupy themselves as they please.

Rorty: Used of a man always in trouble.

Rorys, The: *See* Nicknames of Regiments.

Rosalie: The French linesman's pet name in the War for the bayonet. It originated from a war-song by M. Theodore Botrel, published in the *Bulletin des Armées* in the autumn of 1914. The bayonet is popularly (but erroneously) said to have been invented at Bayonne, and Ste. Rosalie being a favourite patron saint in the South of France, that possibly suggested the name to the writer of the song.

Rosy Lee: Tea. (Rhyming slang.)

Rouen, A Client for: The Army main hospital for venereal disease treatment was at Rouen.

Rouges et Noirs, The: The name of the Concert Party of the First Army. Since the War the *Rouges et Noirs* have given many performances in London. So called from the distinguishing colours of the First Army Red and Black.

Rough, A: A roughrider.

Rough as a Sandbag: A greatly exaggerated story. Also a term for a person who behaves unpleasantly. Uncouth. Objectionable.

Rough House, A: A brawl. Quarrel. Free fight.

Round my Houses: Trousers. (Rhyming slang.)

Route: Always pronounced Rowt, e.g., "rowt march".

Royal Roast and Straight Bake: Roast meat on potatoes. (Navy.)

Royal Standbacks, The: A very old army expression for a regiment imagined by others, for one reason or other, not to have shown particular keenness about going into action.

Royal Tigers, The: *See* Nicknames of Regiments.

Royals, The: *See* Nicknames of Regiments.

Ruby Queen: The Government name for a brand of ration cigarettes, an official "issue" at the front in the War. (*See* Red Hussar.) Also, an occasional nickname for any young nurse or Sister of fresh complexion.

Ruby Red: Head. (Rhyming slang.)

Ruhleben Song, The: Given at a British prisoners-of-war camp-concert in May, 1915, in "Don't Laugh—A revue in Eight Episodes", performed on the occasion. One of its verses and the chorus ran thus:—

"Oh, we're roused up in the morning when the day is gently dawning,
    And we're put to bed before the night's begun,
    And for weeks and weeks on end, we have never seen a friend,
    And we've lost the job our energy had won
    Yes, we've waited in the frost for a parcel that got lost,
    Or a letter that the postmen never bring
    And it isn't beer and skittles, doing work on scanty victuals,
    Yet every man can still get up and sing.
Chorus:
Line up, boys and sing this chorus,
Shout the chorus all you can:
We want the people there, to hear in Leicester Square,
That we've the boys that never get down-hearted.
Back, back again to England!
Then we'll fill a flowing cup
And tell 'em clear and loud, of the Ruhleben crowd,
    That always kept their pecker up."

At Ruhleben, upwards of 4,000 British subjects, civilians, many of whom had been trapped while on holiday in Germany and Belgium by the sudden outbreak of war in August, 1914, were kept prisoners.

Rum Jar: A familiar nickname for a type of German trench-mortar shell. From its shape, somewhat resembling an army rum jar.

Rumble, To: To understand. To grasp the meaning. To find out: to detect.

Run, To: To report or charge anyone with an offence.

Run, To be: To be placed in arrest.

"Run away, Matron's Coming": *See* Nicknames of Regiments.

Runner, A: A messenger or dispatch carrier in action. The duty was often extremely hazardous and great heroism was displayed by the runners on innumerable occasions.

Running Torpedoes: A midshipmans' game. The torpedo—one of the midshipmen—is shot along the length of a smooth table, face downwards, and of course enjoys the performance.

Rupert: A familiar war nickname for a kite or Observation Balloon. Its origin does not seem to be known.

Russians, The Legend of the: During the autumn of 1914, for many weeks extraordinary stories were current all over England that immense Russian forces were being landed in the North of Scotland and passed through by train to the South of England, to be thence transhipped to France to reinforce the hard pressed Allied armies on the Western Front. Hundreds of people declared they had seen the Russians. Sir Basil Thomson says this in regard to the Russians in England in his book, "Queer People" (p. 37). "The landing was described by eye-witnesses at Leith, Aberdeen, and Glasgow: they stamped the snow out of their boots and called hoarsely for vodka at Carlisle and Berwick-on-Tweed: they jammed the penny-in-the-slot machines with a rouble at Durham: four of them were billeted on a lady at Crewe, who herself described the difficulty of cooking for Slavonic appetites". The facts, which did not come out for some months afterwards, were these. A considerable number of Russian officers and their soldier-servants arrived in this country to purchase munitions, or to be posted as attaches to staffs at the front, Just at that time the War Office were changing the localities of Territorial camps, and to secure secrecy, the trains travelled at night with blinds drawn, not even the engine-drivers knowing what they were carrying. Meanwhile, railway officials in the North had written to friends in England, and mentioned as an interesting detail, that some Russians (the before-mentioned officers and their servants) were travelling on their lines. The friends talked, and at once popular imagination and rumour connected the troop trains with the Russians, and so the story of a huge army of Russians passing through England spread and became exaggerated. The authorities, promptly realizing that the news might be useful in its effect on the enemy, did not contradict it: indeed they did everything to help it on. It was promptly taken up by German spies and agents in England—a letter from the spy, Karl Lody, later shot at the Tower, intercepted by the police, contained full information about the Russians and was duly forwarded to its destination, and for some time gave the German Headquarters Staff considerable anxiety.

Rust Buckles, The: See Nicknames of Regiments.

S.M., The: The Sergeant-Major.

Saida: (*Arabic*), Good day! Greeting to you! In common use as a colloquial phrase among troops on Eastern front.

Saida Bint: A "glad-eye" girl. A prostitute, Similarly an Eastern Front term.

St. George for England: The signal made by Vice-Admiral Sir Roger Keyes on the eve of the Zeebrugge attack. Replied to by the *Vindictive's* Captain with "May he give the Dragon's tail a dammed good twist". "Incidentally", says Captain Carpenter, V.C., of the *Vindictive* in his story of the attack, "my signalman substituted the word 'darned', and when corrected spelled 'damned' as 'dammed,' as a compromise".

Salamander: The name of a type of Sopwith aeroplane, the first to have the fuselage armoured.

Salinent, The: The Ypres Salient—invariable so termed. On Shooter's Hill, the 8th milestone from London bears the following inscription on the western side:—

130 miles to
Ypres.
In Defending
The Salient
Our Casualties
Were
90,000 killed
70,000 missing
410,000 wounded.

Sally Booze: Army vernacular for the village of Sailly la Bourse.

Salt Beef Squire, A: An old Navy term for a Warrant Officer.

Salt Horse, A: A non-specialist Naval Officer—one not a Gunnery or Torpedo Officer. (Salt Horse was the name in the old-time sailing men of war period for salt beef.)

Saltash Luck: A thorough wetting (Navy.)

Salkvo, A: A Salvation Army Hut. By permission of the authorities in the War, various religious bodies the Y.M.C.A. and others, maintained establishments for the rest and recreation of the men behind the lines.

Sam Brown: The officers' field service belt carrying revolver, etc. From its inventor, General Sir Sam Browne, V.C., of Indian Mutiny fame.

Sammies, The: A name in the war for the U.S. Army troops serving in Europe. On America joining the Allies, a *Daily News* correspondent, shortly before the first U.S. troops arrived, protested against the application to them of the name "Yankees"; "Do not call them Yankees, none of them like it". *Punch* thereupon (June 13th, 1917), suggested Sammies—"As at term of distinction and endearment ... after their Uncle". The name was adopted popularly in England, only, however, to be dropped after a time. Said an American General in France: "If there is one thing the American soldier dislikes, it is to be called a 'Sammy'!" The U.S. Troops called themselves "Doughboys". (*q.v.*) In the British Army "Yanks" was the usual term and the Americans were quite content with that.

Sammy, To: To clean equipment.

San Fairy Ann: No matter. It's all the same. A wilful perversion of the French "ça ne fait rien". (Sometimes also Aunt Mary Ann!)

Sand Storm: A soup of boiled maize so called from its brownish colour.

Sandbags, The: *See* Nicknames of Regiments.

Sandstorm Medals: Egyptian Army decorations.

Sang Bon: (*French*—Cinq bon). Very good indeed. Five times good. A "Nap hand".

Sankey, A: A five-franc note (*French*—cinq.)

Sankey's Horse: *See* Nicknames of Regiments.

Sappers, The: *See* Nicknames of Regiments.

Sarga: Sergeant.

Saucy Greens, The: *See* Nicknames of Regiments.

Saucy Pompeys, The: *See* Nicknames of Regiments.

Saucy Seventh, The: *See* Nicknames of Regiments.

Saucy Sixth, The: *See* Nicknames of Regiments.

Sausage, A: A German. A Kite Balloon—From its shape. A type of German heavy trench-mortar bomb—from its shape.

Sausage Hill, To go to: To be taken prisoner, "Sausage Hill" being generic term for a German prison camp.

Savage Rabbits, To do: A Tank Corps expression for waiting in readiness before action. From a phrase used by General Elles in February, 1918. The tanks, he said, would lie in wait for a certain time and then "emerge like savage rabbits from their holes and fall on the enemy's flanks".

Sawmill, The: The operating theatre of a hospital.

Scaldings: Make way there! An old Navy expression equivalent to "Gangway!" (*q.v.*). A warning called out by men carrying hot food along the decks from the galley to the mess-table.

Scaly Back: A sailor.

Scapa Flow: The now historic Grand Fleet anchorage in the Orkneys. These lines are from a song in the Grand Fleet.

"Faith, a little bit of garbage fell from out the sky one day,
    And flopped into the Ocean, in a spot up Scotland way,

And when their Lordships saw it—oh, it looked so bleak: and bare,
They said, 'This is the spot, we'll have a naval base up there!'
So they littered it with colliers, to make the matlos work,
And with depôt ships and Oilers, so destroyers shouldn't shirk,
They guarded it with mines and nets, with gates to come and go,
And when they bad it finished—sure they called it "Scapa Flow".

Scarlet Lancers, The: *See* Nicknames of Regiments.

Scarlet Runners: Battalion despatch carriers in action. From the red brassards that they wore.

Scene Shifter, The: The nickname of a big gun in action on the Arras sector in 1917. From the damage it inflicted on the enemy's line, its shells altering the "scenery" front.

Schooner on the Rocks: Baked meat on potatoes. A joint baked in a "sea of batter". (Navy.)

Scooch: Rum.

Scooters: A name given to the C.M.B., Coastal Motor Boats, a type of craft auxiliary vessels introduced in 1915, a development of the racing motor boat. They rendered notable service particularly off the Belgian Coast and with the Dover Patrol in blocking Zeebrugge and Ostend.

Scorching your Eyes out, The Sun's: A Service waking call at reveille—regardless of the time of year—in winter long before sunrise.

Scotch Pegs: Legs. (Rhyming slang.)

Scotch up, To: To follow up an attack.

Scran: Bread: food: rations. (Navy.)

Scran Bag: The receptacle on board ship, in charge of the Master-at-Arms, for any article, boots, clothing, etc., found lying about and impounded for redemption. The money paid goes towards providing soap for washing paint.

Scrap of Paper: A broken pledge. A term now a by-word throughout the world. From the expression used by the German Chancellor, Herr von Bethmann Hollweg, to the British Ambassador in Berlin by way of excusing the violation of Belgian neutrality, at the historic interview in August, 1914, on Sir Edward Goschen stating that England was bound to defend Belgium and would do so. "The step taken by His Majesty's Government, is terrible to a degree: just for the word neutrality—a word which in war-time has so often been disregarded—just for a Scrap of Paper, Great Britain is going to make war on a kindred nation, which desires nothing better than to be friends with her". A very effective recruiting poster early in the War showed a representation draft of the original Treaty of 1839 guaranteeing the Independence of Belgium, with the seals of the signatory Powers including that of Prussia. The conversation between the German Chancellor and the British Ambassador was in German, and the Chancellor used the words: "Ein stückchen papier", as an emphatic colloquialism. It has been suggested that in rending this in English, when penning his despatch, Sir Edward Goschen Anglicized the expression through a recollection of Sardou's play, "A Scrap of Paper", a private performance of which, as it happened, he had witnessed a short time before.

Scrappy: Nickname for a Farrier.

Scrounge, To: To appropriate: annex without leave: steal, or acquire by doubtful means: cadge. Derived from a North-country word "Scringe"—to search about, glean, rummage, pilfer.

Scrub and Wash Clothes: A substitute expression in reading aloud for a word suddenly come upon which the reader cannot pronounce. (Navy.)

Scrubbed Hammock Face, To Have a: To look gloomy. (Navy.) *Cf.* "Sea Boot Face".

Scruffy: Dirty: slovenly: untidy in appearance.

Scuppered: To be killed. Dead. Originally a sea phrase. A man killed in action or falling in heavy weather would naturally roll into the scuppers at the side of the deck as the ship heeled. Also: Scattered, Demoralized.

Sea Boot Face, To Have a: To look gloomy. *Cf.* "Scrubbed Hammock Face".

Sea Pheasant: Bloater. (Navy.)

Seam Squirrel: A louse.

Send for Mary Ann: (*French*—ça ne fait rien): No matter: never mind.

Send it Down David: *See* David.

Serge: Tunic.

Sergeant Major, The: The Crown in the game of "Crown and Anchor" Suggested by the crown on a Company Sergeant Major's sleeve.

Sergeant Major's Tea: Tea with sugar and milk, or a dash of rum, in it. An expression current among the rank and file, suggested by a prevalent opinion that Sergeant Majors had a way of securing such extras for themselves.

Set, To Have Someone: To get the better of: to take at a disadvantage: to get a man convicted.

Set the Swede Down: To have a nap.

Seven, All in the: A matter of course: something to be expected. In allusion to the soldier's term of service with the Colours—e.g., "There's nothing in that—it all comes in my seven".

Seven and Sixpennies, The: *See* Nicknames of Regiments.

Seven Pennyworth, A: Seven days C.B.—Confinement to barracks.

Sewed in his Blanket: Dead and buried.

Sexton Blake: The Provost Sergeant. (Suggested by the name of a detective of popular fiction.)

Shackles: Soup: stew.

Sham the Doctor, To: To malinger.

Shanky: Thrifty: close-fisted.

Shark, To: To steal.

Shave, A: A rumour. A report of unknown or doubtful origin. (An old Service term.)

Shawl: A greatcoat.

Sheavo (or Sheevo): A row: a free fight. Also an entertainment. A Navy term over a hundred years old. In the earlier from "Chevaux", the phrase occurs in a letter of May 6th, 1798, from Lieut. Charles Cathcart, quoted in the Navy Records Society's *Naval Miscellany*, Vol. I., p. 271. "We have just left Gibraltar … Sir John Orde gave a grand chevaux to which he was so good as to invite me".

Shebo: Soap. (Navy.)

Sheeny: A careful, extra economical man.

Sheet, On the: On the "Crime Sheet": charged with an offence: up for trial.

Shell Proof, A: A sarcastic term for a braggart or fool-hardy fellow.

Shell Shock: The popular term in the War for an obscure form of nervous disease prevalent in the Army. It was officially adopted in 1916 and applied to all forms of psycho-neurosis; although by neurologists the term was limited to cases of concussion or commotion of the brain, directly caused by shell explosion. Often due to fatigue, anxiety and emotional instability from prolonged strain, resulting in final break-down, precipitated by a shell-burst near the sufferer. Owing to the number of claims for gratuity for "Shell Shock", allowable as a battle-casualty, Army Form W 3436 was issued requiring evidence by eye-witnesses of the proximity of a soldier to the bursting shell. One result recorded at Base hospitals was that dread of a return to service in the trenches induced the development of a form of shell-shock among high-ly strung men, in the form of hysteria, tremors, convulsions, paralysis, blindness, deafness, etc. It was stated in the House of Lords in 1920, that in the early days of the War, before Shell Shock was fully under-stood, death sentences for cowardice and desertion were passed and executed on men, who in the light of later experience were suffering from shell-shock and really not responsible for their actions. Since the war, the term has been officially abolished, in favour of the technical term "Psycho-neurosis", owing, among other reasons, to widespread abuses, through men unjustifiably posing as "Shell shock victims" to attract public sympathy.

Shemozzle: A row: a quarrel. A misfortune. Also meaning an affair of any sort—e.g., "We hurried up, but the whole shemozzle was over". (East-end Bookmakers slang originally.)

Shemozzle, To: To make off: to get out of the way—e.g., "We saw the M.P.s (Military Police) coming, so we shemozzled".

Shicker: Drunk.

Shiner: *See* Nicknames.

Shiners, The: *See* Nicknames of Regiments.

Shiny Seventh, The: *See* Nicknames of Regiments.

Ship of Troy, The: The transport *River Clyde* of Gallipoli landing fame. (*See* Horse of Troy.)

Shock Absorber: An Air Force familiar term for the Observer in an aeroplane.

Shock Troops: (*German*—Stoss-truppen). The name given by the Germans to special forces of picked men, selected from various divisions and organized in independent formations for forlorn-hope service: introduced in 1916. (*See* Storm Troops.) The term was used colloquially among our men for units of varying composition employed on "stunt" attacks. Also, a name for themselves adopted in certain corps who were specially trained and kept in seclusion for a proposed descent on the enemy on the Belgian coast. (*See* Hush Hush Operation.)

Shocks: Army vernacular for the French town of Choques near Bethune.

Shoey: Shoeing Smith.

Shooting Gallery, The: The Front Line.

Shooting Iron: A rifle: revolver: any firearm.

Shop, The: The Royal Military Academy, Woolwich.

Shop, Top of the: No. 99 in the game of "Crown and Anchor".

Short Horn, The: An Air Force nickname for a type of Maurice Farman biplane, without front elevator and with short skids. Given to differentiate it from the Maurice Farman "Long Horn" or "Mechanical Cow" biplane (*q.v.*).

'Shot, The: Army vernacular for Aldershot.

Shot at Down, To be: Used as a jesting expression colloquially of anyone in a scrape.

Shot up the Back, To be: To be found out: to be put out of action.

Shout the Odds, To: To talk too much: to brag: to grumble.

Shovel Engineer: Artificer Engineer. (Navy.)

Show, A: Used of any attack, action, raid, etc.

Show a Leg: Rouse out! Turn out! Get up! Originally the bo'sun's mate's shout on board ship when calling hands in the morning:—"Show a leg, Show a leg, or a pusser's stocking!" Dating from the time when women were allowed to live on hoard ship, ostensibly as sailors' wives. A leg clad in a stocking put over the side of a hammock, indicated that the occupant was a women who was allowed to remain until the men had cleared out. The call "Show a Leg!" was taken up in the Army many years ago as a barrack-room corporal's call on reveille sounding, and in the War was widely used.

Show Kit, To: To go sick.

Shrap: Shrapnel:—"The man-killing projectile", as it has been called. A shell filled with bullets, time-fused to burst in front of its target and shower down its bullets. The name commemorates the inventor, General Henry Shrapnel, R.A., Inspector of Artillery, early in the Nineteenth Century.

Shrewdy, A: A trickster. A cunning fellow.

Shut your Face: Shut up: Hold your tongue.

Sicker, The: The Medical Officer's report.

Side, Over the: Absent without leave. (Navy.)

Signs—Army Corps; Divisional: Introduced during 1916 as a ready method at the Front of locally recognizing and distinguishing units, *personnel*, transport, etc., of the various Armies, Corps and Divisions, and for making the identification of these difficult to the enemy. The Signs and Badges adopted were of a variety of different forms and types, in most cases specially designed to have a distinctive meaning for all connected with each organization. Some Divisional Signs, for instance, had a territorial significance, such as the Thistle and the St. Andrew's Cross, the badges of the 9th and 52nd Scottish Divisions; the Green Stripe and the Shamrock of the 10th and 16th Irish Divisions; the Red Hand of the 36th Ulster Division; the White and Red Roses of the Yorkshire and Lancashire Division; the Wat Tyler's Sword and the White Tower of the 56th and 58th London Divisions. Some badges bad reference to persons of influence or distinction who had raised the Division or commanded it; portions of the family heraldic bearings of these figuring in the Sign. Thus, the 8th Army had as its Sign the "Horn of the Hunter" from the family arms of General Sir A. Hunter-Weston who commanded it; the 9th Corps, a Bow and Arrow, from the crest of General Sir A. Hamilton Gordon its first commander; the 4th Division, a Ram's Head, from the family crest of its commander, General Sir William Lambton. Lord Derby's crest figured as the Sign of the 30th Division, which Lord Derby had been instrumental in raising. Certain Divisions in the course of their career adopted Signs to commemorate exploits in which they had borne a special part—e.g., the "Umbrella turned inside out" Sign of the 54th Division, adopted to commemorate its part in the capture of the Turkish "Umbrella Hill" position at Gaza in November, 1917; and the "Key" of the 75th Division, commemorating the taking of Nebi Samwil in November, 1917, the key of the Jerusalem defence system. Some Signs again were devised in punning allusion to their commander's names; such as that of the 17th Corps, commanded by General Sir T. D'O. Snow, a Polar Bear standing on an Iceberg, with above, the Seven Stars of the constellation of the Great Bear; that of the 19th Corps, commanded by General Sir Herbert Watts, three "? ? ?"—notes of interrogation (What's)—the "M" and Three Battle Axes of the 18th Corps, commanded by General Sir Ivor Maxse. Among other Divisional

Signs of interest were:—the "Eye", adopted by the Guards' Division; the "Problem figure" from the 14th Proposition of the First Book of Euclid, of the 14th Division; the "A.T.N." Sign of the 18th Division. (the number being suggested by the rapid pronunciation of the three letters); the three "7's" (joined like the legs in the Manx arms) of the 21st Division; the four "8's" of the 32nd Division; the double-three Domino of the 33rd Division; the Bee of the 60th Division; the Pelican of the 62nd Division; the "Broken Spur" of the 74th Division, adopted in memory of it having been converted from Yeomanry into an Infantry Division for service on Gallipoli and in Egypt and Palestine. The Australian and Canadian Divisions had mostly signs of geometrical pattern, and the New Zealanders displayed their Silver Fern Badge. [The above are typical examples taken at random from Captain Wheeler-Holohan's monograph "Divisional and other Signs"]. A very comprehensive collection of these signs and badges may be seen at the Imperial War Museum, South Kensington. Divisional signs, it may be added, replaced the earlier and original system of identification by numerals, as this was found to be giving information to the enemy.

Silent Deaths, The: A familiar name at the Front for night patrol parties lurking in No Man's Land, armed with trench daggers to surprise German patrols suddenly and silently, usually accounting for every man.

Silent Susan, A: A name for a type of German high velocity shell.

Silver Bullets: Mr. Lloyd George's celebrated phrase as Chancellor of the Exchequer in the autumn of 1914, at a public meeting, calling on the Mayors of the United Kingdom to invite subscriptions, etc., in aid of the prosecution of the War.

Sims' Circus: A nickname given to the American flotilla of destroyers sent over first on America coming into the War. (From the name of the distinguished America admiral in command of the U.S. naval forces in European waters during the War.)

Sister Susie, A: A woman doing Army work of any sort. Primarily a Red Cross worker. From a war-time popular song "Sister Susie's sewing shirts for Soldiers".

Six and Two's, The: *See* Nicknames of Regiments.

Six Cylinder Hat: A jesting term for a species of non-regulation big cap affected by many dispatch carrying cyclists.

Six Upon Four: An old navy term for short ration allowance, dating from sailing ship days when, on provisions running low, six men had to subsist on the usual allowance for four.

Skater: An old Army word for a N.C.O.'s chevron.

Skates, To Put on: To Hurry Up. Also to evade duty, To desert.

Skein, A: A glass of beer.

Skilly: Stew.

Skin, A: A horse: mule.

179

Skin and Blister: Sister. (Rhyming slang.)

Skin, Next of: Service colloquial for "Next of Kin", in regard to which periodical declarations in event of casualty are called for.

Skin off your Nose! Here's to the: Your good health!

Skindles: The name given to a restaurant at Poperinghe. In humorous allusion to the well-known fashionable resort at Maidenhead.

Skint, To be: Hard up.

Skipper, The: Captain R.N.

Skipper's Doggie: Midshipman acting as captain's A.D.C.

Skit: Beer.

Skive, To: To dodge a duty or fatigue.

Skoff: Food.

Skoff, To: To eat.

Skolka, To: To sell. To bargain. A Russian word meaning "How much", or "How many". Used in Murmansk and North Russia in the War, in connection with the secret trafficking that took place in Army food, rations of rum, canteen stores, etc., between many of our men and the inhabitants. "Skolkering", as the traffic was called, became so prevalent that the authorities made it a military "crime" involving severe punishment.

Skoosh: Sweetheart.

Skrimshanker, A: A ne'er-do-we'el: a shirker: a "rotter". A very old Army term.

Sky Pilot: A chaplain.

Sky the Towel, To: To give in.

Slacker, A: A term used by the Press in the War of any man who appeared to be hanging back from military service.

Slashers, The: *See* Nicknames of Regiments.

Sling One's Service About, To: To brag.

Sling the Hatchet, To: To talk plausible.

Slingers: Tea or coffee with bread soaked in it. Dumplings.

Slip One's Wind, To: To die. (Navy.)

Sloosh: A wash.

Slushy: Ship's cook. (Navy.)

Smoke, The: London. (Originally tramp's slang.)

Snaffled, To be: To be caught; cut off. (Air Force.)

Snake Charmer, A: A bugler. A Highland piper.

Snappers, The: *See* Nicknames of Regiments.

Snarge, A: Any ugly or unpleasant person.

Snifter: Good. Satisfactory.

Snip, A: A certainty; an easy job. A tailor. (*See also* Nicknames.)

Sniperscope: A periscope device, attachable to a rifle and enabling a man to fire over the parapet while keeping himself under cover.

Sniping: The art of accurate marksmanship from concealment. In the War, for the first year the Germans had things all their own way, employing expert sharpshooters, with sporting rifles fitted with telescopic sights, etc., causing us cruel losses particularly in officers. In one battalion no fewer than eighteen officers were so killed in one day. In spite of all efforts it was not until the "S.O.S." Course (*q.v.*) was organized in 1916, and the training of snipers undertaken on a scientific basis with special appliances, that mastery over the enemy was achieved. Trench counter-sniping was followed by battlefield sniping to keep down enemy fire while captured positions were consolidated, and deal with machine guns and artillery. In one action in 1918 a single sniper put a whole German battery out of action, accounting for every officer and man, one by one. The term is upwards of 150 years old, dating from the American War of Independence. A letter of George Selwyn of 1782 (Hist. MSS. Commission, 15th Report, p. 621) speaks of men being "popped at or sniped, as they call it". In the Burmese War of 1824 a military report states: "Several Sepoys were killed and wounded by the enemy's snipers". The term definitely established itself in military parlance in the Boer War. It is a curious historic fact that the institution of regular regimental snipers was first proposed in the 17th Century by General Monk, Duke of Albermarle, when Commander-in-Chief of the Army in the reign of Charles II.

Snish: Ammunition.

Snob: The regimental boot repairer or maker. Also in the Navy, the name for a man earning extra money by repairing shipmates' boots in spare time.

Snob Shop, The: The regimental boot repairer or maker's workshop.

Snotty, A: A midshipman. An origin for the word is suggested by "Taffrail" as follows. "A 'snot rag', as every schoolboy knows, is the slang term for a pocket handkerchief, and the term 'snotty', as applied to midshipmen, came in at a time when the Lords Commissioners of the Admiralty order that the young gentlemen should wear three buttons on the sleeves of their full dress round-jackets. The buttons, according to certain ribald persons who wished to cast ridicule upon the midshipmen, were placed there to prevent their wearers from putting the sleeves of their garments to the use generally delegated to pocket handkerchiefs. It was nothing but a libel of course, but the nickname still survives and will remain till the crack of doom".

Snout, To: To bear a grudge against.

Snow: Money. Silver.

Soak, To: To catch out. To "have one set" (*q.v.*). To be told off for some piece of undesired work—e.g., "soaked" for a fatigue.

Soap and Baccy Pay: Victualling Paymaster R.N.

Soap and Water: Daughter. (Rhyming slang.)

Sock a Boot into: To take advantage of someone's misfortunes.

Sock into, To put a: To stop: to silence—e.g., Used to anyone making a noise: "Shut up, put a sock into it—i.e., "Gag yourself". Originating possibly among men in hospital wearied of a gramophone's music.

Soft Number, A: An easy job.

Soldier: A familiar term for a Marine Officer on board ship.

Soldier On: A colloquial expression of encouragement. e.g., "Soldier on, chum, everything has got an end".

Soldier, To: To clean equipment, pipe-clay belts, etc. (An old Army term.)

Soldier's Friend: The rifle. Also a familiar name for the metal polish used for cleaning brass buttons, etc.

Soldier's Wind, A: An old Navy expression for a breeze favourable either way, in which anyone could manage a sailing boat.

Solo Flight, A: An Airman's term for flying single-handed.

"Something to Hang Things On": A soldier's humorous expression for himself; in allusion to the paraphernalia of his heavy marching order kit.

S.O.S. Course: The term on the Western Front for the "Sniping, Observation and Scouting" course of training at the Sniping Schools established in 1916. In 1914–15 the Germans were very successful, having an ample supply of good telescopic sights and men skilled in the use of them, recruited from amongst the *Jäger* of their game-forests. The matter was seriously taken up by a number of officers, prominent amongst whom were the late Major Hesketh Pritchard, D.S.O., M.C., and in 1915–16 sniping schools were established and telescopes and telescopic sights were collected, largely as voluntary contributions from civilian owners over the Empire. These were distributed to men and officers, who were trained to make use of them. In 1917 these schools were expanded so as to give training with all types of telescopic sights (about eighteen patterns were then in use in France), in observation, together with instruction in map-reading and photograph interpretation, intelligence details and reconnaissance reports, scouting, etc. The schools were re-named "S.O. and S." schools (Scouting, Observation and Sniping Schools). One school was organized for each of our Armies in France and most of the Army Corps also started "junior" Sniping Schools as well. By that time a complete ascendancy had been gained over the German Snipers, which was held till the conclusion of hostilities, a result obtained as much by good organization as by skilful use of weapons. Great ingenuity was shown by the British Snipers in all the ruses of war, and the Highland gillies, African big-game hunters, Canadian back-woodsmen and British gamekeepers and poachers easily showed themselves more than a match for the East Prussian and Galician *Jäger.* It was at the same time quite as much by proving themselves true scouts and observers—that is, collectors of first-hand information—that the sniping officers and their men proved their value.

Souvenir, A: A trophy. Something to take home from the Front. Many stories are told of the eagerness of men to get hold of souvenirs. An officer describes on incident in this connection. It was after Neuve Chapelle in March, 1915, "A big British soldier with a horribly smashed leg came crawling round a trench with a German helmet hanging from his teeth by its strap. As he neared the teller of the story, the man snapped out, 'Got my souvenir, sir'!" The experiences of the "Old Contemptibles" of the original British Expeditionary Force in regard to "souvenirs" from the point of view of the French local people, as keepsakes, began immediately on our men landing in France. Everybody pestered them for "souvenirs" in the shape of some article of their equipment. The result is thus described by Major Corbett Smith in his "Retreat from Mons". "Before a week had elapsed very few had any buttons left. It is a mystery how they kept their trousers up. Regimental badges and caps were much appreciated, especially the Gunners' letters. It did not take long for the quick-witted French girls to discover that "R.F.A." was obviously intended to represent the Triple Entente, Russie, France, Angleterre. When these units eventually rolled up at their destination it was found that about half the men had lost not only all their buttons and badges, but their caps as well, getting in exchange some horrible provincial product in the shape of a rakish tweed cap. Bits of tape and string held coats and trousers together".

Souvenir, To: To steal.

Spad: A familiar term from the initials S.P.A.D. (Société Pour Aviation et ses Dérivés) a type of single-seater biplane.

Spades, The: The Divisional Concert Party of the 12th (Eastern) Division.

Spanish Knight Trick, The: A trench trap-device worked on the lines of the mediaeval portcullis for cutting off enemy trench raiders by dropping a barrier in their rear.

Spare General, A: A term used by way of sarcasm: used of some overbearing or conceited superior.

Spare Parts: A sarcastic term used for anyone incompetent, or not the kind of person wanted.

Spare, To Look: To be idle: not engaged on any particular job.

Sparks: A wireless telegraphy operator.

Sparks, To get the: To "set" or fix the aim of a machine-gun; on some point of an enemy trench after dark, by firing into the wire-entanglement and noting where the sparks fly off as the bullets cut the wire.

Spassiba: Russian for "Thanks". Adopted as a colloquialism among the troops serving in North Russia.

Specialists: A familiar term for officers and men trained for any particular work, such as bombers, Lewis gunners, etc. Also occasionally used sarcastically of men pleading other employment in order to evade ordinary duty. Similarly used in the Navy familiarly for gunnery, torpedo officers and others.

Spike: *See* Nicknames.

Spin, Up for a: Brought up for a reprimand for some minor offence. (Of an N.C.O.)

Spit and Polish: A Service expression, usually for parade or show-off smartness as opposed to utility. Originally a colloquial term in allusion to the cleaning of brass-work, buttons, decorative details, etc.

Spit Ball: Hand-grenade. (U.S. Army.)

Splice the Main Brace, To: To serve out an extra issue of grog on any special occasion, after heavy exertion, at festivities, etc.

Splinters, The: One of the most popular Concert Parties at the Front, and one of those that continued in existence after the Armistice. "The Splinters" appeared at a London Music Hall in 1923.

Spokey: Wheelwright. Also *see* Nicknames.

Spook, A: An artillery signaller.

Sports Ship, The: A familiar name for the SS. *Borodino* (officially M.F.A. No. 6) chartered in October, 1914, at the instance of the Admiralty by the Junior Army and Navy Stores, as Officers' Supply Ship to the Grand Fleet at Scapa. Boxing competitions, theatrical performances, concerts, billiard matches, etc., were held on board, while the ship at the same time served as a floating multiple-stores establishment with departments on up-to-date lines.

Sportsman's Battalion, The: The 23rd and 24th Battalions of the Royal Fusiliers. Raised by Mrs. E. Cunliffe-Owen (now Mrs. Cunliffe-Stamford). They were remarkable in 1914 as being permitted to recruit men up to 45 years of age, which enabled many men, whom the recruiting officials would not accept as being over the regulation military age, to get into uniform. The battalions, as originally raised, comprised a large number of Mining Engineers, Ranchers, Planters, etc., as well as country gentlemen and farmers. Both battalions did excellent service in France and in East Africa, where the casualties from the climate were very severe.

Sprang: Tea. Drink.

Springboks, The: The South African contingent in the War. From their badge, the Colonial emblem of a springbok antelope.

Springers, The: *See* Nicknames of Regiments.

Spruce, To: To lie. To deceive.

Spud: An Irishman. A potato. *See* Nicknames.

Spud Adjutant: An Orderly Corporal. In allusion to his duty in superintending the party carrying rations (potatoes) from the cook-house.

Spud Practice: Peeling Potatoes.

Spun Yarn Tricks: Underhand dealing.

Spurlos Versenkt: Gone entirely. Disappeared. Specifically—sunk without trace, with all on board. A notorious German phrase of the War that has become historic. Originating through the publication of an intercepted secret telegraphic despatch sent in May, 1917, by the German Chargé d'Affaires in the Argentine, Count Luxburg, in cypher through the Swedish Minister at Buenos Aires to Berlin, recommending that German submarines should be ordered to sink Argentine vessels as well as neutrals "without leaving a trace".

Squad Halt: Salt. (Rhyming slang.)

Square, The: An Army term for the drill or parade ground. In general, the Barrack Square.

Square Bit, A: A sweetheart: A "Best Girl".

Square Dinkum: True. Straightforward. Correct. (*See* Dinkum.)

Square Piece (Square Pusher), A: A respectable young woman. (*See* Pusher). Also Square Pushers, civilian boots.

Square Pushing, to Go: To "walk out" with a girl.

Square, To be Pushed Off the: To be dismissed recruits' preliminary drill. (*See* Square.)

Square Tack: *See* Square Pusher.

Squarehead, A: A German. In its origin an old seafarers' term, suggested probably by the somewhat square shape of the typical Teutonic skull. The close-cropped hair of the German soldier on active service, noticed among prisoners, accentuated the idea of squareness, and gave the term currency at the Front in the War. The Squarehead or Nordic type of skull (*brachy-cephalic*) is a recognized form in anthropology, in contradistinction to the Longhead (*dolicho-cephalic*) type. Says a British authority on the subject: "A very big proportion of the German people are Squareheads. The Saxons are nearly always Nordic, and quite a large proportion of the Prussian aristocracy also. These distinctions as they bear on the habits of the racial types have a bearing also on the callings they choose and the effects of those callings on physique and long life. The great majority of the police are of the Nordic type: so are soldiers and sailors. The Squarehead is almost extinct in these islands. Perhaps, very roughly, one person in 10,000 is an English Squarehead. But it is a very interesting fact that our murderers, in the majority of cases, are square-headed; and in the United States the proportion of murderers of the square-headed type is extraordinarily high."

Squeegee Band: A made-up amateur band formed among the men on board ship with any available instruments. (A Squeegee is an implement used for drying decks.)

Staff: Staff-Sergeant.

Staff Crawl: Colloquialism for an inspection tour round the trenches by a General with his staff.

Staffordshire Knots, The: *See* Nicknames of Regiments.

Stagger Juice: Any intoxicant.

Stall, To Put up a: To mislead: To deceive.

Stand at Ease: Cheese. (Rhyming Slang.)

Stand By, The: The order warning men, not actually on duty, to keep ready for immediate action. The "Periods of Vigilance" (*q.v.*), when no man was to be absent from the immediate vicinity of his post, were familiarly known as "Stand By's". Colloquially used among the rank and file, also by way of giving warning of the approach of anyone considered for any reason a suspicious character.

Stand-to, The: The usual term for a special Danger Period in the trenches shortly before dawn, when an enemy attack was most to be expected. It lasted till daylight, all men manning the parapet ready for instant action. "Stand to your Arms" was the full order. From its regularity of procedure. "Stand-to" became a recognized expression for a definite point of time—e.g., "It was just before Stand-to that the affair happened". "Stand-down" was the corresponding order at the end of the Danger Period, used in like manner as an expression for a definite point of time.

Stand-up Prayers: A bluejacket's expression for Divine Service on board ship under makeshift conditions, when for any reason Service in the customary form was impracticable.

Star of the Line, The: *See* Nicknames of Regiments.

Stealth Raid: A trench raid usually carried out by infantry alone, without support from artillery, trench-mortars or machine-guns, the object being to surprise an enemy post, do as much damage as possible and return before effective resistance could be organized.

Steam Bo'sun: Artificer-Engineer. (Navy.)

Steam Roller, The: The phrase popularly applied in England to the Russian Army at the outset of the War, in anticipation of the overpowering effect of its vast numerical strength. As a newspaper article put it: "The Russian Army with its immense numbers of men, when at length it opens active hostilities, will move with the heavy, resistless, crushing effect of a steam-roller". Like other newspaper phrases the term was taken by the Services and used in a derogatory sense, e.g., for one instance: "That fellow's a Steam Roller, he's very sure—but always half-an-hour behind everybody else!"

Steamer in Him, To have a: To be the worse for drink. (Navy.)

Steelbacks, The: *See* Nicknames of Regiments.

Steerage Hammock, A: A meat roly-poly. (Navy.)

Stellenbosched, To be: To be superseded; sent back, presumably "under a cloud", from the Front. An expression originating in the

South-African War, from the name of a place in Cape Colony where there was a large standing camp to which officers who had failed at the Front were sent to do duty, as a convenient method of shelving them.

Stick-bomb: A type of trench-mortar bomb attached to a hollow steel rod which passed down the bore of the projectile.

Stick, Got the: An old Army term, used in reference to the most smartly turned-out man at guard-mounting inspection, relieved in consequence from performing his tour of guard-duty, and retained as extra, or reserve man, in the event of any of the guard going sick to remain in barracks and act as orderly until the guard dismounted. Two men of a guard in certain circumstances may be so excused. Stick Wallah; a term for a man scheming to get the Stick and evade guard duty and get a night in bed instead. Such have been known to keep spare kit extra cleaned up for the guard inspection.

Sticks: A drummer.

Sticky Jack, A: A Field Service Green Envelope (*q.v.*), issued for specially private communications, which the sender was permitted to close and stick down, the letter being exempted from censorship by an officer of the sender's unit in the usual way, in virtue of the signed declaration "On Honour" as to its contents which the envelope bore.

Stiff, A: An incorrigible or worthless fellow. An unlucky man: one always in trouble. A dead man.

Sting, To: To borrow—e.g., "He stung me for one shilling".

Stink Bomb, A: A Mustard Gas Shell.

Stinks O.C.: Gas Officer, or Instructor.

Stockbrokers' Battalion: The 10th Battalion of the Royal Fusiliers, raised for the War among members and clerks of the Stock Exchange in August, 1914.

Stocking Footer, A: Any noiselessly approaching projectile. A high velocity shell hitting or bursting without sound of warning.

Stodger: An old nickname of H.M.S. *Warspite*.

Stokers: Cinders or smuts on board ship.

Stone Frigate: Naval Barracks.

Stone Winnick, Gone: Muddled. Daft. An expression among the rank and file used of anyone giving incomprehensible or confused orders.

Stonkered: Put out of action.

Stool Pigeon, A: An informer. In the War applied to the disguised Secret Service agents, often placed among enemy prisoners for the purposes of the Intelligence Department.

Stop a Blast, To: To receive a rebuke or reprimand from a superior.

Stop a Packet, To: To be hit by a bullet: wounded: killed.

Storm Troops: (*German*—Sturm Truppen). Originally the name for certain special formations of picked troops, first employed by the Germans in 1916 in the fighting at Verdun, and comprising men selected from all divisions for leading attacks as a species of "forlorn hope". They were composed of young men, bachelors, or married men without children, and were parcelled out, usually in "Assault Companies", each 100 strong, under command of specially trained officers, with attached squads of bombers, machine gunners and flame-projector men.

Stouch, To: To fight. To thrash.

Straddle, To: A naval term. Range-finding at sea by alternately firing short of and over a target or enemy ship until a direct hit is recorded.

Strafe, To: (*German*—Strafe). To punish. To hit hard. Used in the War with an infinity of meanings and now to some extent ordinary English slang. An attack, heavy bombardment, etc., was always a "strafe". A unit in action which had suffered serious casualties was said to have been "strafed". To hit a thing hard was to "strafe" it. To put a candle out or to kill a flea was to "strafe" it. To be reprimanded was to be "strafed". Also an expression of good humoured contempt, or impatience—e.g., "Oh, Strafe it!"—i.e., "Stop! Shut up!"

Strawboots, The: *See* Nicknames of Regiments.

Stream Line, A: A tall man.

Strength, To Get the: To obtain the actual facts about anything.

Strides: Trousers.

Strike Me Dead: Bread. (Rhyming slang.)

Stripe: The rank chevrons of an N.C.O.

Striper (Two; Two and a Half; Three), A: A Lieutenant; Lieutenant-Commander; Commander, R.N. A Navy colloquial expression.

Stripped: Of an N.C.O. To be deprived of rank chevrons: reduced to the ranks by sentence of court martial.

Stubborns, The: *See* Nicknames of Regiments.

Stumer, A: An expression used commonly to denote a shell that had failed to explode. Also, as a question, "Is that a stumer?" used of German gas-shells, it being a common enemy practice to include gas shells in a salvo of ordinary. The others burst on impact and whether those apparently "dud" were really so, or gas shells about to open and let out the deadly gas, was the question. Also a "rotter". Anyone no good or incompetent. Any kind of failure. Originally, and for many years before the war, commercial and Stock Exchange slang for a dishonoured cheque.

Stunt: Used in the Services in the War colloquially for anything special or elaborate, any operation, demonstration or display, an engagement, action, raid, etc. In particular and primarily an Air Force word for trick-flying or anything difficult and at the same time showy. Originally American college slang dating from about 40 years ago. The innumerable applications of "stunt", often in good humoured contempt, really depend for meaning on the context.

Suds: Ale.

Suicide Club: A term applied usually, more or less in jest, to various "specialist" formations whose duties were, or seemed to be, of an exceptionally risky or dangerous nature, such as Bombers, Machine-gunners, Stretcher-bearers.

Suicide Corner: The name in particular given to a notoriously dangerous point in the Ypres Salient. Elsewhere also the name was given to various places where exceptional risks had to be run.

Sugar: Money.

Sun, In the: Drunk.

Sun's Scorching Your Eyes Out, The: Rouse out. Wake up. The lower-deck and barrack-room early morning summons to get up. Originally Navy, a Bo'sun's mate's expression in calling the hands—e.g., "Heave out, heave out, heave out, show a leg there, show a leg, sun's a-scorching your eyes out!"

Supple Twelfth, The: *See* Nicknames of Regiments.

Surprisers, The: *See* Nicknames of Regiments.

Swak: From the initials S.W.A.K.—i.e., Sealed with a Kiss. A common superscription on the envelopes of letters to sweethearts from sailors and soldiers. Sometimes also S.W.A.N.K.—i.e., Sealed With a Nice Kiss.

Sway All Top-ropes, To: To swagger. (Navy.)

Sweat, An Old: An old soldier. A very old expression.

Sweating on the Top Line: To be in eager anticipation. On the eve of obtaining something much wanted. An expression from the game of "House"; used of a player with four out of five numbers on his top-line filled and anxiously awaiting the call of one more to win.

Sweeps, The: *See* Nicknames of Regiments.

Sweet Fanny Adams: Nothing at all—e.g., "He knows Sweet Fanny Adams about his duty". Also the polite form of a certain vulgar phrase. A very popular *revue* by the Divisional Concert Party of the 42nd Division, given in July, 1913, at Headquarters, had "Sweet Fanny Adams" as its title. (*See* Fanny Adams.)

Swing it Down the Line, To: To procure a good job away from the Front; at a Base, etc.

Swing the Lead, To: To malinger: impose upon: take advantage of.

T.M.: The usual abbreviation for Trench Mortar from the initials. The Germans first employed them in the War in November, 1914. On the British side, the Indian Corps were the first to make and use them, the first of all being a makeshift weapon made of wooden barrel-staves hooped together for throwing bombs improvised out of used bully beef and jam tins. Eventually the Trench Mortar became one of the principal weapons of the War. T.M. batteries were created for trench warfare and T.M. schools of instruction were established. One of the most successful types was the "Stokes" T.M., so named from its inventor.

Tab, A: A Staff Officer. In allusion to a Staff Officer's gorget patch.

189

Tabby, A: A girl.

Tabloid, A: An Air Force nickname for a type of small Sopwith biplane of high speed and rapid climbing powers, a special favourite from its numerous good points, its, as it were, concentrated excellencies.

Tack, On the: A Canteen term for a teetotaller.

Tail, To Get on the: An Air Force expression for an attack on the rear of an opponent.

Tails Up: In good spirits. Keen on fighting. "Tails down"—the reverse. "Tails up" was acquired as a nickname by Air Marshal Sir John Salmond during the War, from his reply on one occasion to the Air Council who sent him a congratulatory message in regard to work done by his men in France:—"All ranks have their tails well up, and the superiority of British over enemy airmen has never been more marked".

Take Eight: You've won, I give in.

Take the Air: To fly. An Air Force expression—e.g., "Are you taking the air this morning, Jones?"

Talk Well Off, To: To brag of one's social position or private means.

Talk Wet, To: To talk at random, foolishly.

Tamasha: (*Hind.*—Tamasha): An entertainment; display; show. Anything exciting.

Tank: The name Tank originated in 1916, being adopted as a "blind" to keep the enemy in the dark while the Tanks were being manufactured. The measures taken succeeded completely, the Germans being taken by surprise, when, in September, 1916, during the Battle of the Somme, the Tanks first made their appearance in the field. The deadlock of trench warfare on the Western Front towards the end of 1915 made the devising of exceptional means for breaking through imperative. The first idea of the Tank came from Colonel E.D. Swinton (Eyewitness) who suggested what he called "a caterpillar tractor machine-gun destroyer for the frontal attack of prepared positions". Mr. Winston Churchill, then First Lord of the Admiralty, took up the project and it was mainly by his energies that it materialized. A joint Admiralty and War Office Committee worked out the design and a firm at Lincoln, Messrs. Foster, then engaged in making water carts for the Western Front to carry water for the troops between the purifying stations and the trenches, was entrusted with the manufacture. To mislead enemy agents in England and maintain secrecy at the works and in the neighbourhood, it was given out that the new queer-looking machines in hand were special mobile water-tanks for the Russians, constructed in that peculiar shape in order to be able to traverse the notoriously bad Russian road-tracks, and the first Tanks completed (without guns) were ostentatiously labelled in Russian characters, "With Care to Petrograd". In due course, the name Tank, after various suggestions in nomenclature, "Land ship", "Land Cruiser", "Land Destroyer", "Trench Tractor", etc., had been considered and rejected, was officially adopted by the War Office. Upwards of 2,820 Tanks (Marks I to V) were sent to the Front in the War:—"Male Tanks", "Female Tanks" and "Whippets". (See these names.) "Char d'Assaut" was the French official name for Tank. The German was "Scbützengrabenvernichtigungsautomobil". According to an American officer, General Barton, the secret about the Tanks was discovered while they were being built by a woman spy, the dancer, Mata Hiri, and made known by her to the Germans. Also, according to the same officer, that piece of espionage was the prime cause of Mata Hiri being shot by the French. Mata Hiri, who in 1916 was in London giving "veil-dances" at places of entertainment, and was advertised by the Press as "a high-class Indian princess who had been a priestess in India and had complete power over enormous snakes", obtained here information as to the purpose for which the Tanks were being made from a young officer whom she had fascinated. After passing her information through Holland to Germany, she went off to Paris, on discovering that Secret Service officers in London were enquiring about her. Then followed, after a short time, arrest, court-martial, and the firing party at Vincennes. Apparently the Germans disbelieved her report about the Tanks for their appearance was a surprise.

Tank Flag, The: A product of the War, originating shortly before the Battle of Cambrai, where the flag made its debût by being displayed on the leading tank, the "Hilda", which headed the advance, 350 tanks taking part. The story of the origin of the flag is as follows. In August, 1917, General Elles and Colonel Hardress-Lloyd decided that the tanks should have Colours of their own. In a little shop at Cassel in Northern France they selected brown, red and green for the colours of the flag, the brown and red symbolizing mud and fire (the fighting spirit); the idea in three colours being that the object of the Tank was to fight its way through mud to the object of the Tank was to fight its way through mud to the green fields behind the enemy's line. The title "Royal" was conferred on the Tank Corps in 1923, the King at the same time assuming the Colonelcy-in-Chief. The badge of the Corps is a Tank surrounded by a laurel wreath, surmounted by an Imperial Crown, and its motto "Fear Nought".

Tank Up, To: To drink hard.

Tanked: Drunk. (Tank is an old Army word for a Canteen.)

Tanky: The Petty Officer or Leading Seaman responsible for a ship's fresh water tanks. The Captain of the Hold. (Navy.)

Tap, A: A wound.

Tap, To Do the: To win at cards.

Tape, To: An Artillery technical term meaning to get the range of a target or battery objective. To mark out the ground with white tape for a night assembly of troops before an attack: or the line for a new trench.

Taped, Got You: A common expression in the War meaning "I know what sort of fellow you are", "I see through you", "I have got you marked". In allusion to the marking out of ground with tape as above. The expression is said also to have been current in the Midlands long before the War with meaning as stated above.

Taps: The Defaulters' call (formerly by beat of drum). The "Last Post" bugle call. (U.S. Army.)

Tar Box, A: A heavy shell. (*See* Coal Box.)

Tarmac, on the: Detailed for flying duty. From the tarmac or asphalt laid down in front of a hangar. An Air Force expression.

Tattenham Corner: A Grand Fleet name for the narrow water-way entrance into the Firth of Forth from May Island to Inchkeith, where German submarines constantly lurked, always passed by the British Fleet *en route* for, or leaving, Rosyth, at full speed.

Tattoo: A very old name, originally "Tap-toe" (close canteens and taverns). Originally also the name for the party sent round beating drums in a garrison to notify that all most return to quarters for the night. The drum-beat as they fell in to start was called the "First Post" and the final drum-beat when they got back to the starting point, the "Last Post". An old drill book of 1701, *The Perfection of Military Discipline after the Newest Method as practiced in England and Ireland, or the Industrious Souldier's Golden Treasury of Knowledge in the Art of Making War*, says this: "The Tattoo or Taptooe": "Used in a Garrison or upon the Rounds both to warn the Souldiers and the Inhabitant when they ought to repair to their Quarters or Guard, or when to shut the Doors so if any Spies be abroad they may be the better distinguished, for when the Taptooe is returned to the body of the Guard a 'Warning Piece' ought to be shot off, after which no person ought to be out of his Quarters or from his post unless the Watch-word be given him".

Taube: (*German*—Taube—dove). The name of the German standard-type monoplane used early in the War. From its pigeon-like appearance in flight, the planes or wings being swept back and curving upwards, and the tail planes pennated and spread out.

Tavarish: Comrade. A Russian word in everyday use in the War among our men serving in North Russia.

Taxi-driver: Aeroplane Pilot. (Air Force.)

Tear Gas: Lachrymatory Gas. A species of German "poison" gas used first at the 2nd Battle of Ypres in 1915. It had the effect of making the eye water profusely, temporarily incapacitating the victim and preventing him using his rifle.

Tear It, To: To disappoint, e.g., "I was for leave but that new order's torn it".

Teddies, The: One of the names for the U.S. troops on the first landing in France; disliked by the Americans equally with "Sammies", and soon dropped.

Teddy Bear: The name given to the shaggy goatskin and fur coats issued for winter wear in the trenches in 1915.

Teddy's Hat: The Crown in the game of "Crown and Anchor" (with reference to King Edward VII).

Tell Off, To: To find fault with. To reprimand.

Tenth Don't Dance, The: An old jibe at the expense of the 10th Hussars, originating in 1823 when the regiment was in Dublin. It had previously been stationed mostly in Brighton or in London and the officers were popularly supposed to look down on provincial society. Shortly after arriving in Dublin, the story goes, they attended a ball given the garrison by the civic authorities, and at it declined to be introduced to the ladies, all pleading "The Tenth don't dance". The incident got into the papers and the phrase became a current jest.

Terps: An interpreter.

Terrier, A: A Territorial. A colloquial term dating from the institution of the Territorial System in 1909.

Theatre Ship, The: The Grand Fleet name for the S.S. *Gourko*, ordinarily a "Beef trip" ship (*q.v.*), on board which, when at Scapa, dramatic performances were given; a stage and auditorium being fitted up within the vessel as required. Cinematograph shows were also given on board. The battleships and cruisers of the Grand Fleet, having to be kept always ready to put to sea at the shortest notice, it was impossible to rig a theatre on board; while, also, the distance from London and want of accommodation ashore at Scapa prevented Metropolitan Concert Parties visiting the Grand Fleet as they did the armies on the Western Front.

Thin Red Line, The: *See* Nicknames of Regiments.

Thistles, The: The Divisional Concert Party of the 9th Scottish Division. From the Divisional Sign—a Thistle.

Thistles-Tops, The: The Divisional Concert Troupe of Pierrots of the 52nd (Lowland) Division, whose badge was a thistle on the St. Andrew's Cross.

Thomasina Atkins: A WAAC, a female Tommy Atkins, a member of the Women's Auxiliary Army Corps (*q.v.*). The term apparently originated from the title of a book describing life in the W.A.A.C.

Three Parts Five Eighths: All but quite drunk.

Three Tens, The: See Nicknames of Regiments.

Thruster, A: An obnoxious, pushing person. A "bounder".

Thumbs Up: Very fit and cheerful. (Among the spectators at gladiatorial combats in the arena in old Roman times, curiously, "thumbs up" had the opposite significance. On the victor appealing for the decision as to his prostrate antagonists's fate to the spectators, if these wanted the man killed they turned their thumbs *up*; if they wished him spared they turned their thumbs *down*.)

Tic Tacs (also Tic Tocs): Signallers. (From the sound of the telegraphic instrument.) Originally a race-course slang name for men posted to signal the odds to bookmakers by code gestures.

Tichborne's Own: *See* Nicknames of Regiments.

Tick, To: To grumble.

Tick Off, To: To reprimand.

Ticket, A: Army discharge certificate. An Airman's certificate as a qualified Pilot.

Ticket, To Work One's: To scheme by malingering or deceit in order to obtain a "ticket" or certificate of discharge.

Ticklers: Jam. From the name of firm of jam manufacturers. A colloquial term in the War for ration or "issue" jam; mostly Plum and Apple, as being practically the only sort that reached the ranks. Also a Navy term for jam. Tickler, A.: A name at the Front for a hand-grenade of an early, crude type, made out of used jam tins, as material ready to hand. In the Navy, a former-day name for a Short Service bluejacket—five years sea-service and seven reserve service (*see* C.I.V., and "Selborne's Light Horse") under the scheme of 1903 for creating the Royal Fleet Reserve. The institution of the term of service happening to coincide in date with the introduction of Tickler's jam as a ration, together with other things, condensed milk, etc., the older long-service bluejackets—who looked down on the jam innovation as being babyish, hinting also that it was an Army dodge for working off surplus South African War stores—gave the name "Ticklers" in derision to the new-comers.

Ticky: Verminous.

Tiddly: Smartly dressed. (Navy.) (*See* Guyvo.) Also applied to a ship of smart appearance—e.g., "The Tiddly *Dido*".

Tiddy Chats: H.M.S. *Chatham.*

Tiffy, A: An artificer. (Navy.)

Ti-ib: (*Arabic*—Tay-ib)—Very good. All right. (A current phrase among men on Eastern Fronts.)

Tigers, The: *See* Nicknames of Regiments.

Timbertown, H.M.S.: The name given to the camp at Groningen in Holland by the men of the Royal Naval Division interned there after the fall of Antwerp.

Timbertown Follies, The: The R.N.D. Concert troupe at Timbertown.

Time On, To Mark: To retain; keep.

Timmynoggy: Otherwise Timonoguy—(originally an old sail-drill period term). A name given to various strop and toggle gadgets on board ship, used in connection with the upper yards to save time in sail drill. A device more or less makeshift, to enable something to be done more expeditiously than would be possible in the ordinary way.

Tin Bellies, The: *See* Nicknames of Regiments.

Tin Fish, A: A torpedo.

Tin Hat: The steel Shrapnel-helmet adopted in the spring of 1916 as the universal wear at the Front, and in London by Special Constables during air raids. *Cf.* "Chapeau de fer", the name in the 14th and 15th Centuries for the soldiers' metal headpieces, in particular one pattern very similar in shape to the Great War "Tin Hat".

Tin Hats: Drunk.

Tin Hat On It, To Put a: To finish. To overdo. To add the last straw. In allusion to the weight and discomfort of the shrapnel-helmet. *Cf.* To put the lid on. To put the Kybosh on.

Tin Lizzy, A: A Ford motor car.

Tin Opener, A: A bayonet. Originating apparently at the time of the South African War when bully-beef rations were first introduced on a large scale.

Tin Pirate: A German submarine.

Tin, They've Opened Another: An expression frequently heard in the War among the men in a depreciatory sense, with reference to some newly arrived draft, or officer.

Tip and Run Raids: A familiar expression for the German North Sea coast bombardment raids.

Tipperary: The chance that a war-correspondent at Boulogne, when the Old Contemptibles landed in August, 1914, quoted the lines he heard the men singing:—

"It's a long way to Tipperary,
  It's a long way to go;
  It's a long way to Tipperary—
  To the sweetest girl I know!
  Good-bye Piccadilly!
  Farewell, Leicester Square!
  It's a long way to Tipperary;
  But my heart's right there!"

started the wide-spread popularity of the song, one of the popular songs of the day. It was written by the late Mr. Henry James Williams of Birmingham (who died in February, 1924), and first came out during 1913, a twelvemonth before the War. Music publishers seized the opportunity to "boom" the song and the whole world forthwith accepted "Tipperary" as the war-song of the British Empire. It became a craze in England. Round London the song was heard in every suburban drawing room, while one newspaper worked out the exact number of yards from Tipperary to Leicester Square. In France, the street urchins welcomed our troops everywhere with cries of "Tipperarie!" and the townsfolk sang the words in both French and English. Finally indeed, when, on the early morning of November 11th 1918, Armistice Day, the 7th Canadian Brigade entered Mons amidst the enthusiastic cheers of the inhabitants, the church chimes, it is related, welcomed them with "Tipperary". Many of the regiments of the New Armies in training adopted it, and the streets and country lanes, as they went along on route marches, resounded with "Tipperary", played by the bands as well as sung, together with "Pack up your troubles in your old kit bag", "Your King and Country want you", and the "Marseillaise", which, as the national air of our French Allies, all England in the autumn of 1914 sang or whistled. A number of the New Army units, on the other hand, did not adopt Tipperary, being, it is said, "shy of singing what they believed was the exclusive property of their comrades at the front, the Old Contemptibles". "Tipperary" was also, in due course, adopted by the Dominion Contingents. The Maoris of the New Zealand Contingent, for example, had even a version of it in their own language, the first verse in Maori running thus:—

"He roa te wa ki Tipirere
He tino mamao,
He roa te wa ke Tipirere
Ki taku Kotiro.
E nohoe pikatiri
Hei kona rehita koea
He mamao rawa Tipirere
Ka tae ahua".

As to the universality of "Tipperary", it may be added that at many ports abroad, at Marseilles and Port Said for instance, on occasions when British transports passed French warships, the bands of the latter almost invariably greeted the British vessels with "Tipperary". The name was also given in March, 1915, to a Flotilla Leader, a large destroyer, H.M.S. *Tipperary*, eventually sunk in the midnight destroyer fighting at Jutland (May 31st, 1916) at the head of the Fourth Flotilla. The song, however, was more in favour among the civilian population than with the troops. "Among men at the Front it was never greatly sung", according to Mr. F.T. Nettleingham of the Royal Flying Corps, the author of "Tommy's Tunes" it was never "Tommy's song". The tune was heard in London in public in 1923, played as a marching tune at the film-show of the "Four Horsemen of the Apocalypse". The following doggerel had really a vogue as wide a any song, and a good deal wider than "Tipperary" ever had. It once, the story goes, disconcerted a British officer who thought to liven his men up on leaving the line, and, with in mind the inspiring effect of the Marseillaise on French soldiers, called on his men for a song. With disconcerting unanimity all promptly struck up:—

"I want to go 'ome,
 I want to go 'ome,
 Jack Johnsons, coal boxes and Minnies, they roar;
 I don't want to go to the trenches no more;
 Send me across the sea,
 Where the Allemand can't get at me.
 Oh, my, I don't want to die,
 I—want to go 'ome!!! "

"Tirpitz": The pig belonging to the German cruiser *Dresden*, sunk by the *Kent* and *Glasgow* off Juan Fernandez Island in 1915. He swam off as the *Dresden* sank, but two sailors of the *Glasgow* dived into the sea and brought him on board. The ship's company fastened a big cardboard Iron Cross on the pig, as one man said, "For sticking to his ship after his shipmates had left", and gave him the name, first "Dennis", the conventional ship's pig name, and then "Tirpitz". Brought to England and kept for a time at Whale Island, he was later sold on behalf of the British Red Cross and fetched a very handsome sum. (*See* Dennis.)

Tirps: The familiar and universal Navy name for the Admiral-in-Chief of the German Navy, von Tirpitz.

Tit-bits: A familiar Air Force term for the R.F.C. weekly *communiqué*.

Tit for Tat: Hat. (Rhyming slang.)

Tizzy Snatcher, A: Assistant Paymaster, R.N.

Toad, A: A name given to a type of German hand grenade, shaped like a flat flask studded round the edge with detonating knobs; the shape suggesting a toad.

Toasting Fork: Bayonet.

Toby, A: The steel shrapnel-helmet.

Toc: The letter "T", as pronounced in the signallers' vernacular for clearness of expression and to prevent misunderstanding.

Toc Emma, A: T.M., the initials for Trench-Mortar rendered in the Signallers' vernacular:—(T—Toc, M—Emma.)

Toc H: The War name for Talbot House, Poperinghe, "Toc" being the signallers' vernacular for the letter "T". The original "Toc H" was opened on December 15th, 1915, being named in memory of Lieutenant Gilbert Talbot of the Rifle Brigade, killed at Hooge in the previous July. A second "Toc H" was opened at Ypres in 1916. The purpose was to provide a place of rest and a social centre for all ranks; an institution equipped with a "quiet room", library, attractive tea-room, a chapel, and a garden. Church of England in foundation and ideals, the resident chaplain and superintendent welcomed all comers, of whatever form of belief and the chapel ever stood open to all, regardless of creed, unobtrusively offering its restful consolation. Poperinghe, as the military metropolis of the Salient during upwards of two years, was visited by thousands of officers and men, for practically every one of whom "Toc H", with its unique atmosphere and surroundings, proved alike a club and a home from home. [The writer of this entry, for one, well remembers tramping into Poperinghe one Sunday afternoon from Dirty Bucket Camp, and how at "Toc H", with a book from the library on "English Cathedrals", as he sat reading on the lawn, he experienced the first respite from war conditions he had been able to obtain for many months, For that he will ever be grateful for Talbot House.] After the Armistice, "Toc H" was transferred by its founder, the Rev. P.H. Clayton, to London, establishing headquarters as "Mark I" at All Hallows, Barking. There it maintains itself as an association pledged "to conquer hate and consecrate humour, its members drawn from all classes of society and devoting themselves to carry into everyday practice the straightforward standard of fair-mindedness, unselfishness, helpfulness, and Christian outlook—termed the four points of our Compass". Toc H obtained its Royal Charter as a self-governing body in 1922. Its chaplains (padres) are of all Christian denominations. The Prince of Wales is patron, and its groups and branches have spread over Great Britain and are spreading over the Empire.

Toffee Apple: A name given to a trench-mortar stick-bomb. From a fancied resemblance to the apples dipped in toffee sold under the name at English country fairs.

Toffee-nosed: Stuck up.

Toke: Food, Bread. (Thieves' slang.)

Tom Cox: A duty shirker. A man who talks arid does nothing. An old Navy term; origin apparently unknown—*Cf.,* "Tom Cox's traverse", to work which brought trouble.

Tom Pepper: A proverbial story-teller. (Navy.)

Tom Thumb: Rum. (Rhyming slang.)

Tommy Atkins: The popular generic name for the British private soldier. In its origin the name dates from August 1815 (Waterloo year), when the War Office issued first "Soldier's Account Book", which every soldier was provided with. The specimen form sent out with the book to show how details should be filled in, bore at the place where a man's signature was required the hypothetical name "Thomas Atkins", (or, alternatively, for illiterate men "Thomas Atkins X his mark") "Thomas Atkins" continued to appear in later editions of the Soldier's Account Book until comparatively recent times. It has now disappeared. A more or less current Service slang name from about 1830, the general of the name "Tommy" for a soldier dates from about fifty years ago. Mr. Kipling's verses finally familiarized it all over the English-speaking world.

Tommy Cooker: The name given to a contrivance for cooking or warming up food or tea, used largely in the trenches during the War, consisting usually of a tin or metal container holding a solidified composition with a wick. Thousands were sent out as gifts during the War, while the men also made them for themselves.

Tommy Waacks: An occasional nickname for the W.A.A.C., the Women's Auxiliary Army Corps. (Later "Queen Mary's".)

Tonics, The: The Concert Party of the 92nd Infantry Brigade.

Tony, A: A Portuguese. The abbreviated form of Antonio; used as a generic term at the Front for the men of the Portuguese Expeditionary Force.

Toot: Money. (Navy.)

Toot, On the: At once; quickly—e.g., "Do it on the toot".

Toot Sweet: A corruption of the French *Tout de suite*. At once: quickly.

Toot Sweeter, A: A high velocity shell. In allusion to its rapidity of approach.

Tooth Pick: Bayonet. Entrenching Tool.

Top Hat Party: A lower deck term in the War for City civilians who entered on board ship in the Navy. (*See* Hostility Men.)

Top of the House: No. 99 in the game of "House".

Top, Over the: In trouble. Charged with a "crime". Ordinarily, of course, the expression on starting for an attack; going over the top of the trench parapet.

Top Traverse, Off One's: Off one's head. Acting crazily.

Topper: *See* Nicknames.

Torpedo Jack (also Torps): Torpedo Lieutenant, R.N.

Toss, To Argue the: To dispute: wrangle: to have too much to say.

Tot Sack, A: A bag; usually a sandbag holding rations for a number of men.

Toto: Vermin: lice. The universal French Army word. Originally a Champagne peasants' word, adopted in place of the ordinary French word "pou" and to some extent taken up by the British on the Western Front.

Touch Lucky, To: To have a stroke of luck.

Touch Out, To: To evade a duty by trickery.

Touch with Death, To: To have a narrow escape.

Toughs, The: *See* Nicknames of Regiments.

Tower Bridge, The: A name given to the huge pit-head mine structure at Loos, taken in September, 1915, the appearance of its two tall, pit-head erections joined by horizontal corridors, suggesting tile Tower Bridge of London. (*See* Crystal Palace.)

Towse, To: To punish. To thrash.

Tractor, A: An aeroplane with the air-screw or propellor in front.

Trade, The: The Submarine Service. "No one knows how the title of 'The Trade' came to be applied to the Submarine Service. Some say that the Cruisers invented it, because they pretend that submarine officers look like unwashed chauffeurs. Others think that it sprang forth by itself, which means that it was coined by the Lower Deck, where they have always the proper names for things. Whatever the truth, the Submarine Service is now 'The Trade'. And if you ask them why, they will answer, 'What else would you call it? The Trade's the Trade, of course!'" Kipling Tales of "the Trade". (*Sea Warfare*—page 97.)

Trades Union, The: *See* Nicknames of Regiments.

Tranchée des Baionettes: One of France's hallowed places in the vicinity of Fort Douaumont, the "key" of the Verdun defence system. At the very height of the German bombardment a relief section of the French 137th Regiment was making its way in single file along a narrow trench when a salvo of heavy shells scored a direct hit and blew in the trench. Every man of the section was buried where he stood. Their bodies are still there, standing upright and not very deep, the muzzle of their rifles and bayonets sticking 15 inches or so out of the ground in a row.

Travelling Circus: An occasional name for a group of machine-guns moving from point to point in the trenches and opening fire for a few rounds at each. Unpopular with the men in the trenches as attracting enemy retaliatory fire on them. Also a name for a Staff tour of inspection around the trenches.

Transport Tale, A: A "tall" story usually of unsavoury kind. An expression meant in a derogatory sense, arising out of the rivalry that existed between the battalion companies and the transport section of units.

Trap Ships: The German Navy Name for the British "Decoy" or "Q" ships. (*See* Baralong Fate.)

Trays: Infantrymen.

Trek, A: A march. A Cape-Dutch word, originally adopted by the Army during the South African War. On trek—on the march. To trek—to march.

Trench Feet: The familiar name for the malady, similar in effect to frost-bite, practically universal in the first winter of the War, as the result of men having to stand in a cramped position and inactive for long periods in flooded trenches which caused stoppage of the circulation of the blood in the lower limbs. Napoleon's men in the Retreat from Moscow suffered similarly, as did our men in the trenches before Sebastopol.

Trench Journals: One of the novel departures of the Great War was the development of journalistic enterprise among number of units, mostly Territorial and "New Army", in the form of "private" corps magazines, mostly started while training in England in 1914 and 1915. Some "died" after the units passed oversea, owing to the impossibility of carrying them on at the Front, but a number survived and most of these are now in the Imperial War Museum Library. The best known of all probably: was the "Wipers Times" of the Ypres Salient which in 1916 with "The Somme Times", and "The Kemmel Times" was amalgamated in the "B.E.F. Times", and at the armistice became "The Better Times". It has come into a second existence as the "Ypres Times", the quarterly journal of the Ypres League (*q.v.*). These are some of the fancy names adopted by various Trench Journals:—"The Duration" and "Salut Poilu", both "run" by the Queen's, Own Yorkshire Dragoons; the "Emergency Ration", the 3rd Corps Cavalry annual; the "Wiggle-Waggle", "Sapper's Solace", "The Wire", "Eyewash", "Spark-lets", journals of R.E. signalling companies; "The Mudlark" of the Bedfords ("published in the trench-es" according to the imprint): the "Carry On", "The Limit", "The Whizz-Bang", "The Strafe" of the 2/5 East Surrey, "The Swell" of the 13th King's Liverpool, "The Dud" of the 7th King's Shropshire, "the Jab", "the Castironical" of the "Cast Iron Sixth", City of London Rifles, "The Bankers' Draft" of the 26th (Bankers) Battalion of the loyal Fusiliers, "The Asuwere" of the 21st London, "The Pow-Wow" the journal of the Universities and Public Schools Brigade, "The Dump", "The Stand Easy", "The Stand-to", "The Wangler", "The Macedonian Stretcher" of the Salonika Stationary Hospital, the celebrated Balkan News and so on with a score of other names. Some of the ships of the Grand Fleet at Scapa and others elsewhere also ran their journals or magazines; among them the "Chronicles of the Q.E." of H.M.S. *Queen Elizabeth*, "The Searchlight" of H.M.S. *Lion*, "The Kia Ora" of H.M.S. *New Zealand*, "The Iron Duke's Magazine" of H.M.S. *Iron Duke*, "Cyclopede" of H.M.S. *Cyclops*, "The Lyre" of the *Athenic*, "The Southampton Echo" of H.M.S: *Southampton*, "The Calliope Clarion" of H.M.S. *Calliope*. The 63rd Royal Naval Division had "The Mudhook", The R.M.A. "The Ypres Times and Tombstones Journal", and the R.N.A.S., "The Ripping Panel", "The Piloteer" and "The Fly Paper".

Trench Ring, A: A finger ring made of any scrap of war material come across, the brass of a shell case, etc. Affected by many men at the Front, Regulars, Territorials and New Army alike as "souvenirs" and often worn in preference to ordinary rings. The aluminium noses of German shells which had failed to burst were in much request for ring metal and a number of accidents occurred to men in handling them.

Trench Waders: The India-rubber or "Gum" thigh boots supplied in the winter after 1914 for men while in the trenches. (*See* Trench Feet.)

Tripe (also Tripehound): A name given to the Sopwith Military tri-plane, mostly used by the Royal Naval Air Force in the Dunkirk area.

Tripe, Up to: No good.

Triple X's, The: *See* Nicknames of Regiments.

Trooper: The official designation for a private in a regiment of Cavalry of the Line.

Trophy: ("Pronounced "troffy".) A dull-witted recruit. A bad drill—a man always in the "awkward squad".

Trossy: Slovenly: dirty.

Trumpet Cleaning, Gone: Dead.

Tube-train, A: A shell passing high overhead and making a heavy rumbling sound.

Tug: *See* Nicknames.

Tumble to it, To (Take a Tumble): To understand: to realize a situation.

Turkey, A: A bluejacket's name for a "Red" Marine (R.M.L.I.).

Turn it in, To: To die.

Tutoring: The term for the system adopted in the War of whenever possible attaching troops newly arrived at the Front for special instruction before going into the Line to troops which had already had trench experience; battalions being usually each allotted to a "tutor battalion" for the officers and men individually to receive instruction in details.

Twerp, A: An unpleasant person.

Twicer, A: A cunning fellow. One given to take by stealth more than his due. A Widower, or Widow, marrying a second time.

Two and a Hook, The: *See* Nicknames of Regiments.

Two by Three: A name (from their size) for a species of Canteen cake.

Two Five Two, To be Put on the: To have one's name entered on the "Crime sheet"—Army Form 252.

Two Fives, The: *See* Nicknames of Regiments.

Two Fours, The: *See* Nicknames of Regiments.

Two Red Feathers, The: *See* Nicknames of Regiments.

Two Tens, The: *See* Nicknames of Regiments.

Two Two's, The: *See* Nicknames of Regiments.

U-Boat: (*German*—Untersee Boot). The familiar name in the War for a German submarine. Over 200 are stated to have been sunk, 178 being recorded as having met their fate in action with British craft of various kinds. Over 3,000 men of the German crews went down in the U-boats. According to official records, 15,313 persons, passengers and crews of Mercantile Marine vessels, lost their lives in the War as victims of the U-Boats.

U.P.S.: The Universities and Public Schools Battalions (18th, 19th, 20th, and 21st Royal Fusiliers). A letter in the *Times* of August 26th, 1914, calling on all Public School marksmen at Bisley between 1898 and 1903 to form a battalion of marksmen started the movement. It resulted in the formation, a little later, of a University and Public Schools Brigade, 5,000 strong, enrolled in eleven days. The London contingent numbered 2,000. The U.P.S. provided the Armies at the Front in April, 1915, with 3,083 officers, Three of the battalions (18th, 19th and 21st) were disbanded in April, 1916, the majority of the men going to cadet schools, and the rest being drafted into other Royal Fusilier battalions. The 20th Battalion served until April, 1918.

Uckeye: All right. (A perversion of the Hindustani word *uchcha*.)

Ullage: An incompetent person. Anything useless. (Navy.) In its original meaning, the remainder after taking out the contents of a cask.

Umpteen: Any unknown number of anything: lots of, e.g., "I didn't count, there were umpteen of them". (Originally signallers' slang.)

Umpty Iddy, To Feel: So so. Not very well. All upside down.

Umpty Poo: (*French*—un petit peu). Just a little more. (An expression in use mostly among military labour gangs, railway workers, etc., by way of incitement to further exertion.)

Uncle Charlie: In heavy marching order with pack on back. (*See* Charley.)

Uncle Ned: Bed. (Rhyming slang.)

Undertaker's Squad, The: Stretcher bearers.

Ungummed (also Unstuck): Superseded. Dismissed. Disrated. (A colloquial equivalent for the French *degommé*.)

Unhealthy: Dangerous. (Used of any locality exposed to enemy fire.)

Unknown Warrior, The: The bringing "home" of the body of an "Unknown Warrior"—soldier, sailor, or airman, whichever it might chance to be—from one of the Fronts and re-interring it in Westminster Abbey as representative of the British Forces in the War was first proposed in 1919, but the idea was rejected by the Cabinet. A year later the Dean and Chapter of the Abbey laid the proposal directly before the King, who desired the Cabinet to reconsider it, expressing his own approval. The Cabinet thereupon took up the idea and arrangements were made. A number of bodies were disinterred at random in various cemeteries on the Western Front, and one taken, again at random. Removed to Boulogne with every honour the French could show, Marshall Foch personally representing the French Army, and escorted by British and French destroyers to Dover, thence, again with every honour, the body was brought to Victoria and to the Cenotaph on November 11th, 1920, the day the permanent Cenotaph was unveiled. Admirals of the Fleet, Field Marshals, and a guard of honour of V.C.'s escorted the coffin, with the Padre's Flag (*q.v.*) over it for pall. At the Cenotaph the King, as Chief Mourner, representing the Empire, laid a wreath on it. Borne then into the Abbey, and laid in the grave in the nave, the King in the course of the funeral service strewed earth from a Flanders battlefield upon the coffin. The grave was kept open for a week, and over a million people in a queue, it was calculated, filed past it. France, Belgium, Italy and America followed suit, France laying her "Unknown Warrior" beneath the Arc de Triomphe.

Unload, To: An Air Force expression meaning to drop bombs.

Unstick, To: An Airman's term for leaving the ground, starting off on a flight.

Up Against the Wall: Under sentence of death.

Up the Line, To Go: To go into the trenches.

Up the Rigging: In a fit of temper. (Navy.)

Ups and Downs, The: *See* Nicknames of Regiments.

Uriahites, The: The Mine Bumping Squadron (*q.v.*) the Third Battle Squadron of the Grand Fleet, sent ahead when the Grand Fleet put to sea to take the risk of being mined for the benefit of the main "Dreadnought" Battle Fleet, which followed immediately in its track. So called as being put "in the forefront of the battle". They were more fortunate in the outcome than the hardly used Uriah of Scripture whom King David so cruelly victimised, as none came to grief while employed as above. (*See* Wobbly Eight.)

V.: Rendered "Vic" in signallers' vernacular for clearness of expression and to avoid misunderstanding.

V and A, The: The Navy familiar name for the Royal Yacht the *Victoria and Albert.*

V.A.D.: Voluntary Aid Detachment A Territorial Women's Corps, formed in 1909 on the creation of the Territorial Force and organized jointly by the Red Cross Society and the Order of St. John, for service with units, the members being trained in First Aid with general nursing work, the care of sick soldiers, etc. In the War, the V.A.D. served both at home and abroad, attached to military hospitals and Red Cross hostels, performing every kind of work, domestic and clerical, as clerks, telephone operators, cooks, typists, and also, on occasion, as motor ambulance drivers. Princess Mary served during the War in the nursing branch of the V.A.D.

V.C. Mixture: Rum. A familiar term for the rum ration sometimes issued before an attack in cold weather or after long exposure under inclement conditions.

V.T.C.: Volunteer Training Corps. An organization for Home Defence in the War, comprising men unfit for the Army, or unable to be spared for whole-time service. Entirely an organization of volunteers at the outset, after the adoption of compulsory military service exempted men were required to join the V.T.C. The training included evening drills and among other exercises trench digging during week-ends, the trenches dug for the defence of London in the event of invasion being largely the work of the V.T.C.

Vamp, To: To eat.

Van Blank: (*French*—Vin Blanc). White wine.

Van Blank Anglais: Whisky.

Vandook: Rifle. (A corruption of Bandook—*q.v.*)

Vein Openers: *See* Nicknames of Regiments.

Vertical Breeze (also Vertical Gust), To Suffer From a: To be nervous. *See* Wind-up.

Vet, The: Medical Officer.

Vetted, To be: To be medically examined.

Vics, The: *See* Nicknames of Regiments.

Victory March, The: The popular name for the ceremonial march in London on July 19th, 1919, of the representative troops of the Allies and the Royal Navy and British Army in celebration of Peace. Also the similar triumphal march in Paris a week ear her on July 14th, the day of the "Fête Nationale".

Victory Medal, The: The Allies War Medal granted to all serving in the British Forces in the War. It is said that the designation was adopted "because it was the one title for a War Medal which the Germans could not copy". Men who serve in the London Forces were specially presented also with a certificate as a testimonial of the thanks of the Metropolis.

Virgin Mary's Bodyguard, The: *See* Nicknames of Regiments.

Vittles: Paymaster for Victualling, R.N.

Vlam: Army colloquial for the town of Vlamertinghe in Flanders.

Vrille: A spinning nose-dive. (Air Force term adopted from the French.)

W.A.F.: Women's Auxiliary Force. An organization of working women formed in 1915 to train classes of girls in useful work of every kind: First Aid, Nursing, Cooking, work in hostels and clubs for serving men, etc. All were volunteers, training in spare time. Converted in 1920 into the Victory Corps to aid ex-service men and their families, and fill gaps in other organizations.

W.A.A.C.: Women's Auxiliary Army Corps. Formed early in 1917 on a suggestion by the Adjutant General, Sir N. Macready, that women employed on Army work should form part of the Army and, be under the War Office, distinct from other women organizations, as an Army Auxiliary Corps. In the outcome, a corps of 1,200 officers and 56,000 women was formed and employed as clerks, waitresses, chauffeurs, etc. Upwards of 9,500 served in France. The W.A.A.C. also drafted contingents to other women organizations, the W.R.A.F. (*q.v.*), etc. In 1918 Queen Mary became Commandant-in-in-Chief and the title of the Corps was changed to Queen Mary's Army Auxiliary Corps.

W.D.R.C.: Women's Defence Relief Corps. Formed in September, 1914, to do men's work and release men for war service.

W.E.C.: Women's Emergency Corps. Formed on the declaration of War by Millicent, Duchess of Sutherland, the Duchess of Marlborough, the Marchioness of Londonderry and the Countesses of Essex and Selborne, to assist generally and co-operate with the authorities.

W.F.C.: Women's Forage Corps. Organised in March, 1917, as auxiliary to the Royal Army Service Corps and employed as hay-balers, rack-makers, thatchers, sheet-repairers, transport-drivers, clerks, etc.

W.L.: Women's Legion. Founded by the Marchioness of Londonderry to supply women for agricultural and horticultural work and as camp cooks, mess attendants, etc.

W.N.L.S.C.: Women's National Land Service Corps. Organized for farm work by the Board of Agriculture, in 1916.

W.R.A.S.: Women's Reserve Ambulance Society. (*See* Green Cross Society.)

W.R.A.F.: Women's Royal Air Force. Organized with drafts from the W.A.A.C. for manufacturing work in connection with the Air Force: dope and fabric making, acetylene welding, meteorological and photographic work, etc. The W.R.A.F. numbered 25,000 at the Armistice. Familiarly known as the "Wrafs" or "Rafs", also the "Penguins" (*q.v.*)

W.R.N.S.: Women's Royal Naval Service. Formed in 1918 under Dame Katharine Furse, G.B.E., with headquarters at the Crystal Palace. The organization supplied every kind of worker: orderlies, clerks, victualling service assistants, cooks, telegraph-operators, store keepers, stewards, painters, depth-charge makers, draughtsmen, sailmakers, etc. It numbered at the Armistice 450 officers and 5,578 women workers. Familiarly known, from the initials, as the Wrens.

W.V.R.: Women's Volunteer Reserve. Formed by Vicountess Castlereagh in March, 1915, to assist other women's organizations, and for agricultural work, hospital gardening, canteen work, etc. There were 40 County Companies in Great Britain and four battalions in Canada, numbering in all at the Armistice over 10,000.

Wad Scoffer: A teetotaller. Bun Eater.

Wads: Gunner, R.N. Also the name given to certain buns or small cakes sold at canteens.

Wall, Up Against the: In serious difficulties. (In allusion to the death penalty, execution by a firing squad.)

Wallah: (*Hind.*—Wala—an adjectival suffix to various Hindustani words in popular Anglo-Indian use, corresponding to the Latin "-arius"). A fellow or man, agent, helper, inhabitant, owner, etc. Used of any person engaged in or connected with any employment. In the War a universal Service colloquialism, e.g., Machine-gun wallah, a machine gunner; bomb-wallah, a bomber; Base-wallah, a man serving at a Base; Rooty-wallah, an orderly distributing bread rations, etc. (*See passim* for other examples.)

Wangle, To: To manage, or contrive, or obtain anything in some sly, roundabout, underhand way. Applicable to anything and everything in any circumstances, e.g., "I wangled a week's extra leave"; "He wangled that out of the quarter-master"; "It looked at one time touch and go with us, but we wangled through somehow". The War gave " wangle" a universal vogue. The origin of the term is the subject of controversy. The English Dialect Dictionary "claims it as an old Oxfordshire folkword, meaning "to adjust or fit in a loose, makeshift manner, to manage under bad conditions". It is also said to be an old engineering workshop word, meaning to coax or manoeuvre anything bulky through a restricted opening, or past an obstacle.

Forty years ago it was a compositor's term for adjusting, or "faking" type-matter to suit convenience. Also, some thirty years ago, in Manchester, a "wangler" was the name for a theatrical placard distributor, who, by means of complimentary tickets or cajolery, got shop-keepers to exhibit his bills. "Wangle" was a term in use in the Navy before the War.

War Baby: Any young subaltern or soldier. A colloquial term. Also, a child born during the War.

War House, The: General Staff slang for the War Office.

War On, There's a: A common phrase at the Front as an expression of impatience, equivalent to "Hurry up", e.g., "Look sharp, don't you know there's a war on!" Also, by way of explanation, or excuse, "You know you can't have that, there's a war on".

Warming the Bell: Putting on the clock. Advancing the time illegitimately for some particular reason. Calling the next watch on board ship before the proper time, for instance. (A bluejacket's expression.)

Wart, A: A midshipman or junior subaltern, "as being", in the words of a certain senior officer, "at once an objectionable and unavoidable excrescence". Also, the single star of rank of a 2nd Lieutenant.

Warwicks: Sixes (at cards). In allusion to the Warwickshire Regiment as the former 6th Foot.

Warwickshire Lads, The: *See* Nicknames of Regiments.

Was Bird, A: A wartime phrase used of any elderly man eager to enlist.

Wash Out, A: A failure. Useless. Cancellation of a signal message. A miss or bad shot. A term of universal application, used of anybody or anything that dissatisfied a speaker: his colonel for instance; an attack that failed; a bad billet; a poor dinner; a watch that stopped; and so on. One young officer, on getting a letter from England, was heard to say: "D—n it, my fiancée's a wash out!" "Wash out" was an old Navy term originally, the order for cleaning the slate in the days when slates were used to take down the words of a signal or message. Later, in the Army, in the days when iron targets were used, a rifle-range order at the end of a squad's practice to obliterate the bullet marks and prepare the, target for the next squad by, blacking over the bull's eye an whitewashing the rest of the target.

Water Cart (or Wagon), On the: A Teetotaller.

Waterloo Day: Pay Day. (An old Army term.)

Waxed, To have Someone: *See* Cold, To Leave One.

Waxy: A saddler.

Waxy Navy, The: The Royal Naval Volunteer Reserve. To distinguish them from the R.N. the men have the three white lines on the collars wavy instead of straight, while the rings of gold lace on the officers' sleeves are similarly "wavy".

Wear, To: To put up with, e.g., "I won't wear it", I won't stand it.

Weary Willie, A: An expression used of any long-distance shell passing apparently slowly, high overhead.

Webs: A Sailor's feet. (Navy.)

Weekly Account: The familiar and very old Navy name for the white patch on a midshipman's collar.

Weekly Account, To Pipeclay a: Used of an account "fudged" to pass an inspecting officer, Just as a dirty belt or pouch might be made to pass muster by being robbed over with pipeclay.

Weeping Willow: Pillow. (Rhyming slang.)

Weighed Off, To be: To be brought up before an officer and punished.

Weight About, To Throw One's: To swagger, to boast to display authority unnecessarily, e.g., of some newly promoted N.C.O., "Now he's put up his stripe, Jones does throw his weight about".

Well Oiled: Considerably under the influence of drink.

Welsh Rarebits, The: The Divisional Concert Party of the 53rd (Welsh) Division.

West, To Go: To die. To be killed. To disappear. To be lost, e.g., "Poor Bill went West yesterday, a sniper got him". "My leave's gone West", i.e., been stopped. "My mess-tin (or anything else down to a bootlace) has gone West", i.e., been lost. As to the origin of the phrase, which the War familiarized widely, various suggestions are extant. One attributes it to the Ancient Egyptians, among whom the West was spoken of as the home of departed spirits, and "to the West" the mourners cry on the banks of the Nile. Another attributes the origin to the North American Indians, who used the expression "gone to meet the setting sun" as synonymous with death. Others bringing it down to within a hundred years ago, as being a current expression in the United States in regard to men, gone prospecting in the then unsettled and dangerous Indian territories in the West beyond the Mississippi, who had not returned—implying that they were dead. The phrase in the English Language, is, as a fact, at least as old as an Early English 14th Century poem with the refrain, "This world is but a vanity", in which the lines occur:—

"Women and mony wilsom wy
  As wynd and watter ar gane west."
Or modernized:
"Women and many a wilful man
  As wind and water are gone west."
Sixteenth and early Seventeenth Century writers used the phrase "goe westward" of malefactors going from trial in the City of London to be

hanged on Tyburn gallows. "Go West", meaning to die, was a common phrase in South Africa thirty years ago, and in the Boer War, as colonial slang among colonial troops was taken up by our men and became a fairly common expression in the Army.

Westoes: West Country ships, i.e., ships commissioned at Devonport. (Navy.)

Weston, My Oath Miss: *See* My Oath, Miss Weston.

Wet: Silly. Wet, to talk nonsense.

Wet One's Commission, One's Stripes, To: To stand treat on promotion.

Wet Triangle, The: A Navy term in the War for Heligoland Bight, the triangular area of sea, bounded on two sides by the Schleswig and Frisian coasts, and on the West, by a line drawn from Horns Reef off the Danish coast to the Dutch Island of Terschelling.

Whacked to the Wide: Tired out.

Whaley: The familiar Navy name for Whale Island in Portsmouth Harbour, the Naval Gunnery School establishment (H.M.S. *Excellent*). "Whale Island" was the name of the mud fiat, converted into an island of solid ground with dumped soil from the excavation of the modern basins and docks at Portsmouth, on which the buildings of tile establishment are sited. From its former-day resemblance at low tide to the back of a whale.

Wheeled Up, To be: To be brought before an officer for an offence.

Whippet, A: The name of a type of small, light Tank, designed to act with cavalry, first used in April, 1918, in the action at Villers Bretonneux. Whippets carried four Hotchkiss guns, with a crew of one Officer and two Other Ranks, and had a speed of about eight miles an hour.

Whistling Percy: A name given in particular to a German 9-inch naval gun of flat trajectory, captured at Cambrai in November, 1917— from the sound made by its shell in flight. (Whistling Willie, Whistling Walter, etc., were names similarly given to various other enemy guns and shells.)

White Feather Maniacs: A name for the young women who during the earlier months of the War went about distributing white feathers to young men not in khaki. In one case, a widely told story goes, a young woman, seeing a youth at tea in a London hotel lounge in plain clothes, offered him a white feather "as a present". "It is my second 'present' to-day", said the youth with a smile. "Really", said the girl. "Another white feather, I suppose?" "Well, no, not exactly", was the reply, as the youth drew from his pocket a small case with the Victoria Cross which the King had that morning presented to him.

White Sheet: Army vernacular for the town of Wytschaete in Flanders.

Whitewashers, The: *See* Nicknames of Regiments.

Whizz-bang, A: The familiar name at the Front for a certain German field gun shell, from the whizz of its approach and the burst being usually practically simultaneous. An Army Field Postcard, bearing printed sentences of personal details, those not applicable to be struck out. Also, the Divisional Concert Party of the 5th Division.

Wig-wag: To transmit a message by waving flags. The action of so signalling; also the message itself, and the flag used.

Wild Macraes: *See* Nicknames of Regiments.

Wilkie Bards: A pack of cards. (Rhyming slang). (From the name of the well-known comedian.)

Willie, Big and Little: Names given the Kaiser and German Crown Prince in a series of cartoons which appeared in the *Daily Mirror* during the War. The names soon became popular, and were applied to a variety of objects. For instance, two experimental tanks, which were begun on about August, 1915, were so named. "Little Willie" first "moved" on September 8th, but got no further than the experimental stage. "Big Willie" first "moved" in January, 1916 and so satisfactorily that it became the prototype of the Mark I Tank.

Win, To: To steal.

Wind Fight, A: A colloquial War time expression for a false alarm. Sometimes caused by a look-out in a fit of nerves opening rapid fire in the dark on an imaginary enemy, the adjoining posts thereupon taking up the fire and then others, until the firing spread for miles. One "wind fight" over a wide area on the Western Front is said to have been started by a young soldier fresh from England suddenly, in the dark, blazing off rapid fire at a pollard willow stump, taking it for the leader of an enemy attack. Lord Wolseley in "The Story of a Soldier's Life" (vol. I., p. 180) says this, referring to his experiences in the field: "By night even the most courageous often think they see an approaching enemy or other dangers which have no existence except in their own heated imagination. I have many times known the bravest soldiers on a dark night make absolute fools of themselves ... Stones become men creeping towards you, and a few scrubby bushes are by the heated imagination easily mistaken for bodies of the enemy."

Wind Jammer, A: An Inspecting Officer. An officer given to stopping men's leave. Any unpopular officer.

Wind Stick: Aeroplane control lever. (*See* Joy Stick.)

Wind Up, To Have the: To be nervous: to be over anxious. To put the wind up: to frighten. Originally an airman's expression probably. (*See* Vertical Gust.)

Windy: Nervous. Cowardly.

Windy Corner: A familiar name in the War for any place specially dangerous or trying to the nerves on account of enemy fire, On the Western Front one of these was the notorious "Windy Corner", near the Menin Gate of Ypres. A certain area of sea at the Battle of Jutland, where the enemy's salvoes at one period fell thick and fast, was also afterwards spoken of as "Windy Corner".

Winger, To Do a: To take unfair advantage of in a bargain.

Winkle Pin: Bayonet.

Winkle, To: To capture individual prisoners by stealth. To creep stealthily out at night and get behind the enemy's line in order to surprise and pounce on a dug-out or trench, and pick out from there under bayonet compulsion two or three men for bringing away to be questioned by the Intelligence Department. Usually carried out by a small party, known as "winkling". The homely method to picking out winkles from their shells with a pin would suggest the term. Also, to commit petty larceny, to steal, e.g., "Somebody got into our hut last night and winkled everything".

Winnie: Quinine.

Winning the War, Anyway it's: A sarcastic expression of discontent or weariness over anything displeasing to a speaker as seeming unnecessary. For instance, on some minor routine order coming round, such as "blankets will henceforth be folded to show the edges and not as heretofore to conceal them", a man would exclaim, "Ah, well, I suppose anyway it's winning the war!"

Wipe Up, To: To steal.

Wipers: Army vernacular and the universal name at the Front, for Ypres—Yperen in Flemish. This coincidence may be noted. The well-known "Ypres Tower" at Winchelsea in Sussex, according to tradition built by an named after William de Ypres, Earl of Kent, in the time of King Stephen, has, it is said, always been known as "Wipers Tower" (vol. I., p. 614) tells this story: "Lady X told us a good story of—visiting a hospital. She was talking to a soldier who constantly brought "Wipers" into his tale. Each time—said, 'Ypres' rather sharply to correct the Tommy's pronunciation, and when she had gone the Tommy was asked how he had got on. He said that she was a nice homely woman and very kind, but it was very bad that she was troubled with such bad hiccups. Lady X told the story well, making 'Ypres' into a sort of hiccup each time."

Wipers Express, A: A nickname among men present at the Second Battle of Ypres for tile huge German 42-cm shell, from the noise as it rumbled overhead resembling the passing of a train. Wrote an officer of the Indian Corps in France: "The sound of these enormous projectiles resembled nothing so much as an express train tearing through the air, a resemblance which was in fact embodied in the name by which they were known, that of the 'Wipers Express'". A hole made by one of them in the ground near Ypres measured 72 feet across by 48 feet deep.

Wipers Times: *See* Trench Journals,

Wire, To be on the: To be missing. A familiar expression used of any-body wanted, who cannot be found.

Wise, To Give the: To give a secret warning.

Wise, To Put: To inform. To forewarn. A general Service expression often used in the War in particular of the taking round the trenches of newly arrived officers and N.C.O.'s for instruction, "to put them wise" as to the position and local conditions. (Probably of American origin.)

Wobbly Eight, The: A Grand Fleet nickname for the original "Third Battle Squadron". The eight old battle-ships of the *King Edward VII.* class. (*See* Behemoths, Mine Bumping Squadron, and Uriahites.)

Wolfe's Own: *See* Nicknames of Regiments.

Women of the Empire, Earl Haig's Thanks to the: Earl Haig, in his "Final Despatch" of March 21st, 1919, paid this tribute to the Women of the Empire: "No survey of the features of the War would be com-plete without some reference to the part played by the women serving with the British Armies in France. Grouped also under the Adjutant General's Branch of the General Staff, Queen Alexandra's Imperial Military Nursing Service, the Nursing Sisters of the Canadian Army Medical Corps, and of the Australian. New Zealand, South African and Territorial Force Nursing Services and the British Red Cross Society, have maintained and embellished a fine tradition of loyalty and efficien-cy. These services have been reinforced by members of the Voluntary Aid Departments from the British Isles, the Overseas Dominions and the United States of America, who have vied with their professional sis-ter in cheerfully enduring fatigue in time of stress and gallantly facing danger and death. Women in the British Red Cross and other organi-zations have driven ambulances throughout the War, undeterred by discomfort and hardships. Women have ministered to the comfort of the troops in huts and canteens. Finally, Queen. Mary's Auxiliary Army Corps, recruited on a wider basis, responded to the call for drafts, and by the aid they gave to our declining man-power contributed materially to the success of our arms."

Women of the Empire, the King's Thanks to the: On June 29th, 1918, in reply to the "Address of Homage" offered to his Majesty and the Queen on the occasion of their Silver Wedding, the King expressed his "Thanks to the Women Workers of the Empire" in the following terms:—"When the history of our Country's share in the War is written, no chapter will be more remarkable than that relating to the range and extent of women's participation. The service has been rendered only at the cost of self-sacrifice and endurance. Women have readily worked for long hours and under trying conditions in our factories and elsewhere to produce the supplies of munitions which were urgently needed at the Front and to maintain the essential services of the Country. As nurses and V.A.D. Workers, they have laboured in hospital for the care of the sick and wounded with even more than the accustomed devotion which has characterized our Red Cross Services since the days of the Crimean War. They have often faced cheerfully and courageously great risk, both at home and overseas, in carrying on their work, and the Women's Army has its own Roll of Honour of those who have lost their lives in the service of the country. Some have even fallen under the fire of the enemy. Of all these we think to-day with reverent pride".

Wonkey: Jumpy. Nervous. An Air Force term for anyone displaying undue nervousness, suggesting loss of nerve.

Wood Butcher, A: An aircraft artificer's term for a carpenter—not necessarily implying an inexpert workman.

Wood in the Hole, Put a Piece of: Shut the door.

Woodbine, A: A name among Overseas and Colonial Troops for a British soldier, from "Tommy's" partiality for cigarettes of the well-known "Woodbine" brand.

Woodbines, The Packet of: The nickname among men at the Dardanelles for the five-funnelled Russian cruiser *Askold*, present there in the Allied Fleet. Suggested by the five cigarettes in a packet of "Woodbines". The nickname was also in vogue earlier among naval men who had met the ship.

Wooden Overcoat, A: A coffin.

Woodspoiler: A carpenter. (Navy.)

Woolly Bear: A name for a shell (Shrapnel) giving off thick white smoke on bursting.

Work Back, To: To use up, e.g., "That stuff lying about there has all got to be worked back".

Work It: Keep it.

Working One's Ticket: Malingering with a view to obtaining a discharge certificate.

Wrafs, The: The Women's Royal Air Force. (*See* W.R.A.F. Suggested by the initials.)

Wrens, The: The Women's Royal Naval Service. (*See* W.R.N.S. Suggested by initials.)

Write off: An Air Force expression for a complete and hopeless aeroplane crash, the number of the machine being in consequence struck out or "written off" the books.

Wozzer, The: The name among the Australians in Egypt for the street "Haret el Wazza" in Cairo, a low neighbourhood. Two encounters there in 1915 between police and native mobs were given the name of the "Battles of the Wozzer".

X Ships: The name given to certain specially designed vessels in the War, built at Lord Fisher's instance, for landing troops in Northern Germany. They were of shallow draught, with twin motors, burning shale-oil and having a speed of six knots. One of them, "X 222", armed with two 12 pr. Guns was employed in the Channel and Irish Sea on Anti-submarine service.

Xaroshie: Very good: quite right. A Russian word (the "x" being pronounced like "ch" in loch), in colloquial use among troops in North Russia.

Y. Emma (also Y), The: Y.M.C.A. Canteen—(Emma, the letter "M" as pronounced by signallers, being a familiar colloquial substitute for "M"—e.g., "I'm going to the "Y Emma" (or "to the Y").

Y Gun: A species of two-barrelled gun of howitzer type in the shape of a "Y", mounted on board destroyers on anti-submarine service, for discharging two depth-charges at once, firing them to about 50 yards on each side of the vessel.

Yachting, To Go: To be absent without leave. (Navy.)

Yack-a-Poeser, A: A cup of tea flavoured with rum.

Ya-Inta: Hallo! Hi, you there! An Arabic expression in use on Eastern Fronts in the War.

Yallah: Go on. Get on with it. An Arabic word used on Eastern Fronts.

Yank, To: To jerk suddenly on a lever or cord.

Yanks, The: The Army name for the U.S. troops on the Western Front. (The name Yankee originally came into general use about 1700 for any white inhabitants of the Northern Settlements. It is really the Red Indian pronunciation of the French word "Anglais" (English)—Yengees, Yanghis, Yankees.)

Yapper, A: A windbag. A chatterer.

Yard Arm, Looking after One's Own: Considering one's own interests first. (Navy.)

Yard Arms, To Square Yards With: To settle accounts. To bring to an issue. To have it out with anyone. (Navy.)

Yaw, To: A naval term adopted in the War into the Air Force. To sway horizontally, or swing, an aeroplane, pivoting on its axis, alternately to right and left off the line of its flight, in a sort of see-saw motion. A ship "yaws" when her head from unsteady steering swings or falls away, deviating from her former course. In Ballistics the oscillation of the point of a projectile about the axis of flight.

Yellow Cross Shell: A mustard-gas shell, from the mark on the shell.

Yellow Diamonds, The: The Concert Party of the Tyneside Scottish Battalion of the Northumberland Fusiliers.

Yellow Peril, A: A cigarette.

Yimkin: Perhaps. An Arabic word used colloquially among troops on the Eastern Fronts.

Yob, A: Anyone easily made a fool of East End slang.

You and Me: Tea. (Rhyming slang.)

Youkanski Canaries, The: The Concert Party of H.M.S. *Intrepid*, when serving at Youkanski on the Murman Coast, North Russia.

Young Bucks, The: *See* Nicknames of Regiments.

Young Buffs, The: *See* Nicknames of Regiments.

Ypres Day: October 31st, the Anniversary Day observed by the "Ypres League" by paying a special visit to lay wreaths at the foot of the Cenotaph and attending a special Memorial Service in Westminster Abbey held beside the Ypres Flag.

Ypres League, The: Founded in 1920 by Field Marshal the Earl of Ypres (Lord French) and Lord Plumer and open to all with relatives or friends who served or died in the Salient, "In order that they may have a record of that service for themselves and their descendants and belong to the comradeship of those who understand and remember all that Ypres meant in suffering and endurance". The King is Patron-in-Chief of the League, and the Prince of Wales and Princess Beatrice, Patrons. Comradeship and the rendering of assistance to ex-soldiers, sailors and airmen or their descendants, the creation of an Ypres Defence Memorial and the endowment of a Pilgrimage Centre at Ypres, are among objects of the League.

Z Day: The official term for the date fixed for any important operation, the letter "Z", as a contraction for "Zero", being adopted for secrecy in lieu of naming beforehand the exact date. The days immediately preceding were medicated by the preceding letters of the alphabet— e.g., The opening of the main attack of the Battle of the Somme was fixed for June 29th, and notified beforehand as "Z Day". The four days for the preliminary bombardment, June 25th to 28th were referred to in communications simply as "V", "W", "X", and "Y" days, no calendar dates being given.

Zepp, A: A Zeppelin airship. From the name of Count Zeppelin the German cavalry officer who invented the rigid dirigible airship. He was celebrated as a daring officer in the Franco-Prussian War of 1870–1, and according to a story told in France he got the first idea for his airship from documents found in a chateau in Alsace, the residence of a French scientist of the day, on the occasion of a raid that he made on the chateau, with a party of Uhlans. He began experimenting with dirigible airships on retirement from the service many years afterwards, and after repeated failures and exhausting his private fortune, by means of popular propaganda he induced the Prussian Government to subsidize the further efforts which eventually produced the perfected bomb-dropping Zeppelin of the Great War.

Zeppelin in a Cloud: Sausage and mashed potatoes.

Zero (Zero Hour): The term for the time officially appointed for the opening of an attack, kept secret at headquarters and meanwhile referred to as "zero", the actual time being finally made known to the troops to be employed only at the latest possible moment before the attack. Minutes before "zero" were designated "Zero *minus*—", and minutes after "Zero *Plus*—", e.g., Zero being 3.20 a.m., 3.05 would be stated as Zero *minus* 15, and 3.30 a.m. as Zero *plus* 10.

Zero, To: A marksman's term. To ascertain by experimental testing the peculiarities of a rifle at known ranges and set the sights to suit the marksman's individual idiosyncrasies in aiming. Zero being known, allowances for deflection, etc., at various ranges would be calculated readily.

Zig-zag: A French colloquial descriptive expression; used mostly among civilians in the war area in Northern France.

Zig-zag To: An anti-submarine attack device. To steer an erratic course by constantly shifting helm; an evolution used in the War by all ships, so as to render submarine attack difficult, and as a precaution in traversing danger areas.

Zob: The name of a form of gamble in the Services, sometimes adopted alternatively to tossing for drunks—akin to the ancient Italian game "Morra", now prohibited. With the hand in three positions. The hand closed, stands for a stone; open for a piece of paper; with two fingers extended for a pair of scissors. The stone blunts or "beats" the scissors; the scissors cut or "beat" the paper: the paper envelopes, or "beats" the stone. The players call "Zob, Zob, Zippety", compare hands and so decide the winner. According to one story, an old fashioned senior officer visiting a ward-room on board ship found the officers "Zobbing" for drinks. His report, mis-transcribed, reached the authorities and represented that he had found "British officers sobbing for drinks".

Zoom, To: Air Force slang. To make an aeroplane, flying level at speed, dive sharply and then suddenly point upwards and as it were leap up, climbing steeply by impetus alone, the engine being shut off.

Zouave, to Play the: To show off. To affect an ultra-military manner or appearance. To swagger. An occasional colloquialism at the Front in the War. In allusion to the "side" that the Zouave regiments of the French army are often credited with putting on as *corps d'élite* of world-wide fame. The Zouaves, as a corps, originated about 1835 during the French conquest of Algeria, as native "friendlies", and take their name from the village of Zouavia in Algeria, where the first of them were enrolled. The corps was converted later into a purely French unit, uniformed in Oriental fashion. Quartered ordinarily in Algeria, the Zouaves have taken a distinguished part in all the wars in which France has been engaged since the Crimea. There were also so-called Papal Zouaves in the Vatican Army until 1870, among them curiously a Glasgow Zouave regiment and also a corps of Zouaves of Antibes who obtained a certain reputation. The British West India Regiment wears a Zouave type of uniform, adopted, it is said, at the instance of Queen Victoria in 1858, Her Majesty having been struck by the picturesque appearance of the Zouaves of the French Imperial Guard whom she had seen during her visit with the Prince Consort to Napoleon III in Paris.

Zubian, H.M.S.: A composite name given to a certain composite destroyer. The *Zulu* and the *Nubian*, two destroyers of the Dover Patrol, were mined and seriously damaged, one in the forepart of the vessel, the other aft, The undamaged halves of each were put together as a single ship and the name *Zubian*, combining both original names was officially given to the vessel. German secret agents in England, it is told, hearing that a destroyer called the *Zubian* was in commission, of the building of which they could find nothing, took it that the *Zubian* represented a new special class and spent a large sum in vainly trying to get plans of the class.

"Tommy" by Rudyard Kipling, written in 1890

I went into a public 'ouse to get a pint o'beer,
The publican 'e up an' sez, "We serve no red-coats here."
The girls be'ind the bar they laughed an' giggled fit to die,
I outs into the street again an' to myself sez I:

> *O it's Tommy this, an' Tommy that, an' "Tommy, go away";*
> *But it's "Thank you, Mister Atkins", when the band begins to play,*
> *The band begins to play, my boys, the band begins to play,*
> *O it's "Thank you, Mr. Atkins", when the band begins to play.*

I went into a theatre as sober as could be,
They gave a drunk civilian room, but 'adn't none for me;
They sent me to the gallery or round the music 'alls,
But when it comes to fightin', Lord! they'll shove me in the stalls!

> *For it's Tommy this, an' Tommy that, an' "Tommy, wait outside";*
> *But it's "Special train for Atkins" when the trooper's on the tide,*
> *The troopship's on the tide, my boys, the troopship's on the tide,*
> *O it's "Special train for Atkins" when the trooper's on the tide.*

Yes, makin' mock o' uniforms that guard you while you sleep
Is cheaper than them uniforms, an' they're starvation cheap;
An' hustlin' drunken soldiers when they're goin' large a bit
Is five times better business than paradin' in full kit.

> *Then it's Tommy this, an' Tommy that, an' "Tommy how's yer soul?"*
> *But it's "Thin red line of 'eroes" when the drums begin to roll,*
> *The drums begin to roll, my boys, the drums begin to roll,*
> *O it's "Thin red line of 'eroes" when the drums begin to roll.*

We aren't no thin red 'eroes, nor we aren't no blackguards too,
But single men in barricks, most remarkable like you;
An' if sometimes our conduck isn't all your fancy paints:
Why, single men in barricks don't grow into plaster saints;

> *While it's Tommy this, an' Tommy that, an "Tommy, fall be'ind",*
> *But it's "Please to walk in front, sir", when there's trouble in the wind,*
> *There's trouble in the wind, my boys, there's trouble in the wind,*
> *O it's "Please to walk in front, sir", when there's trouble in the wind.*

You talk o' better food for us, an' schools, an' fires an' all:
We'll wait for extry rations if you treat us rational.
Don't mess about the cook-room slops, but prove it to our face
The Widow's Uniform is not the soldier-man's disgrace.

> *For it's Tommy this, an' Tommy that, an' "Chuck him out, the brute!"*
> *But it's "Saviour of 'is country", when the guns begin to shoot;*
> *Yes it's Tommy this, an' Tommy that, an' anything you please;*
> *But Tommy ain't a bloomin' fool – you bet that Tommy sees!*

Lightning Source UK Ltd.
Milton Keynes UK
UKHW022014131118
332288UK00004B/83/P